# Online Communication

## Linking Technology, Identity, and Culture

**LEA'S COMMUNICATION SERIES**
*Jennings Bryant / Dolf Zillmann, General Editors*

Selected titles in the series include:

**Greene** • Message Production: Advances in Communication Theory

**Petronio** • Balancing the Secrets of Private Disclosures

**Riffe/Lacy/Fico** • Analyzing Media Messages: Using Quantitative Content Analysis in Research

**Shepherd/Rothenbuhler** • Communication and Community

**Wicks** • Understanding Audiences: Learning to Use the Media Constructively

For a complete list of titles in LEA's Communication Series, please contact Lawrence Erlbaum Associates, Publishers.

# Online Communication

## Linking Technology, Identity, and Culture

Andrew F. Wood
*San José State University*

Matthew J. Smith
*Indiana University South Bend*

LEA LAWRENCE ERLBAUM ASSOCIATES, PUBLISHERS
2001 MAHWAH, NEW JERSEY LONDON

Lawrence Erlbaum Associates, Inc., Publishers
10 Industrial Avenue
Mahwah, NJ 07430

Cover design by Kathryn Houghtaling Lacey, based on an original design by Andrew Wood

**Library of Congress Cataloging-in-Publication Data**

Wood, Andrew F.
Online communication : linking technology, identity, and culture / Andrew F. Wood
Matthew J. Smith.
p. cm.
Includes bibliographical references and index.
ISBN 0-8058-3731-0 (pbk. : alk. paper)
1. Information technology--Social aspects. 2. Communication and technology. 3. Communication--Social aspects. 4. Internet--Social aspects. 5. Social interaction. I. Smith, Matthew J. II. Title.
HM851 .W66 2001
302.2--dc21

00-067730
CIP

Books published by Lawrence Erlbaum Associates are printed on acid-free paper, and their bindings are chosen for strength and durability.

Printed in the United States of America
10 9 8 7 6 5 4 3 2

For my wife and daughter,
Jenny and Vienna,
my family in the valley and over the Hill . . .

—Andy

---

For my wife, Susan, who teaches me about
communication every day
that we share our lives online and off.

—Matt

# Brief Contents

## Part I: The Internet as Social Technology



## Part II: The Self Among Others



## Part III: Internet Culture and Critique

# DETAILED CONTENTS

## Part III: Internet Culture and Critique

# PREFACE

When someone says, "I'm going online," where are they going? Early in the 21st century, when so much of the globe is mapped and so much geography charted, is there really a new place to be visited on the World Wide Web? We think so. Considering online communication as a metaphorical journey involves adopting many of the same words and images that we use in other excursions. We borrow ideas from our physical interactions to make sense of communication through computer networks. Using the Internet, we *send* mail, we *visit* libraries, we even *surf*. Yet, these words alone limit our understanding of online communication, so we must employ new ones. *Uploading, downloading, pinging, networking*—these relatively new words hint at a new world of human interaction that emerged with the popularization of the Internet. As you can guess, hundreds of books promise to make sense of this new world. The problem is that most of these books try to explore online communication as merely a site of new technologies. Few attempt the synthesis of technology, identity, and culture that we feel can place the Internet in human perspective. This book is our attempt to fill that void.

*Online Communication* aims to help you conceptualize the human uses of the Internet by examining the emerging theories that offer explanations for what people are doing with this technology, socially and communicatively. Now, for some people, *theory* is a dirty word. It suggests lofty and vague treatises, far beyond the grasp of the average person. Theory, however, has gotten a bad rap. When explained with accessible language and concrete examples, as we have tried to do here, theory helps us to see how processes tend to function in a variety of occurrences rather than in just one case. The value to using theory when approaching the Internet is this: Understanding how communication processes function in general will allow you to apply them to recognizing specific instances of these occurrences in your own life.

Over the last several years, a great deal has been written about the effects of computers on human communication. Journalists have made it the focus of their human interest stories, critics have cited it as the root cause of declines in society, and scholars have examined its effects on everything from the way we think to the way we relate to others. In order to establish some sense of coherence in addressing this body of information, we have organized this book into three general sections with 10 more specifically themed chapters. What follows, then, is a brief overview of those sections, chapters, and other key features you will encounter in reading *Online Communication*.

The first section of this book includes two chapters that serve as introductions to both the technologies of the Internet Age and their social implications. Beginning with chapter 1, we introduce computer-mediated communication (CMC) as a subject of academic research and a fascinating site where we may examine contemporary trends in society. We examine CMC as a blurring of two types of interaction, immediacy and mediation, in order to challenge the assumption that communication aided by computer networks is necessarily less personal and less powerful than traditional modes of human discourse. We then identify the technological and social features that distinguish five common forms of CMC: electronic mail (e-mail), bulletin boards systems (BBS), Internet relay chat (IRC), multi-user domains (MUDs), and the World Wide Web (WWW). We conclude this chapter with an in-depth examination of the dominant metaphor used in conjunction with the Internet, *cyberspace*, and we consider the origins and implications of this frequently invoked term.

In chapter 2, we focus our attention further on the technology of online communication, including a brief history of network computer technology as a social force. Starting with 19th-century thinking machines, we cover the modern evolution of cybernetic devices that influence our interaction with people and the environment. We provide specific insight on the Internet's evolution from a military command and control network to the Web as a kind of cybernetic organism. We then address the essential characteristics that distinguish the Internet from other interpersonal and mass communication contexts by reviewing five key features setting it apart: packet-switching, multimedia, interactivity, synchronicity, and hypertextuality.

The second major section of the book considers issues of online identity, taking into account how people construct presentations of self within a social environment. We begin with the construction of online identity in chapter 3. This chapter opens with a discussion of the phenomenon of telepresence, that is, the degree of realism one perceives through a given medium. We then turn to the role of theatrical metaphors in several scholarly studies of Internet usage and explain how qualities of role-taking and play are evident in online interactions. We also examine the degree to which online identities can be anonymous, and we raise warnings that the Information Age presents dangers to one's individual identity, online and in real life, in the forms of shadow identities and identity fraud, respectively.

Because personal identity affects interpersonal communication, we next turn to questions of establishing online relationships in chapter 4. Scholarly arguments contend that there are three distinct perspectives here: one that asserts CMC fosters an impersonal environment that is hostile to relationships; another that says CMC can sustain interpersonal relationships that are comparable to those negotiated face to face; and yet another that suggests CMC presents a hyperpersonal context where people uncomfortable or unsuccessful in other contexts can excel at relating. In addition to a variety of theories associated with each of these perspectives, we also deal with relationship issues such as the online conflicts known as *flame wars* and infidelity in the form of *cyberaffairs*.

Our consideration of identity continues in chapter 5, where we consider how people address their own well-being through computer-mediated channels. Herein, we consider the controversial concept of Internet Addiction Disorder, presenting the cases for and against the existence of this communication-based problem. Thereafter, we also discuss ways in which people seek the aid of others in various forms of online therapy, such as virtual support groups. Accordingly, we review the types of messages that people typically exchange in these venues and pause to consider the possible shortfalls of these mediated dialogues as well.

The last chapter in our section on creating the self among others, chapter 6, reflects on the growth of the social aggregate itself, the so-called virtual community. We examine several historical precedents for today's virtual communities, including the imagined communities created by the mass media and the fan communities. We define the virtual community in terms of essential qualities and examine what standards and sanctions are in place to regulate the social behavior of good Internet citizens, or *netizens*.

Our third and final section addresses issues of how the Internet has affected our culture and how people have responded to those changes with critiques. For example, in chapter 7, we turn to the corporate side of online communication and its impact on the information economy. Initially, we focus on the use of computer networks to enforce corporate discipline. We then turn our attention to methods in which corporations employ online communication to survey and influence the behaviors of consumers with techniques such as "cookies," voluntary data submission, and data mining. Along with discipline, we study the diffusion of innovation through computer technology in corporate environments, paying particular attention to the roles of interaction and diversity as factors that influence the pace of computer-mediated change at work. Finally, we evaluate the trend of corporate convergence and the creation of mega-media whose embrace of online communication promise to change fundamentally the ways we entertain and educate ourselves. We conclude this chapter with a study of how online-savvy corporations are redrawing the economic geography of the United States.

Chapter 8 addresses another question of culture shift, and the critiques that accompany it, when it examines the question of whether a digital divide exists beyond the media hype. We examine this divide along demographic dimensions such as gender, race, and class. We then turn to governmental and community-based efforts to close the digital divide, studying grass-roots efforts like NetDay and educational movements that strive to enhance information literacy alongside more traditional competencies. We also explore recent critiques of the digital divide as an artificial problem that obscures more significant concerns. We conclude with a reminder that the theorized gap between information haves and have-nots may be debatable in the United States, but this divide is undeniable around the world.

Chapter 9 offers a response to the argument that online communication merely provides another site where the same old powers-that-be exercise control over our lives. To explore this possibility, we discuss the notion of discursive resistance through which individuals and groups employ online communication to critique economic and social systems while proposing new ones. This notion challenges us to theorize cyber*space* as a site to challenge dominant *places* of power. Although we offer case studies of ways in which online communication provides disenfranchised folks a chance to gain a voice in public life, we also note the rise of Web-based hate groups who employ the same freedoms for more insidious goals.

Chapter 10 concludes the volume with a study of the ways in which popular culture artifacts such as books and films attempt to make sense of the increasing role computer technologies play in our lives. This analysis begins with the "cyberpunk" movement and its literary antecedents dating back to Mary Shelley's

*Frankenstein.* Studying cyberpunk, we reveal consistently appearing themes in literary evaluations of computer technology including fears that human beings may become obsolete in comparison with the machine. Turning to film, we see similar trends in movies ranging from Lang's (1926) *Metropolis* to the Wachowski brothers' (1999) *The Matrix.* Although books and films may not represent "high" culture, they do manage to provide powerful insight into the ways in which we struggle to make sense of online communication.

In addition to the contents of the chapters themselves, two special components of *Online Communication* merit special attention: "Hyperlinks" and "Online Communication and the Law." Throughout this text, you will find material that has been set apart from the text in a stylized box and labeled a "Hyperlink." If you are familiar with the Web, then you know that a hyperlink is a specially marked symbol (in the form of either words or images on the computer screen) that when clicked with a mouse will "jump" to another site on the Web. Clicking a hyperlink is like following a tangent, a line of thought that is related to, but somewhat "off course" from the direction of a conversation. As you will see, our Hyperlinks perform a similar function in that they present information and indicate topics related to, but not explored in as much depth as those themes addressed in each chapter. However, we hope you will find the insights presented in these asides will serve as bases for discussion in your classroom, around your dinner table, in a chat room, and wherever else you might find your own conversations "jumping," as it were, to online communication.

Along with Hyperlinks, we have placed a section entitled "Online Communication and the Law" at the conclusion of each chapter. Although this book is not geared for pre-law students, we have found that our attempt to provide a synthesis of technology, identity, and culture demanded some attention to the legal ramifications of the issues raised in this text. The belief by many Internet advocates that "information wants to be free"—illustrated by the fierce debate inspired by the Napster case—has met fierce response by artists seeking to protect their labor, corporations seeking to protect their profits, and parents seeking to protect their children. Similarly, the belief by many Internet observers that this medium should be regulated and taxed raises troubling questions: Who has the authority to monitor online content and seek revenue from Internet-based sales? The city, the state, the nation, or some other entity? Given that the Internet is not "based" in any locality, it is hard to imagine where it may be defined as a legal entity. These are good times to be an Internet lawyer! Thus, we tackle thorny legal issues that emerge from our chapters' topics such as one's right to "flame" other Internet users, a company's obligation to make online services available to the disabled, and the legal definition of "Internet time." If any of these topics seem entirely new to you, don't worry. They won't be for long. Ideally, the introduction of these special sections—Hyperlinks and Online Communication and the Law—will provoke some stimulating conversations among your colleagues.

## ACKNOWLEDGMENTS

In getting to the point where we could share our perspective of this material, we had considerable help along the way. First, we would like to thank our respective universities, San José State University and Indiana University South Bend, as well as our colleagues at each institution for their support while we were drafting this text, including secretarial support from Cookie Galvan and Patricia Loredo. Second, we are grateful to several anonymous reviewers and John T. Morrison of Rollins College whose insights helped us to refine our prose. Third, we owe our gratitude to our editor, Linda Bathgate, and the staff of Lawrence Erlbaum Associates for their confidence in this project. Fourth, we want to acknowledge the faculty of our alma mater, Ohio University, who helped encourage our scholarly efforts by guiding, challenging, and mentoring us through many intellectual, personal, and professional obstacles. Finally, we thank our students—particularly the participants in a San José State University summer course and Alex Kramer, Stephanie Flaharty, Toni Adams, and Megan Malugani who offered critical advice to draft versions of this book. Our students guide us and inspire us to try great things. We hope this volume does the same for them.

*—Andy and Matt*

# PART I

# THE INTERNET AS SOCIAL TECHNOLOGY

The growing impact that the Internet has on our lives is increasingly difficult to ignore. Even those who might claim to be "computer illiterate" are likely to encounter the direct or indirect effects that the Internet has had on the society in which we live. For example, pick up *The Wall Street Journal* and you are likely to see that the stock market has risen or fallen in correspondence with the successes and failures of Internet-based companies. Begin a term project by doing some research, and you are likely to find that the campus library has all but abandoned card catalogues in favor of a quicker, more space-efficient electronic system, one that is probably accessible from your dorm room or home. Turn to your classmates and ask if they or someone they know has ever made a friend or a date of someone who they met online, and they will probably cite an acquaintance or two. Without having to look much farther than the world around you, you are likely to find the ever-increasing influence of the Internet in the realms of economics, academics, and personal relationships, among many others.

Despite its pervasiveness in our lives, however, how much do you really understand the Internet? Here, we are not asking about your knowledge of the programming languages and hardware configurations that make the Internet function. Our colleagues in computer science best explain those technical matters. Rather, we are asking about your understanding of the human uses (and misuses) of that technology in social terms. This first part of the book provides some insights for addressing this question. In the next two chapters, you will read about the social character of the Internet, that is, how people have conceptualized and used the various Internet technologies in accord with or in consideration of one another. The communicative, historical, and linguistic concepts that we introduce in this part of the book form a foundation for the discussions we build on in subsequent chapters. Furthermore, they testify to the growing breadth and depth of the technology's effects on human thought and action.

# CHAPTER 1

# USING TECHNOLOGY TO COMMUNICATE IN NEW WAYS

*The Internet is like a giant jellyfish. You can't step on it. You can't go around it. You've got to get through it.*

—*John Evans (Borenstein, 2000)*

At the heart of this book rests a basic assumption: Communicating in computer-mediated contexts is somehow different than any other form of communication. Software engineer Ellen Ullman (1996) describes encounters in which these differences have been made apparent to her. She regularly communicates with her fellow computer programmers and her supervisors through her computer. Over the years, she reports that she has acclimated to the shortness and arrogance that many of her colleagues seem to convey in their correspondence. Such behavior is, of course, not restricted to online interaction. However, what has struck Ullman more are the contrasts she has noted between mediated and face-to-face interactions with her co-workers. Two examples illustrate Ullman's keen perceptions.

On one occasion, Ullman found herself up one night and decided to send a message to a colleague. He happened to be awake as well and after reading her message wrote back to inquire why she was up so late. The two exchanged cordial messages that night, and yet the next day when they attended a corporate meeting together, Ullman was unsure about how to approach him. They had, after all, been friendly with one another just hours before, and yet in the office setting, she questioned, "in what way am I permitted to *know* him? And which set of us is the more real: the sleepless ones online, or these bodies in the daylight?" (p. 6).

On another occasion, Ullman had struck up a romantic relationship with a fellow programmer. For quite a while, the two communicated exclusively through exchanges of electronic mail (e-mail). He would send her a message, she would reply, and so forth. This continued on with increasing frequency, until they were writing to one another almost every waking hour. Eventually, the couple decided to meet for dinner, and when they did, Ullman noticed something unusual about their conversation. "One talks, stops; then the other replies, stops. An hour later, we are still in this rhythm. With a shock, I realize that we have finally gone out to dinner only to *exchange e-mail*" (p. 17).

The questions and patterns that Ullman developed as a practitioner of computer-mediated communication (CMC) did not fully emerge until she saw the assumptions of one form of interaction contrasted with another. What she had learned to accept as norms in the world of computer-mediation seemed odd, uncomfortable to her in real life. Some people report a similar feeling of dissonance when working in just the opposite manner, coming from the familiar practices of face-to-face interaction to the subtle distinctions associated with CMC. Either way, people like Ullman, and perhaps you, are aware that some things about the online experience are different.

In this chapter, we examine CMC to understand the experience of online interaction. Naturally, this requires an overview of just what CMC is, and how it fits within the field of communication studies and popular culture. Following this discussion, we examine CMC as a blurring between immediate and mediated communication. As is seen here, this process of blurring holds important implications for our conceptions of self and society. The question remains, however: How do we communicate differently in this medium than through other traditional modes of interaction? Answering that, we explore popular components of online communication, including e-mail, bulletin board systems (BBS), internet relay chat (IRC), multiuser domains (MUDs), and the World Wide Web (WWW). The third major section of this chapter introduces the study of cyberspace as a metaphoric means to understanding CMC. To that end, we explore the meaning of the word and the location of the *cyberspace* experience before extending our study to the alternative metaphors for our online interactions. We conclude with a reminder that dominant spatial metaphors for CMC may limit our understanding of this environment.

## WHAT IS COMPUTER-MEDIATED COMMUNICATION?

In this section, we begin to explore CMC as an integration of computer technology with our everyday lives. We define computer-mediated communication as the study of how human behaviors are maintained or altered by exchange of information through machines. How do we study this process? By pulling on the insights of a variety of researchers and commentators. In the field of communication studies, most scholars avoid setting up disciplinary boundaries so rigid that we miss out on fascinating human phenomena simply because they don't "fit" artificial boundaries. We do not want to neglect the contributions allied fields like psychology, sociology, and composition studies (to name but a few) have to offer. Even within an area of research as specific as CMC, we must not lose sight of how this mode of human interaction affects so many parts of our lives as to be almost ever present. Nonetheless, it is all too easy for us to blur the distinction between our chosen focus of study and the larger forces of technology shaping our lives. Doing so, we risk making this text an unmanageable mess. For the sake of simplicity, therefore, we propose that our study is limited to the analysis of those technologies that serve more or less directly to mediate intentional human communication.

Here's an example: Although nuclear power plants—each with many computer processors and terminals—remain a significant component to the U.S. energy system, these sites would not play a significant role in the study of CMC. We talk about nuclear power plants—their potentials and their threats—but we seldom talk though them. The presence of computer technology, therefore, does not constitute the only required component for our analysis. We choose, instead, to focus on those technologies that help individuals and groups relate one to another in some fashion, for good or for ill.

As you might guess, the primary focus of our work is the Internet—that network of networks. Although we learn more about the Internet later in this chapter, it is important to know at this point a key distinction we make between the chips and channels that comprise this medium. Although the architecture of computer devices that aid the transmission of digitized information around the world is itself a fascinating topic, such an inquiry is beyond the scope of this book. Rather, we have chosen to focus on the channels of communication made possible by the Internet, on what has been called the "space within [the] lines" where human beings exert individual will, conduct business, and form communities. In this way, the emergence of telephony in the 19th century seems quite analogous to our study of contemporary computer technologies. The principle of mediated discourse—whether mainly by way of telephone or through the more sophisticated technologies of today's desktop computers—inspires careful examination because of its potential to alter human interaction without the need for physical presence.

## WHY STUDY CMC?

Certainly the student of communication can find plenty of other phenomena to explore, such as small-group interaction, corporate culture building, and health care discourse. However, we focus on CMC because of its impact on all of those contexts. Many student "study teams" find online chat rooms to be more convenient than face-to-face interaction. Many corporate offices streamline internal communication with e-mail. Many patients use the Web to inform themselves about their medical options. In each case, the introduction of online media changes day-to-day life and alters, to some degree, how we relate to each other.

We approach these topics with a desire to understand the blurring of technology with our everyday lives. We study the sophisticated ways in which computer technology—the microchips that process information and execute commands and the software that allows human beings to employ this technology—is integrated into our physical environments, interpersonal relationships, and even senses of personal identity. Although technology has always played a role in social life, the power of computer technology offers a new dimension to this theme. Where computing devices were once rare, expensive, and so complicated as to require expert attention at all times, the computers we use are more subtly embedded in our lives. Our use of telephones, cars, microwave ovens, and even clothing increasingly requires some use of computer technology. Thus, when we study CMC, we don't just explore the use of technology in communication; we study the blurring of technology with our everyday lives.

Thus far, we have identified CMC as the study of how human behaviors are maintained or altered through exchange of information through machines, and we have positioned CMC research within the realm of communication studies. Our next step is to examine a key component of communicating online, the distinction between immediacy and mediation. As we discover, computer-mediated interaction increasingly appears to blur any distinction between these terms.

## IMMEDIACY VERSUS MEDIATION

Think back to Ullman's narratives. She felt tension regarding a colleague with whom she had communicated all night through the Internet. She felt connected, close to her co-worker. But when they met the next day, neither had a framework to orient their face-to-face relationship with their online one. One reason to explain this conundrum is the blurring of immediate and mediated communication they experienced. In this section, we explore these terms more closely before discussing their impact on society, self, and reality.

**Immediate communication** refers to a process where messages are transmitted more or less directly, without the aid of exterior technology. **Mediated communication** separates the communicators through some technology—from the simplest types like paper to the most sophisticated kind of computer device like a wireless Web unit. When you stop by your professor's office to ask a question and he or she answers you, you both are engaging in immediate communication. When you send your professor an e-mail and he or she responds, even within a few seconds, you both are experiencing mediated communication. After all, regardless of how quickly the interaction takes place, this communication could not occur without the mediation of some technology. The proliferation of mediating technologies raises the question: What kind of academic community emerges if most of your interactions with colleagues and professors are mediated in some way? On a larger level, what kind of culture arises from a mediated society?

### Mediated Society

History records many critics who feared that too much mediation, either through bureaucracy or technology (or both) would lead to social collapse. Think back to stories you might have heard of Greek philosophers pleading their cases before tribunals of their peers. One such man, Socrates, stood in a court of law. He was said to be 70 years old, a gadfly who taught the young to disobey their elders and question the social norms of his day. He spoke without notes or script. There was no mechanical device to record his words. Like his student, Plato, Socrates would argue that ideas hewn from truth should be spoken simply and not mediated by devices, whether they are mechanical ones or rhetorical ones (Stone, 1988).

After the death of Socrates, forced to commit suicide after being judged guilty in the Athenian court, Plato would go on to argue that even the art of writing should be feared, lest his society lose the power of memory to store culture. Plato argued that words mediated by the technology of writing could be used to deceive masses of people. The democratic nature of ideas fixed onto paper that could be freely interchanged would, he feared, replace the careful and wise debate that he felt was so lacking in the trial of Socrates.

Plato believed that the true self could not be defined by text. A person must speak his or her mind directly to confront the problems of society and maintain one's personal ideals. And yet, today, we are surrounded by devices designed to capture, compose, and alter our words and, by extension, ourselves. Some theorists suggest that ours is an age of over-saturation, that our machines and media have begun to overwhelm us with too many choices. Kenneth Gergen (1991) described the resulting impact as **multiphrenia**—the experience in which our identities are defined and shaped by too many choices of self-expression. We turn, therefore, to the role of self in an increasingly mediated society.

## Mediated Self

The mediated self constructs a sense of "who I am" through interaction with others through various media. In an oral culture, a person speaks and is judged according to that speech. His or her narrative is communicated without mediation. Community members don't need to sift through layer after layer of image and artifice to get a sense of the speaker. Compare this immediate culture to a mediated one such as that experienced in contemporary America. A speaker, such as a political candidate, is mediated by almost countless technologies such as edited speeches, camera shots, and Web sites. Every technology communicates a slightly different version of the political candidate so that, after a while, it's hard to discern whether a real person resides underneath the political spin. To illustrate the power of mediated communication in a comical sense, we recall a 1970s *Doonesbury* comic in which a character asked a political figure, "If we turned off the cameras, would you cease to exist?" In the shift from voice to text, from human to machine as mediator of our ideas, we face remarkable new challenges. The most important challenge, in a world in which more and more of our messages are mediated, is to sustain a coherent sense of personal identity.

How did this explosion of mediated selves began? In exploring this question, we delve deeper into the implications of using technological innovation as the sole force that drives and shapes human communities. With the emergence of writing, immediacy became no longer necessary for discourse. In other words, a person's presence was not necessary in order to feel a person's influence. One could inflict a law or tax or faith-justified expectation without the requirement of physical presence. As handwriting became supplanted by machine writing, when moveable type replaced hand-copying of words, it became even easier to manufacture and mass produce words that simulated ideas, that themselves simulated human interaction. For monks and visionaries, the written word could unite isolated peoples into global faith or political organization.

Consider the example of the *Declaration of Independence*. Here, we see a text used as a distance weapon against a king. You might imagine the power of that document from the stirring speeches delivered before its completion during those sweltering summer days in 1776 Philadelphia. Surely those ideas uttered by visionaries such as Benjamin Franklin, John Adams, and Thomas Jefferson propelled a nascent nation to war with a global power, Great Britain. Yet, for the majority of revolutionaries, the message embodied by that declaration was delivered in paper form, or read second-hand. Yet, across the vast distances of the colonies from Maine to Georgia, an army was raised and a superior force defeated. Clearly, the technology of writing served to mediate that message in ways that would have been feared by Socrates and Plato. No longer would men and women of intellect debate face to face. Aided by technology and its power to mediate human experience, individuals would form nations and overthrow tyrants without ever seeing one another in person. Somewhere beyond those human constructions lies "reality," untouched by human will. But in an increasingly mediated world, even reality becomes subject to manipulation.

## Mediated Reality

Beyond our sense of self and society, mediated communication even affects our perception of the world around us. In *Orality and Literacy*, Walter J. Ong (1982) argues that the technologies of communication influence our thought processes and, by extension, our cultures. In making his case, Ong concentrates on the influence of one of the earliest technologies of communication—writing. He notes that cultures without writing systems privilege the sense of hearing as a tool for interpreting reality. Knowledge within these cultures is community-based and people tend to construct their identities in relation to the community, dependent as they are on contact with each other for information. In contrast, print cultures encourage more individuality and less connectiveness to the community among their participants. Literacy led to people looking for information in the relatively isolated exercise of reading rather than through face-to-face interaction. The dominant sense in literate cultures, as you might imagine, is sight, not hearing. However, the proliferation of electronic media in the twentieth century heralded a turn in Ong's estimation. Radio and even television favor the sense of hearing over sight.

Ong calls this turn **secondary orality**—a shift in the way we perceive reality that evokes a more communal culture. The work of another noted scholar, Marshall McLuhan (1964), concurs with Ong's. McLuhan saw the same trend toward what he called a "global village," consisting of people who shared common experiences through mediated messages rather than immediate interaction. We can look to how people turned to electronic media during events such as the assassination of President John F. Kennedy, the explosion of the space shuttle Challenger, and the death of Princess Diana for examples of how we were able to share events collectively rather than individually. Mediated through this secondary orality, these events evoke a sense of connected culture, even as they shape our perception of each tragedy as somehow connected to our lives. In a mediated world that has the power to appear immediate, "you are there."

So far, we've identified CMC as a means to understand human interaction through mediating technologies, and we have examined the blurring of immediacy and mediation as powerful influences on society, self, and reality. We've approached these dimensions from an historical overview to argue that today's debates about the implications e-mail, virtual reality, and the Internet are hardly new—As long as humans have used technology to relate to each other, essential questions of self and truth have emerged.

Tom Standage's (1998) book, *The Victorian Internet*, illustrates that advances in communication—the Internet in the 20th century, the telegraph in the 19th, for example—tend to provoke similar questions among us. Indeed, although the devices are different, the question has largely been the same since the days of Socrates. Shall our ideas lose their fidelity—their apparent truth as perceived by others—when communication becomes more and more mediated by technology? Can text and image serve with spoken words toward the goal of identification and human community? Or, perhaps, do these simulations of human interaction deprive us of some key part of ourselves? Consider these questions as we explore corporate, therapeutic, and alternative uses of CMC throughout the book. In chapter 2, we go beyond immediacy and mediation to explore other characteristics of online communication. But, we now shift our emphasis toward an overview of the various technologies through which we communicate online.

## HOW DO WE COMMUNICATE THROUGH CMC?

What constitutes interaction on the Internet today is not the same as what it was a decade ago. In fact, people are always finding new ways to use the communication media around them. It was not so long ago that people thought of the telephone as a technology used exclusively for the exchange of oral symbols. You would dial the number of a person or business across the country and expect to talk to a person on the other end of the line. If, however, the topic of your conversation involved discussing anything printed, such as a legal contract, you would have to wait until it arrived through traditional mail-handling services. However, the proliferation of the facsimile machine (fax) throughout the 1970s and 1980s (Walker, Tames, Man, & Freeman, 1996) allowed people to transmit written materials and even images over the same telephone lines they used for speaking (albeit they would not allow you to speak and send a fax at the same time). The fax machine changed our thinking about telephony as a technology for more than just vocal presentation. Now we also know it as a tool for communicating documents—and even electronic signatures—as well.

The Internet has had a similar history. At one time, interaction over it was largely limited to text-based exchanges. E-mail, BBS, MUDs, and IRCs are forms for the exchange of textual messages. The use of words alone is still a popular means of online communication, but now people can also share images and sounds through their computers as well. The innovations brought by the introduction of the World Wide Web over the last decade has broadened the sensory data that people can share over the Internet. Scholars have examined communication in each of these five forms of CMC.

### Electronic Mail

E-mail is perhaps the most popular and familiar channel for communicating through the Internet. Like its ancestor, the much slower paper-based "snail-mail" routed through traditional postal means, e-mail involves the exchange of textual messages between two or more parties. Unlike its ancestor, e-mail arrives much more quickly and seems to express meaning in a notably variant fashion.

Judith Yaross Lee (1996) explains that people approach e-mail as a "hybrid medium," uniting rhetorical elements of both spoken and written communication. This results in a form of communication "between the telephone and the letter" (p. 277). The practice of writing e-mail eschews the formality of traditional text. In this regard, e-mail is like the telephone in that there is a quality of orality, of transcribing the message as though one were uttering it from one's lips. And yet e-mail is obviously like the letter because of the dominance of type in its presentation. Consider, for instance, the informal text of the following:

```
Bruce:
How about February 19? That's a Saturday. Unless you're
planning to visit Susan, we could get together, have
lunch, see your apartment, show me the wilds of Gotham,
etc.
MK
```

As you can see, the person who **posted**, or sent, this message wrote in a fashion that was far more conversational than the conventions of formal letter writing would dictate (i.e., a formal salutation like Dear Mr. Esposito). Through their practice, people have made the writing of e-mail a less formal, albeit no less textual, mode for communication.

## HYPERLINK: CHAIN MAIL AND THE PROLIFERATION OF INTERNET HOAXES

> I'm an attorney, and I know the law. This thing is for real. Rest assured AOL and Intel will follow through with their promises for fear of facing an multimillion dollar class action suit similar to the one filed by PepsiCo against General Electric not too long ago. I'll be damned if we're all going to help them out with their e-mail beta test without getting a little something for our time. . . .
>
> For every person that you forward this e-mail to, Microsoft will pay you $203.15, for every person that you sent it to that forwards it on, Microsoft will pay you $156.29 and for every third person that receives it, you will be paid $17.65 . . .

Perhaps you have received a solicitation like this yourself from a family member, friend, or colleague. Whether it's getting money from Microsoft or free computers from IBM, e-mail chain letters promise their recipients riches and good fortune just for doing what they might be in the process of doing anyway: sending along more mail. Unfortunately, messages such as these are all-too-often hoaxes (Emery, 1999).

Electronic chain letters are fascinating rhetorical documents whose credibility is largely reliant on the number of "forwards" they have enjoyed rather than the quality of arguments they offer. Some of the claims, such as the one that says Microsoft will give you money just for forwarding an e-mail message, may seem more credible to someone who regularly uses e-mail than they would to an outside observer. It is, after all, difficult to argue with dozens (if not hundreds) of people, some of whom you know, who are willing to take the chance that the claims just might not be false and have already forwarded the message.

Electronic chain letters might also owe their popularity to another aspect of the technology. Unlike their paper-bound predecessors, electronic chain letters are much easier to forward. With a few clicks of your keyboard, dozens of acquaintances can receive the same promising news without the unnecessary hassles of photocopying the message and paying postage to mail it. However easy it might be to forward such messages, it is unlikely that person-to-person e-mail will ever catch on as a valued (and hence financially rewarding) marketing tool. As the wise have often counseled: Any promises that seem too good to be true, probably are.

## Bulletin Board Systems

A variant of e-mail called a bulletin board system (BBS) is also a form for text-based communication, but distinguished by the size of the audience it attempts to reach and the technological manner in which messages are read. In a BBS, individual contributors send messages to a single computer address. The program then posts these individual messages that visitors can access and read at their discretion. In this manner, a BBS functions like the kiosks or wall-mounted boards you see around your college campus covered with public announcements for fraternal rushes and credit card offers. Unlike these cluttered presentations, however, a BBS organizes incoming materials so that subsequent messages responding to previous messages are ordered one right after another. Such an aggregate is called a **thread** and each can continue to extend for as long as contributors continue to send in submissions. Interestingly, these threads practice a type of hypertext in that contributions layer on and reflect back on one another.

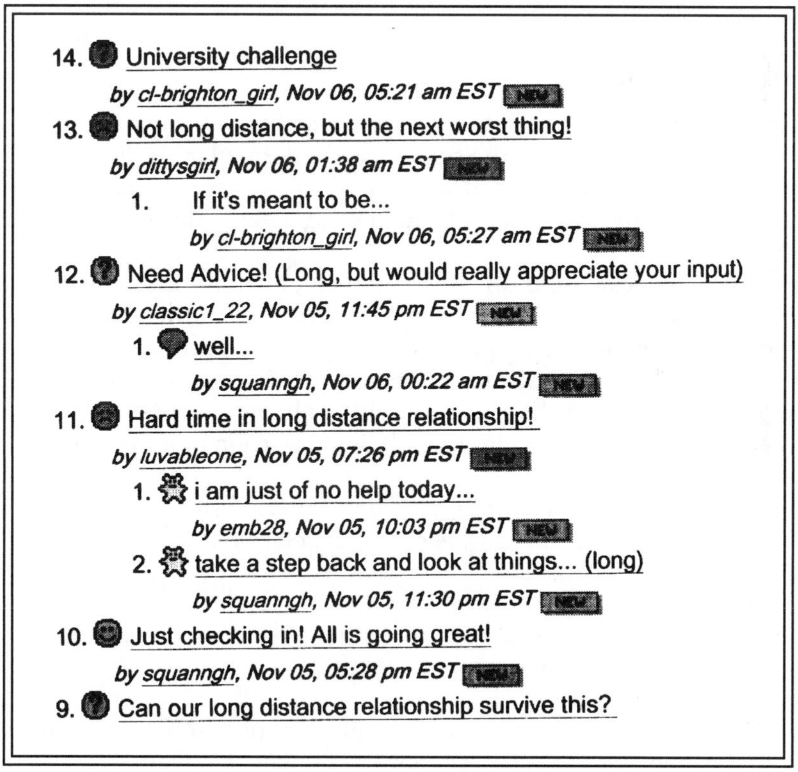


Fig. 1.1. A typical newsgroup screen capture.

Most BBS are organized around a topic of special interest, ranging from the practical (e.g., sci.electronics) to the entertaining (e.g., rec.humor). Such special interest groups are called **newsgroups**, and people participating in them have developed a flow for interaction therein. Nancy K. Baym (1997) reports that contributors to rec.arts.tv.soaps are among those BBS groups that keep streams of conversation going by adapting to the technology. In responding to a previously posted message, the custom of cutting and pasting the relevant parts of that message as a point of departure of one's own has arisen. This is not, however, merely a mechanical response. Baym notes that the comments are cut to minimal length, suggesting that people are aware of the expectation that they will cite the ideas of others but that they will do so with brevity.

Another text-based form, the listserv, communicates with a wider audience, just as a BBS does. A **listserv** is a service one registers for in which messages sent to a central e-mail address are forwarded directly to subscribers. Unlike the BBS, then, messages are not stored in a central archive awaiting the individual to access it, but routed by a computer to each individual subscriber's mailbox. A number of organizations are experimenting with listservs and offer to send periodic newsletters to your e-mail address announcing their products and services. You may have even had a course in which the instructor used a listserv for messages to be exchanged among all the members of your class. As such examples illustrate, a key distinction between the BBS/listserv and e-mail, then, is that these messages are written as a public rather than personal address.

## Internet Relay Chat

Unlike e-mail or a newsgroup, IRC occurs in real time. Like a newsgroup, IRCs are often thematic, addressing the concerns of a particular audience. For instance, iVillage.com, a Web site directed at women, features chat programs for issues such as parenting, beauty, and career, to name but a few. Similar chat rooms exist throughout the Internet.

Although people can "pair off" and conduct a turn-by-turn conversation using chat programs, some of the most popular forums for chatting, including those on iVillage.com, are frequented by groups of people who participate in the conversation at the same time. Because most systems post comments in the order in which they are received, a given discussion might get buried amidst the stream of contributions being offered. Consider the following portion of an IRC log:

> **Goldbricker:** Well, SoSon, what's the solution?
> **fieldmaus:** What's "bolderdash" really mean?
> **sheri22:** I think JimmEE comment was out of line. How would he feel if I said that to him?
> **SoSon:** I think we should try to concentrate more on education and less on punishment.

In typical conversation, one would expect "SoSon" to have the next turn and be able to reply to "Goldbricker's" inquiry. However, because the system posts contributions in the order in which they arrive, by the time SoSon begins to write a reply, other contributors have already sent their messages.

Susan Herring (1999) cites that these violations of traditional turn-taking behaviors create a lack of conversation coherence. Yet, despite the seeming confusion that comes with chatting, it continues to be popular. Why? Herring suggests that participants in these forums have found the heightened interactivity and play of language particularly attractive. And in order to cope with the potential incoherence of the numerous exchanges, they have adapted to the situation, developing new communication strategies. For instance, although the conversational overlap in the previous example would be ill-suited to effective communication if everyone in the same physical space were attempting to talk at the same time, overlap seems to work in the typewritten environment. Because it takes less time to read than to type, overlap is actually a very efficient strategy. If everyone had to wait on each person to type a response, people would spend a lot more time than is apparently necessary in developing their online conversations. Moreover, despite the influx of multiple messages, people seem to be able to keep track of their particular thread in the conversation because of the textual record that is preserved as contribution after contribution is displayed on the screen.

## Multiuser Domains

Another form of synchronous, text-based interaction occurs in a MUD. Originally called multiuser dungeons because they were inspired by the fantasy role-playing game "Dungeons and Dragons," MUDs have inspired a plethora of acronyms, each suggesting some specialized quality of its approach to the concept. These include MUDs object-oriented (MOO), multiuser shared hallucination (MUSH), and multiuser character kingdom (MUCK), among others. What is common among all these permutations is that they are efforts toward text-based virtual realities in which participants interact with an environment, objects, and other participants. Constructed of nothing more than the words on the computer screen and the user's imagination, everything about a MUD is invented, although it is all rule-governed by the administering program. Nonetheless, participants enjoy a great deal of freedom in adopting roles, in indicating movement through the virtual environment that they read about on the screen, and conversing with their fellow participants in a MUD.

The experience of MUDding could look something like the following. Imagine you are seated at your computer screen and at the ">" prompt, you type in various commands:

```
>look
Hallway
There are stairs leading upward to the east. There is
an unmarked door to the west.
>east
A large ballroom is at the top of these stairs. A crys-
tal chandelier hangs from the ceiling and Gershwin
tunes are playing from an old phonograph in the cor-
ner.
Gumba is here.
>say hello Gumba
You say "hello Gumba"
Gumba says "welcome to my party"
```

Although they certainly might sound like nothing more than a video game with words instead of pictures, Pavel Curtis (1997) argues that the virtual reality of MUDs are social phenomena. Accordingly, he identifies three factors that distinguish MUDs from other simulations:

1. MUDs do not have a predetermined end goal. MUDs are ongoing adventures unlike video games that have a final level to be achieved.
2. MUDs allow users to add to the richness of the environment by contributing new spaces and objects that become an ongoing part of the administrating program.
3. MUDs typically have more than one user connected at any given time, all of whom are communicating in real time.

These factors contribute to a virtual environment in which people construct identities, relationships, and whole worlds using text. For these reasons, a number of researchers have investigated MUDs. The results of much of that information are presented in chapters of this book dealing with identity, relationships, and community.

## World Wide Web

The World Wide Web, often referred to as simply "the Web" or abbreviated WWW, is increasingly becoming a **portal** to the other forms of CMC. That is, people begin their Internet excursions to pick up mail from their e-mail accounts, check out the latest newsgroup messages, or meet some friends in a chat room through the Web. This experience begins when they launch their **browser**, a program that downloads instructions taken from the Internet and displays them on their desktop computer as text, images, animation, and sounds. Mosaic was the first widely available browser, although today Netscape Navigator and Microsoft Explorer command a majority of this software market. Perhaps because it is a much more graphical interface, people have lately been turning to this form of CMC as a way into the other, more text-based forms.

Like the other forms discussed thus far, the Web also possesses communicative properties based on its technological abilities and the social practices that have emerged through the use of it. One of the rhetorical effects of the Web has been the ways in which the globally accessible messages posted to it address particular audiences. Ananda Mitra (1997) found that the choice of words and the use of imagery on a Web site indicated whether it was aimed at an ingroup audience of like-minded individuals or an outgroup audience of people unfamiliar with one's culture or ideas. In his review of sites related to the nation of India, Mitra noted that the Web designers were careful to use the multimedia cues available to them in order to distinguish which audience they were attempting to communicate with, an ingroup of Indian nationals or an outgroup of international visitors. For example, a page that prominently features a map of India is directed to an outgroup audience, one that would not be as familiar with the geographically inspired icon as an Indian would. As Mitra notes, designers use a number of the Web's technological features, including formatting, language, multimedia, and hypertext, to make the distinction to an intended audience.

As can be seen from this brief review, each of the forms of CMC in this section exhibit not only functional differences based on their technological properties, but also communicative differences based on their social applications. Regardless of the distinct forms CMC may take, there are qualities of online interaction that are hauntingly familiar and yet notably different than other contexts. Although we more fully explore these similarities and differences in the coming chapters, we turn now to attempts to make sense of the context through language, for it is in articulating how people talk about the Internet that we may begin to better understand its effects.

## HYPERLINK: COMPUTER ANXIETY

If you were fortunate enough to grow up with a computer in your home or in your school, you probably don't give much thought to the intimidation those who are less familiar with the technology might feel. Yet, before they can ever experience the Internet, many people must first deal with feelings of apprehension. Communication scholars have studied apprehension, the fear or anxiety about real or anticipated interactions, in many contexts, most notably as it is experienced by public speakers (McCroskey, 1978). However, the same sensations that accompany "stage fright" in the public context can occur to someone anticipating the computer-mediated context as well, resulting in what is commonly known as **computer anxiety**. In fact, as many as 55% of Americans may suffer some degree of computer anxiety (cited in Williams, 1994).

Computer anxiety may manifest itself in a number of ways. According to Larry D. Rosen, Deborah C. Sears, and Michelle M. Weil (1987), a team of researchers who have investigated ways to measure and counter computer anxiety, three manifestations are possible. Those who possess some apprehension about computers "may display anxiety about computers, may have negative attitudes about computers, or may engage in disabling self-critical dialogues when interacting with computers" (p. 177). You may know different people who actively avoid new technologies, criticize them, or express doubts about their own competence when confronted with them: "I just don't understand computers."

Craig R. Scott and Steven C. Rockwell (1997) found that there was a remedy for those coping with computer anxiety. In a study that examined the relationship among communication apprehension, writing apprehension, and computer anxiety, they found that experience was a strong predicator of future technology use. In other words, the more experience people had with the technology, the less apprehensive they felt about using it. In learning to communicate successfully with others using the Internet, then, it is important for those of us with an interest in CMC to understand that people who are ill at ease with technology require our patience and guidance in coming online. Helping them to acquire the skills necessary to operate technology is a first step in extending the communicative potential of the computer to others.

In this section, we have outlined five commonly employed tools to mediate our communication: e-mail, bulletin boards systems, Internet relay chat, multiuser domains, and the World Wide Web. We conclude this chapter with an analysis of another kind of mediation—the use of language and, specifically, metaphor to intercede between ourselves and the machines we use.

## COMPREHENDING THE INTERNET THROUGH LANGUAGE

According to the Judeo-Christian tradition, the first project God assigns to mortals is to name things:

> And out of the ground the Lord God formed every beast of the field, and every fowl of the air; and brought them unto Adam to see what he would call them: and whatsoever Adam called every living creature, that was the name thereof. (Genesis 2:19)

Ever since that divine commission, humankind has been about the business of naming. It is through naming, or more broadly taken, language, that humanity has been able to explain the mundane elements of the world around us (e.g., *cattle, water, underwear*) and to make some sense of the intangible world of constructs that allow us express our spiritual and social beliefs (i.e., *peace, justice, equity*). Language grants us a certain degree of control over the phenomena of experience, for at the very least language allows us to identify what some thing is.

When encountering anything for which we do not already have a term, we will turn to metaphor in order to draw a comparison between the new phenomenon and a familiar thing. Just consider how children go about explaining experiences in their lives by pulling on the resources of their limited vocabularies when they do not yet have a more defining term. In such cases, a small child might laugh and call for the attention of a "funny face" not yet possessing the vocabulary to label someone a "clown."

In like manner, adults, trying to make sense of the many new technologies of the last century have often turned to metaphor to make sense of the often fantastic inventions they have encountered. As you've probably seen in period films or cartoons, people at the turn of the 20th century used the phrase "horseless carriage" to describe the automobile. A carriage was a familiar mode for transportation and referencing it as a means for explaining the automobile helped people explain the function and composition of the machine. More recently, people have used metaphor to describe computer technology as well. Microsoft chose to label their operating system "windows" in part because the boxes it projected on one's computer screen looked a bit like the rectangular structures on most homes. Perhaps more important than the visual analogy, however, was the fact that "windows" were familiar, unthreatening objects in most people's experience.

As just noted, language allows us to grasp the tangible and the intangible. In attempting to explain the complexities of online interaction, language has again relied on metaphor to make sense of the Internet. A good number of these metaphors have attempted to relate the ethereal qualities of the Internet to more grounded concepts of space. Of the terms bandied about in the last decade or so, none exhibits this quality better than that of *cyberspace*. As discussed in the following sections, coming to an understanding of how to think about electronic forum for interaction and how to express our experiences within them is influenced by our choice of metaphor.

## DEFINING CYBERSPACE

You are likely to have heard the term *cyberspace* used in conjunction with the Internet. However, despite its popularity among media reports and marketers, just where this term comes from and what it means is less commonly known. The *cyber* in *cyberspace* comes from the Greek for "steersman" (*kubernetes*) and carries with it the connotation of control. In desiring to communicate that same sense of control, Norbert Weiner (1954) established the precedent of making *cyber* a prefix when he first adopted it to christen a field of study he called "cybernetics"—the science of automatic control systems. **Cybernetics** concerns itself with the quality of controlled feedback in systems like machines (such as when your automobile's dash board indicates a low fuel tank) and societies (such as when a family must compensate for a member's death). We learn more about the role of cybernetics in the history of communication technology in chapter 2.

For now, it is important to recall that William Gibson (1984) borrowed from Wiener when he coined the word, *cyberspace*. In his science fiction novel *Neuromancer*, Gibson defined *cyberspace* in the following manner:

> Cyberspace. A consensual hallucination experienced daily by billions of legitimate operators, in every nation, by children being taught mathematical concepts. . . . A graphic representation of data abstracted from the banks of every computer in the human system. Unthinkable complexity. Lines of light ranged in the nonspace of the mind, clusters and constellations of data. Like city lights, receding. (p. 51)

Interestingly, Gibson was writing a prophetic description of what the Internet might be like almost a decade before the introduction of the technology that would make any truly "graphic representation" of the World Wide Web possible. According to a later interview, Gibson's inspiration for cyberspace came after witnessing children playing with video games. "These kids clearly *believed* in the space games projected," he said, noting that they seemed "to develop a belief that there's some kind of *actual space* behind the screen, someplace you can't see but you know is there" (cited in McCaffery, 1992, p. 272).

Gibson's term seemed to catch on once people began to note the similarities between Gibson's imaginary plane and what can be experienced in various online interactions. Ever since, people have used it to describe "where" online interaction seems to occur. In due course it has contributed a new affix to the English language, allowing its practitioners to indicate computer mediation in everything from *cyberlaw* to *cybersex*.

### Finding Cyberspace

Of where the phrase *cyberspace* comes from is far easier to define than what cyberspace is. One possibility is that cyberspace is merely the "consensual hallucination" that Gibson first dubbed it. Indeed, some have compared cyberspace to the nonlinear reality of mind-altering drugs (Bromberg, 1996), whereas others have concluded that cyberspace takes the mind to the next level of human consciousness (Rushkoff, 1994). However, such hallucinatory analogies carry with them the implication of an apparition without substance or effect. Such imagery belies the impact that electronic encounters have on people beyond cyberspace. Shawn P. Wilbur (1997) deftly argues that although the Web may be the product of ethereal contact, people still find their lives affected by their encounters in cyberspace:

> The deepest roots of virtuality seem to reach back into a religious world view where power and goodness are united in virtue. And the characteristic of the virtual is that it is able to produce effects, or to produce itself as an effect even in the absence of "real effects." The air of the miraculous that clings to virtue helps to obscure the distinction between real effects of power and/or goodness and effects that are as good as real. (pp. 9–10)

To the chat room participant, for instance, the effect of building a relationship online can be every bit as meaningful and rewarding as building one face to face (Rheingold, 1993). We must consider, then, that engaging others in the context of virtual reality is more than a substanceless hallucination.

Howard Rheingold (1993) proposes a less psychedelic definition. He contends that cyberspace is "the conceptual space where words, human relationships, data, wealth, and power are manifested by people using CMC technology" (p. 5). Conceiving of cyberspace as a "conceptual space" is among the most useful ways to explain to a geographically oriented culture where the Internet is to be found. With disparate parts of its whole situated in computer systems around the globe, the only "place" where cyberspace could be situated is within conceptual space. And yet what happens "there" is typically consensual, an experience built on interaction. Let us agree to a working definition of cyberspace that defines it as more than a hallucination, and is more likely a "consensual, conceptual space."

### HYPERLINK: GET A (REAL) LIFE

Throughout this book, we use the term **real life** to distinguish human behavior that occurs without the aid of computer mediation from that which occurs online. Cybercultural enthusiasts sometimes use the abbreviation IRL for "in real life" to express the same concept. Calling offline interaction "real" might be something of a misnomer because many people who communicate via the Internet consider the effects of online interaction just as impactful as those one might encounter in a face-to-face scenario. The argument goes that if offline interaction is real, than online interaction must be unreal, and thus meaningless. We do not intend to perpetuate a negative connotation in our selection; however, "real life" has been embraced by the scholarly literature, and so even though it is not without its faults, we use it herein for consistency.

## Extending the Metaphor

Why is it that the better part of society has embraced the metaphor of space rather than any other? After all, wouldn't something like cyber*library* be a better descriptor of the Internet's information-rich contents? Perhaps if all the Internet did was foster the flow of information and not facilitate interaction among people, any other metaphor might have dominated, and yet it is space that presently influences our interpretation of the Internet. The reasons may be that a sense of space has always been particularly important to people. Space has been instrumental in helping people make sense of the world around them and in enabling their interactions with others.

Once again, we know that the Greeks were among the earliest people who used space to express both tangible and intangible meanings. For example, the Athenian citizens would often gather in a large open plaza called the **Agora**. Here they would exchange ideas, debate politics, and conduct business. Thus the Agora became an important meeting space for Greek culture. Some cyberculturalists have likened the Internet to a modern day Agora where people go to meet one another (O'Leary & Brasher, 1996). But the Greek contribution to the importance of space also included the use of conceptual space as well. As discussed earlier, the Greeks expected public speakers to deliver their speeches without the benefit of manuscripts or notes. This led some teachers of rhetoric to develop elaborate systems for memorization.

One popular method had students memorize their speeches by relating parts of their presentation to parts of a visualized house. Within each room of the house students were to place another part of the speech. As one spoke, one was to visualize walking through the structure, open doors to various rooms along the way. As one opened these metaphorical doors, the messages within them were to stand revealed in one's memory and then to be expressed in one's speech. From early on in Western society, then, the concept of space was of particular importance for both social and intellectual purposes.

Metaphors dealing with space have, of course, continued on from the classical period through to the modern period. In medieval times Dante Alighieri's classic trilogy, *The Divine Comedy*, depicted the conceptual realms of hell, purgatory, and heaven as geographic spaces. Each of the three books chronicles Alighieri's journeys through multiple layers of punishment, repentance, and ecstasy. For instance, in *The Inferno*, Alighieri links each of the descending levels of hell to worse and worse crimes, beginning with those who indulged in emotional and physical pleasures on the upper level and ending with the treacherous on the very bottom. Such an arrangement suggests that the intangible world of religious doctrine could be understood through geographic metaphor.

In America, space has been a driving metaphor since the foundation of the colonies. For almost three centuries, the notion of "manifest destiny" dictated that America push back the physical space of the western frontier until the land had been claimed from sea to shining sea. And when America ran out of land to discover, it turned its attention to the "final frontier" of space. More recently, the notion of a frontier has been applied to the metaphoric frontiers of medicine and the inner space of human biology.

Similarly, the Internet has been conceptualized as a frontier. Anthologies with titles like *High Noon on the Electronic Frontier* (Benedikt, 1991). and *Cyberspace: First*

*Steps* (Ludlow, 1996), underscore the role that the spatial metaphor has played in our conception of the Internet, but then so has a lot of more popular usage. To some, claiming domain names on the World Wide Web harkens back to the land rushes of the American west. To others, the lack of rules governing social behavior has been compared to the lawlessness of the Wild West.

Even beyond frontier imagery, other spatial conceptions of the Internet have influenced how we think of it. Another popularized spatial analogy is that of the "Information Superhighway," a transportation analogy used by the Clinton administration to suggest the manner in which space is transcended by the Internet. Even the way people talk about using the Internet is correlated with space. "Surfing" has emerged as a popular descriptor of the process of interacting with the network. In reality, a surfer is physically located in a wave in the ocean. In like manner then, Internet surfers ride the waves on an ocean of information. However, although surfing is reminiscent of a physical activity, the metaphor is actually borrowed from the practice of flipping through channels of television, whose screen is similar but whose function is different than the computer's. As Steven Johnson (1997) explains, surfing suggests a rather passive activity, one he would preferably trade in for a more active term. His choice? Navigating. Why? Johnson cites that navigating suggests the same sense of the oceanic voyage, but one in which the traveler is making more conscious decisions about direction than a surfer at the mercy of the waves. Interestingly, both surfing and navigating are connected notions of space.

Finally, John Perry Barlow (1995) offers a rationale for this preoccupation with space. He theorized that a collective loss of our sense of community has set many of us on a quest to find a place to belong. For generations, people lived in small communities where they behaved in relationship to one other. Our increasingly depersonalized urban centers have left many people feeling alone and created in them a longing for the simpler communities of past generations. The Internet, it seems, is the forum, and hence the place, where people have turned to find their sense of community once again.

## A Critique of the Spatial Metaphor

Because it helps us to comprehend, to some degree, the daunting complexity of the phenomenon, you might not think that the spatial metaphor for framing the online environment would raise objections. And yet David J. Gunkel and Ann Hetzel Gunkel (1997) warn that "the activity of naming is never a matter of 'mere words.' It is one of the primary mechanisms of appropriation and control" (p. 132). In particular, Gunkel and Gunkel are concerned with the rhetoric of cyberspace as a "new world" awaiting conquest, promising wealth, and offering utopia. They remind us that previous "discoveries" of new worlds, such as the voyages of Christopher Columbus to North America, served to perpetuate existing frames of reference more than introduce new ones. As in that historic case, the discovery of America brought more changes on the native people and geography than it did on Europe, most notably by instigating the virtual genocide of the native peoples.

Gunkel and Gunkel want for us to consider how our conception of a metaphor could limit our perceptions of and responses to the network of networks. "Naming is always an exercise of power and must therefore be taken seriously" (p. 133), they note. Getting too accustomed to the notion of cyberspace as a new world has the potential to limit our thinking into what this new context for interaction could be and should not be. The new worlds of Columbus' voyage, of the later push toward America's western frontier, and of the more recent mission to outer space have carried with them some sense of moving over terrain, of tapping into riches, and of finding a better place.

In the case of cyberspace, Gunkel and Gunkel indicate that these three dimensions could foreclose some of the potential within the online experience. For instance, grounding ourselves in a three-dimensional analogy like the geographically situated "new world" could foreclose the possibility of perceiving the Internet in more fluid, nonphysical terms. Also, if the benefits of the new world are conceptualized as economic boons (a la Columbus' quest for gold and spices), alternative conceptions of social and cultural configurations could be lost. Cyberspace might be a space for socializing and not just pillaging. Finally, perceiving it as an unpolluted utopia, where all society's ills can be solved, ignores the lessons of the past, when other new lands and new media were promised to solve humanity's problems.

## CHAPTER SUMMARY

As this section demonstrates, the language we use to understand the Internet is both helpful and contested. Clearly, the final word on what online interaction is and is not has yet to be uttered, but as students of the emerging cyberculture, we must be sensitive to how the choices we make influences how we experience it. Throughout this chapter, we have provided you tools for gaining a deeper sensitivity toward online communication. Exploring the emerging field of CMC, we have identified the continuum of mediation and immediacy as a primary axis to understanding society, self, and reality in the contemporary world. We have also toured some of the tools through which our relationships are increasingly mediated. Finally, we have surveyed the role of cyberspace in making sense of online communication. At this point, we are ready to examine on an historical and functional level the next question that animates this section: Just how do these tools work?

### Online Communication and the Law

This section will appear at the conclusion of each chapter in this book. We include these sorts of discussions because legal definitions and challenges to various forms of CMC, in corporate and personal contexts, affect more than courtroom participants. Future decisions about online communication may very well affect us all.

Reading a book like this, you are probably willing to accept the claim that Internet communication is unique, that it merits special study. But does that mean that our experiences in the "real world" are so radically altered in the

Internet Age? Before you answer, consider a recent court case that established a legal precedent for the concept of **Internet time**. In this case, Mark Schlack decided to leave his job at EarthWeb for a promising position at ITworld.com. Schlack's former company sued him for violating a clause in his contract that stipulated that he could not join another company that competes with EarthWeb for one full year.

These sorts of "noncompete" clauses are typical in most industries and almost always upheld in court cases. However, District Court Judge William H. Pauley III ruled in favor of Schlack. Writing in *The New York Times*, Carl S. Kaplan (1999) explained that Pauley's decision adds legal standing to the notion of Internet time—that a year in the information industry is equivalent to "several generations, if not an eternity" (n.p.). You may not be an information technology expert, but you can surely relate to Schlack's predicament: Internet communication seems to foster so much change, so much innovation, that stepping away from this environment for a year would result in a culture clash on your return.

## Glossary

**Agora**: An open meeting space within the Greek city of Athens, commonly used for transacting all kinds of social exchanges.

**Browser**: A software program that interprets information from the Internet and displays it as text, images, animation, and sounds (e.g., Mosaic, Netscape Navigator, Microsoft Explorer).

**Bulletin Board Systems (BBS)**: A publicly accessible collection of organized messages posted by various contributors.

**Computer-mediated communication (CMC)**: The study of the ways in which human behaviors are maintained or altered by exchange of information through machines.

**Computer anxiety**: Fear of using or considering using computer technology.

**Cybernetics**: The science of automatic control systems.

**Cyberspace**: The consensual, conceptual space where online interaction occurs.

**Immediate communication**: "Live," face-to-face human interaction.

**Listservs**: A type of e-mail in which one posts messages to and receives messages from others through a program that delivers to all those who subscribe to it.

**Mediated communication**: Human interaction that is aided by some exterior technology such as print, radio, or the Internet.

**Multiphrenia**: Conception of human identity as being splintered because of overlapping technological and cultural forces.

**Newsgroup**: Any one of the BBS groups devoted to a particular topic (e.g., alt .culture).

**Portal**: A starting point for one's Internet excursion.

**Post**: The act of putting a message onto the Internet.

**Real life**: Human behavior occurring in contexts other than those involving computer mediation.
**Secondary orality**: The perceptual return to privileging spoken rather than written discourse as the dominant sense for interpreting the social world.
**Thread**: A series of e-mail messages posted to a BBS that follows a particular line of conversation.
**World Wide Web**: Network of documents, pictures, sounds, and other "texts" organized in a point-and-click method that mirrors most desktop computers.

## Topics for Discussion

1. Keep a journal over a 24-hour period of how long you spend involved in Internet communication. Rank order your activities. They might include the following: chatting with friends, conducting research, paying bills, or just "surfing" for entertainment. What are your primary reasons for going online?
2. Have you, like Ellen Ullman, noticed distinctions in the way you interact with people online versus in real life? Identify an important message you have communicated to a friend or loved one. Write a brief explanation of how the context you chose, face to face or mediated, affected the message. As part of your response, consider how the message might have been affected if you switched contexts (i.e., sent the news via e-mail rather than face to face).
3. Make a list of 10 people who are most important to you. Would you describe the majority of your interactions with them as immediate or mediated? Do you think that a majority of mediated relationships might adversely affect your emotional well-being?
4. What other metaphors for the Internet have you heard or could you substitute for those involving space? Either identify another you are familiar with or create you own and write a paragraph in which you relate your metaphor to certain Internet phenomena. Consider what your metaphor reveals particularly well about online interaction and what it might obscure about it.

## REFERENCES

Barlow, J. P. (1995, March–April). Is there a there in cyberspace? *Utne Reader*, pp. 52–56.
Baym, N. K. (1997). Interpreting soap operas and creating community: Inside an electronic fan culture. In S. Kiesler (Ed.), *Culture of the Internet* (pp. 103–120). Mahwah, NJ: Lawrence Erlbaum Associates.
Benedikt, M. (Ed.). (1991). *Cyberspace: First steps*. Cambridge, MA: MIT Press.
Bromberg, H. (1996). Are MUDs communities? Identity, belonging, and consciousness in virtual worlds. In R. Shields (Ed.), *Cultures of Internet: Virtual spaces, real histories, living bodies* (pp. 143–152). Thousand Oaks, CA: Sage.

Borenstein, D. (2000). *Quoteland.com.* <http://www.quoteland.com>.

Curtis, P. (1997). MUDding: Social phenomena in text-based virtual realities. In S. Kiesler (Ed.), *Culture of the Internet* (pp. 121–142). Mahwah, NJ: Lawrence Erlbaum Associates.

Emery, D. (1999, July 13). *Current Internet hoaxes.* <http://urbanlegends.about.com/library/bl>.

Gergen, K. (1991). *The saturated self: Dilemmas of identity in contemporary life.* New York: Basic Books.

Gibson, W. (1984). *Neuromancer.* New York: Ace Books.

Gunkel, D. J., & Gunkel, A. H. (1997). Virtual geographies: The new worlds of cyberspace. *Critical Studies in Mass Communication, 14,* 123–137.

Herring, S. (1999). Interactional coherence in CMC. *Journal of Computer-Mediated Communication,* 4(4), <http://www.ascusc.org/jcmc/vol4/issue4/herring.html#USER>.

Johnson, S. (1997). *Interface culture: How new technology transforms the way we create and communicate.* San Francisco: HarperCollins.

Kaplan, C. S. (1999, November 5). In internet time, a year is much too long, judge finds. *The New York Times.* <http://www.nytimes.com/library/tech/99/11/cyber/cyberlaw/05law.html>.

Lee, J. Y. (1996). Charting the codes of cyberspace: A rhetoric of electronic mail. In L. Strate, R. Jacobson, & S. B. Gibson (Eds.), *Communication and cyberspace: Social interaction in an electronic environment* (pp. 275–296). Cresskill, NJ: Hampton Press.

Ludlow, P. (Ed.). (1996). *High noon on the electronic frontier: Conceptual issues in cyberspace.* Cambridge, MA: MIT Press.

McCaffery, L. (1992). *Storming the reality studio: A casebook of cyberpunk and postmodern fiction.* Durham, NC: Duke University Press.

McCroskey, J. C. (1978). Validity of the PRCA as an index of oral communication apprehension. *Communication Monographs, 45,* 194–203.

McLuhan, M. (1964). *Understanding media: The extension of man.* New York: Routledge.

Mitra, A. (1997). Diasporic Web sites: In group and outgroup discourse. *Critical Studies in Mass Communication, 14,* 158–181.

O'Leary, S. D., & Brasher, B. E. (1996). The unknown god of the Internet: Religious communication from the ancient agora to the virtual forum. In C. Ess (Ed.), *Philosophical perspectives on computer-mediated communication* (pp. 233–269). Albany: State University of New York Press.

Ong, W. J. (1982). *Orality and literacy: The technologizing of the word.* New York: Routledge.

Rheingold, H. (1993). *The virtual community: Homesteading on the electronic frontier.* Reading, MA: Addison-Wesley.

Rosen, L. D., Sears, D. C., & Weil, M. M. (1987). Computerphobia. *Behavior Research Methods, Instruments, & Computers, 19,* 167–179.

Rushkoff, D. (1994). *Cyberia: Life in the trenches of hyperspace.* San Francisco: HarperCollins.

Scott, C. R., & Rockwell, S. C. (1997). The effect of communication, writing, and technology apprehension on likelihood to use new communication technologies. *Communication Education, 46,* 29–43.

Standage, T. (1998). *The victorian internet.* New York: Berkley Books.

Stone, I. F. (1988). *The trial of Socrates.* Boston: Little, Brown and Company.

Ullman, E. (1996). Come in, CQ: The body on the wire. In L. Cherny & E. R. Wise (Eds.), *Wired women: Gender and new realities in cyberspace* (pp. 3–23). Seattle, WA: Seal Press.

Walker, R., Tames, R. Man, J., & Freeman, C. (1996). *Inventions that changed the world.* New York: Reader's Digest.

Weiner, N. (1954). *The human use of human beings: Cybernetics and society.* Boston: Houghton Mifflin.

Wilbur, S. P. (1997). An archaeology of cyberspaces: Virtuality, community, identity. In D. Poster (Ed.), *Internet culture* (pp. 5–22). New York: Routledge.

Williams, S. (1994, June 12). Technophobes: Victims of electronic progress. *Mobile Register,* p. 9E.

# CHAPTER 2

# UNDERSTANDING HOW NEW COMMUNICATION TECHNOLOGIES WORK

*I used to think that cyberspace was fifty years away. What I thought was fifty years away, was only ten years away. And what I thought was ten years away. . . . it was already here. I just wasn't aware of it yet.*

*—Bruce Sterling (Borenstein, 2000)*

| | |
|---|---|
| Joe Fox: | You're crazy about him— |
| Kathleen Kelly: | Yes. I am. |
| Joe Fox: | Then why don't you run off with him? What are you waiting for? |
| Kathleen Kelly: | I don't actually know him. |
| Joe Fox: | Really? |
| Kathleen Kelly: | We only know each other—oh, God, you're not going to believe this— |
| Joe Fox: | Let me guess. From the Internet. |
| Kathleen Kelly: | Yes. |
| Joe Fox: | You've got mail. |
| Kathleen Kelly: | Yes. |
| Joe Fox: | Very powerful words. |
| Kathleen Kelly: | Yes. |

If you saw the 1998 Tom Hanks/Meg Ryan film, *You've Got Mail* in a movie theater, you can reasonably claim to have been present at a defining moment in popular culture—when it became apparent to a critical mass of people that computer technology wasn't just for folks in white lab coats anymore. Certainly, the notion that people may research papers, entertain themselves, and even make friends online was hardly revolutionary in 1998. At least two generations of audiences had become comfortable with computers in their lives—most obviously with video games (Bennahum, 1998). Moreover, the Internet had been a popular phenomenon for years prior to the release of *You've Got Mail*. But, for many people, the site of America's favorite sweetheart couple falling in love by the music of tapping keystrokes served as a wakeup call: Computer technology increasingly shapes human interaction.

It is little surprise that *You've Got Mail* centered on a love–hate relationship between individuals who represent different channels of human communication. In the film, Kathleen Kelly (Meg Ryan) runs a small bookstore and offers her customers immediate and individualized attention. Enter Joe Fox (Tom Hanks), whose Barnes and Noble-style conglomerate threatens to run Kathleen's tiny shop out of business. Joe's store is so big and its computer-mediated database of books is so impressive that its customers are likely to find whatever reading material they desire. However, the size of Joe's store means that his customers risk losing the individual attention they would find in Kathleen's shop. Two technologies of human interaction—one small and personal, the other vast and impersonal—clash in *You've Got Mail*. The struggle of Kathleen and Joe resonates with many of us because they mirror the struggles we face to make sense of CMC as a set of tools in our everyday lives.

This chapter offers a bookend of sorts to the previous chapter's introduction to the role of computer technology in human communication. Having introduced the tools of CMC, both functional and metaphoric, it is appropriate that we examine more closely how these tools work. In this chapter, we place computer technology in an historical context, surveying the emergence of online communication from the perspective of cybernetics. We then step beyond chapter 1's exploration of mediated and immediate communication to overview five qualities that distinguish Internet technology from other forms of communication: packet-switching, multimedia, interactivity, synchronicity, and hypertextuality. These functions help explain how CMC works to blur the distinction between mediation and immediacy.

Throughout this chapter, we approach computer technology as important—critical, even—to understanding a relationship like that of Kathleen and Joe's in *You've Got Mail*. But before we go further, it is important to remember that even the most modern romance cannot be explained by computer technology alone. As we hasten to explore technology as a force that shapes identity and culture, we must not fall into the trap of technological determinism. **Technological determinism** assumes that our growing ability to alter or replace nature provides a central reason for most personal and social trends. A technologically determinist perspective on an historical event, say World War I, would focus primarily on the innovations in killing machines like the machine gun and the use of mustard gas to explain what some critics viewed as the dehumanization of the 20th century. Certainly, technology plays a key role in social innovation—and crisis. However, in this text, we approach technology as merely one key component to understanding identity and culture, preferring to view human experience as an intersection of all three. Indeed, as we begin our brief history of cybernetic technology, we find that personality and cultural assumptions played significant roles in the evolution of what would become the Internet.

## A BRIEF HISTORY OF CYBERNETIC TECHNOLOGY

Charting the development of mediating technologies in human history is a subject deserving of several volumes, so substantial has been their influence on societies. And yet it is beyond the scope of this book to delve too deeply, too specifically into much more than a review of the most significant highlights of the story in establishing the forerunners to today's mediating technologies. Thus, although the history of computers encompasses everything from the mechanical adding machines of yesteryear to tomorrow's visions of computers that abandon silicon for more subtle architectures that mimic human DNA, it will suffice to say that the history of computers is a narrative of human beings seeking to employ technology to alter their worlds. To understand this history within our limited space, then, we explore a brief narrative beginning with conceptions of thinking machines, continuing through to cybernetic devices, and arriving at today's Internet as a contemporary cybernetic organism.

## THINKING MACHINES IN THE 19TH CENTURY

Some of the earliest mechanical calculating machines mirrored the processes of ancient clock makers and loom designers. Yet Charles Babbage (1791–1871), perhaps more than anyone, introduced these machines to nonscientists. Here, it is important to remember that during the height of Britain's Age of Empire, scientists and planners could easily be compared to modern rock stars. During the 19th century, their clever mechanical devices and globe-girdling plans employed science as a civilizing force earned them popular acclaim. But it was Babbage, however, who generally receives credit for striving to develop a device that remarkably resembles the modern computer—**the analytical engine**. As Shurkin (1984) explains in this book, *Engines of the Mind*, Babbage was a dabbler whose interests ranged in the scientific study of whether some beggars were really poor (or just faking it) to inquiries into which types of paper and ink made for the most comfortable reading experience.

Babbage's lifelong obsession, however, was his dream to create a steam-driven machine that would compute tables and formulas. Like today's computers, his analytical engine would consist of "memory" (columns of wheels with engraved numbers) and a form of "central processing unit" that manipulated the numbers with the aid of punch cards. As it turned out, Babbage's engine was too sophisticated to be produced; his mechanics required tools that had not been invented yet. But his engine is at the heart of today's thinking machines.

You can imagine how these calculating machines might have worked by picturing a mechanical loom such as the **Jacquard Loom**. This device offered a means for a weaver to mass produce patterns of cloth by punching holes in cards. The hooks would guide the thread only where there were holes in the cards, leaving the empty sections alone:

> The data—the description of the pattern—were coded in terms of a binary alphabet represented by the holes and "nonholes" in the cards; thus the communication between weaver and weaving machine used a language, as all communication does, and the cards formed the channel of communication for this language. (Moreau, 1984, p. 14)

Whether these devices were mechanical or electrical, in the case of the room-filling vacuum tube computers of the early to mid-20th century, the principle was the same. Computers could manipulate data—manifested in the form of cards or electrons—according to the desires of their users.

## CYBERNETIC DEVICES IN THE EARLY 20TH CENTURY

Throughout the 19th- and early 20th-century evolution of computers, critics feared their potential to rid human beings of their capacity to act with purpose within some ethical framework. Here again, technological determinism is at work. For many, the mechanized warfare of World War I confirmed their worst fears, that centuries of the industrial revolution had wrought nothing less than the end of civilization. It is, therefore, fascinating to observe how the introduction of cybernetic devices in the next global conflict would occur simultaneously with a renewed attention to the process through which individual and cultural narratives affect technological innovation.

You may recall our definition of CMC as the study of how human behaviors are maintained or altered by the exchange of information through machines. From this perspective, cybernetics helps us understand the process through which that exchange takes place. As discussed in chapter 1, cybernetics is the science of automatic control systems. The study of cybernetics can range from the most complicated phenomena like the process of atmosphere renewal to the most apparently simple devices, like the thermostat you probably have in your home or office. As you know, a thermostat receives input in the form of a preset temperature, generally "programmed" by turning a dial or setting a switch. If the temperature in your room slips below that preset number of degrees, the thermostat sends that message to the central heating system in your home or building to increase the energy used to heat your space. If the degree of heat in your room rises above a certain level, however, the thermostat instructs the heater to shut down. This all might sound most mechanical—and, to be sure, machines are essential to the process—but the heart of cybernetics is the manner through which physical devices and natural forces are controlled and altered by human agency.

Norbert Weiner (1954) is a scientist and writer who popularized the study of cybernetics with his book, *The Human Use of Human Beings*. Weiner's work with cybernetics began with the efforts of anti-aircraft gunners who wanted to build machines that would help them plot and anticipate the movements of enemy aircraft. Weiner helped develop devices that would provide feedback to the weapons so that when a gun missed its target, it could compensate. After missing the plane with its first round, the gun would adjust for distance, wind velocity, the acceleration of its target, and various other factors before firing another round. This time, after firing twice, the machine would have a more accurate "fix" on its target—teaching itself how to respond to changing environmental and human factors. Unfortunately for the pilot of the enemy aircraft, the machine would learn quickly and eventually (within seconds) hit its target.

Recalling the example of the thermostat, you can see a similar principle: Machines can alter their behavior according to the programs of their operators. Of course, if you have ever been in a room where the thermostat didn't work properly (or if you can imagine yourself in the unhappy position of being a pilot in the sights of a computer-mediated weapon), you recognize that human computer interaction goes both ways. In a cybernetic environment, computers and humans share information to alter each other's behavior. Perhaps one of the most significant impacts of Weiner's work is a more sophisticated concept of information. From the perspective of cybernetics, **information** is an exchange of data necessary for one system to influence the behavior of another system.

As a student of communication, you might find that definition of information to be somewhat strange. After all, from a more common perspective, information is simply a container for our messages. One of the authors of this book used to think it quite clever to play on the implied breakdown of the word to describe communication as the process of putting facts *in formation*. Weiner's approach, however, emphasizes the challenge of communication scholars to identify their topics. Do we study the process through which data—facts, sounds, gestures—are transmitted as an engineer would study the efficient movement of words through telephone lines? Or, instead, do we study the human choices and social consequences that shape our communicative acts? The cybernetics-oriented definition of information allows a middle ground central to the foundation of this book. We approach CMC as a study defined not only by its range of interests, but also its perspective on human discourse where individuals and technology shape each other in surprising ways.

### HYPERLINK: "WHAT'S THE DIFFERENCE ENGINE?"

Before Charles Babbage's experiments with the analytical engine, he imagined a simpler mechanical device that would solve certain equations. His "difference engine" provides a central character of sorts for a book of the same name, written by Gibson and Sterling (1991). In the book, Victorian scientists develop a difference engine that can be used to predict and potentially control the movements of ordinary people. The authors provide a nightmarish vision of the power of this steam-driven thinking machine:

> Paper-thin faces billow like sails, twisting, yawning, tumbling through the empty streets, human faces that are borrowed masks and lenses for a peering Eye. And when a given face has served its purpose, it crumbles, frail as ash, bursting into a dry foam of data.

The "Peering Eye" is the machine that surveys all human conduct through its acquisition of information. The threat, predicted by the *Difference Engine*, is that a machine provided too much information may no longer find human beings to be useful.

In *The Human Use of Human Beings*, Weiner (1954) warned that human beings cannot allow their will and consciences to be controlled by machines. His call to cultivate "fertility of thought" was a reaction to what he viewed as an increasing "massification" of media. In a world in which ideas can be considered interchangeable, where original thoughts are rare, the value of individual opinions becomes random. Human lives, Weiner warned, would become just as random as the "dry foam of data" described by Gibson and Sterling. Do you think that Weiner was simply afraid of the machines he created or, perhaps, was he correct?

## THE INTERNET AS CYBERNETIC ORGANISM

Our understanding of self-regulating machines is essential to understanding the Internet for, in many ways, we are talking about a cybernetic organism. To understand this idea, start with the military goal of **command and control**. This term refers to the notion that information, properly channeled, can ensure that individuals will act as a unit within a framework larger than themselves. To fight fascism in the early 20th century or protect a nation from a nuclear powered foe throughout the Cold War, command and control were essential to the health and continued existence of the United States.

The irony is that a military system of command and control—so useful in World War II when gunners needed the help of machines to keep up with increasingly rapid aircraft—facilitated the evolution of a system that simply could not be controlled: the Internet. The Internet emerged during a period of tremendous fear on the part of the U.S. government. In 1957, the Soviet Union had launched its Sputnik satellite, marking a major victory in the Space Race. Immediately, U.S. policymakers geared up their efforts to "catch up" with the Soviets. The fact that a satellite crafted by the Soviets had virtually free reign over U.S. airspace led some to believe that floating missiles and space-based weapons were not far behind.

Scientists, military planners, and educators needed to pool their efforts. After the Sputnik launch, the United States formed the Advanced Research Projects Agency (ARPA). Among their projects, ARPA scientists envisioned a "Galactic Network" of computers that would not relay on a central system to function. Rather, they would form a network with a common protocol that could respond to changes, even the elimination of individual computers from the network. Although it is inaccurate to say that ARPA scientists sought to create a nuclear war-proof computer network, the Defense Department funding their efforts began to imagine their project could result in one anyway. In 1969, universities made plans to launch **ARPANET**, a network of computers that would draw from each other's resources in a timeshare relationship and provide the foundation for the unbreakable computer network. This innovation was revolutionary because of its ability to facilitate the transmission of overlapping messages with different destinations through the same network.

Of course, the technology being used to move information between computers was so exotic that few civilians could understand it. Zakon (1998) recalls that the company that won the contract to manufacture Interface Message Processors for this network received a congratulatory telegram from Senator Ted Kennedy for their plans to build the *Interfaith* Message Processor, thanking them for their efforts to stimulate religious communication between people with different views of God. Although politicians were slow to grasp the significance of this evolution in computer science, many universities caught on quickly.

The first universities to sign on to the project were UCLA, Stanford, University of California Santa Barbara, and the University of Utah. But dozens and, eventually, hundreds more followed. Throughout the 1970s, their research efforts were being used to test e-mail, newsgroups, and other experimental ways for scientists to interact with one another. During the 1980s, as network researchers experimented on various protocols for moving "packets" of information, ARPANET split into military and civilian components. Before long, people referred to the computer system where computers transfer information simply as the "Internet."

## Hyperlink: Vannevar Bush and His Amazing Memex

Long before there was an Internet and the countless megabytes of data it now contains, a research scientist named Vannevar Bush (1945) envisioned a prototypical hypertextual system for cataloguing information. Writing at the end of World War II, Bush foresaw the need for a better means of keeping track of all the research publications being produced in the wake of so many scientific discoveries during his times. What Bush suggested was a device he called the **memex**. Although the technology to realize such an invention did not yet exist in 1945, Bush theorized that a memex could help people cope with the vast amounts of information that existed on any given topic. In design, it would be housed in a desk-like structure, with screens for displaying data and internal mechanisms for retrieving and archiving it. Information within the memex would be stored on numerous sheets of microform. Most importantly, the reader would have the ability to establish links among various sources of information stored within the memex for future retrieval. Bush indicated that customary systems for cataloguing information were based on arbitrary systems, like alphabetizing. The memex, he contended, operated more like the human mind, which works through associations. For example, a person might associate ice cream with kissing, not because "I" and "K" are near one another in the alphabet, but because she received her first kiss at the Dairy Queen. Bush's memex would allow users to make such idiosyncratic connections among topics.

Although Bush's vision for the memex, per se, was never realized, his ideas were highly influential in the development of hypertext systems and, ultimately, the World Wide Web. Accordingly, someone writing a web page today could create a hyperlink from a mention of her first kiss to the Dairy Queen site. The ability to associate ideas within a rich pool of possible references was prophesied in the 1940s and realized in the 1990s, but the effects of Bush's uninvented invention will impact us throughout the coming century.

## WHAT IS THE INTERNET?

The history and evolution of this network of networks is fascinating. But we cannot proceed without a specific definition of the **Internet**. Here, we borrow from the Federal Networking Council (1995), which proposed a definition that includes three primary elements:

- The Internet is linked together through a global address system.
- The Internet uses a common form of transmission protocol.
- The Internet allows public and private communication.

Let's consider these requirements for an Internet in turn.

First, a global address system ensures that a message can actually reach its destination. Imagine if your address (say, 1600 Pennsylvania Avenue, Washington DC) could be shared by other people, that, instead of there being one site to indicate the placement of that house, there were several. Mail delivery would get pretty complicated! The Internet works because each address in the network refers to only one location.

Second, the Internet requires a common form of transmission. In other words, computers must be able to route their messages through according to consistent rules—just like a driver in California must know that stop signs mean the same thing, even when she or he visits another state. The Internet works because every computer knows the rules of the road.

Finally, the Internet must allow for the layering of communication, both public and private. In other words, the Internet does not simply have one function, but many simultaneous uses. Thus, it is possible for the same Internet connections to facilitate overlapping, but separate, transmissions of information. The same principle is found in the Eisenhower highway system that was planned to serve both the needs of civilian travel and military preparedness. The same stretch of highway that allows the movement of trucks and private cars was also designed, in many places, to serve as landing strips for aircraft in case of war.

Thus, the Internet is a network of computers that allows for the transmission of data for multiple purposes through a common set of protocols according to a global address system. Notice that among these three qualities, "ease of use" cannot be found. For most people during the period of Internet evolution, from 1969 through the 1980s, access to this network of networks required patience with a communication system designed by engineers for engineers. Only with the emergence of the World Wide Web would the Internet become more than a technical marvel.

Up until the 1990s, manipulating information in what had become the Internet required users to comprehend arcane commands. If you wanted to access a file online, you needed to submit a specialized code. There was no such thing as "point and click." Tim Berners-Lee, looking to simplify information exchange between high energy physicists, took the Internet to an entirely new level by proposing the World Wide Web (WWW).

As discussed in chapter 1, the World Wide Web is exciting because of its transformation in how people interact with computers and each other. With the invention of web browsers such as Mosaic, Netscape, and Explorer, the same ease of use that nonscientists came to expect from their desktop computers became available beyond the desktop through the use of a point-and-click interface. The World Wide Web mirrored the Internet in its impact on computer networking. What was, at first, a clever way for scientists to share research soon became—for many users—the primary manifestation of the Internet, just as the Internet outgrew its military ARPANET predecessor.

As with most contemporary computers, you can access the contents of the Web without knowing any programming languages or network protocols. We understand the WWW as a cybernetic organism; it grows and changes as new information is placed within its domains. The Web is hardware and software—machines and codes—but it is also a regulator of human behaviors whose implications are only now being imagined.

## Hyperlink: "A Post-Beige Revolution"

With its "1984" advertisement mocking the plodding predictability of personal computers—their no-nonsense green or black screens, their neutral beige coloring, their orientation toward business and other "practical" concerns, their stupefying complexity—Apple Computer launched a revolution in hardware and software design. Where IBM developed machines-as-tools, Apple offered computers-as-toys. A bright screen that displayed a friendly "hello," icons that represented data in the form of folders, papers, and even a trash can, and a mouse that inspired users to feel like they were physically manipulating their textual environments with a point and click.

These innovations, borrowed from previous experiments in people-friendly graphical user interfaces, were first ridiculed, then studied, and ultimately copied by any computer company that planned to last beyond the 1980s. But imitation spelled doom for Apple, a company that fell prey to a host of internal and external faults. By the mid-1990s, Apple computer was seen as a device for a particularly small brand of holdouts, those idealists who had not "given in" to the Wintel empire of Microsoft Windows and Intel processors. Even the development of a very fast Power PC chip could not turn the company's fortunes. Apple's flamboyant and notoriously thin-skinned co-founder, Steve Jobs, had long previously left the company, shoved aside through a combination of corporate politics and his own hubris. Market share had slipped from more than 10% to less than 6%, making Apple Computer an also-ran in an industry of giants.

In desperation, Apple begged Jobs to return as interim chief executive officer, to turn around the company that was launched with a "hello." Within months, Apple introduced the iMac—a computer designed with a faster processor, easier Internet configuration, and (most importantly) a radically new look from any other machine on the market. The first iMacs featured a somewhat turquoise shell and see-through covering; the mouse looked like a flying saucer. Combined with an ambitious advertising campaign ("Think Different") and a revitalized sales strategy, the iMac was the top-selling computer through retail and mail-order channels in the 1998 holiday season, according to *The New York Times* ("Apple's iMac," 1999). In an interview with Jobs, *Time Digital's* Chris Taylor (1999) struggled to make sense of the popularity of this machine, finally asking, "Would you call it postmodern?" Jobs simply responded: "I call it post-beige."

## WHAT ARE SOME CHARACTERISTICS OF ONLINE COMMUNICATION?

Thus far, we have surveyed a brief history of computer technology from the perspective of cybernetics, exploring the evolution of the Internet as a feedback mechanism that grows so rapidly and in so many intriguing ways that it is hard not to imagine it as a living organism. Consuming resources, responding to change, and generating offspring, the Internet may not be alive in a literal sense, but it displays characteristics that are certainly vibrant. In this section, we explore the question of whether the Internet might be seen as a new kind of mass medium—or maybe an entirely new form of communication. We then outline five characteristics of the Internet that help explain the ways in which CMC assists and alters contemporary communication.

Morris and Ogan (1996) suggest that the Internet represents a new form of mass medium. They note that traditional mass media like newspapers and television have promoted an affiliation between the producers of messages and the audience for those messages characterized as a one-to-many relationship. As an example, Dan Rather speaks to millions of Americans every night on the evening news. The Internet may be looked on a mass medium that adds one-to-one (as in e-mail), many-to-many (as in listservs), and many-to-one (as in corporate Web sites) to the mix. Viewing the Internet as a mass medium does help explain some aspects of what happens online. For instance, a traditional mass media theory like uses and gratification, can help to explain why people visit particular sites on the World Wide Web (Kaye & Medoff, 1999). However, limiting one's view of the Internet to that of only a mass medium, and relying only on the pre-established theories of mass media, would fall short of addressing the interpersonal aspects that are present online.

In contrast to the Internet as mass medium approach, J. Michael Metz (1994) suggests that CMC "is a field of theoretical study in its own right, not merely a channel to study within other theoretical contexts" (p. 33). Metz's point is well taken. In recent years, the field of communication studies has grown increasingly aware that context factors into the ways that messages are produced and interpreted. Such emerging contexts exhibit qualities that help distinguish them from more traditional areas of study like interpersonal, organizational, or mass communication. Thus, scholars have begun offering specialized courses in health, family, and, of course, CMC. As is seen in this and the following chapters, elements of CMC could be taught in an interpersonal, organizational, or mass communication classroom. And yet the qualities that distinguish computer-mediated from other contexts for communication might not be fully addressed in any one of those courses.

Many scholars would agree that there are some telling distinctions between other forms of human communication and that conducted on the Internet. One of them is Sheizaf Rafaeli, who identifies five qualities that distinguish the Internet from other forms of communication (Newhagen & Rafaeli, 1996). These distinctions are packet-switching, multimedia, interactivity, synchronicity, and hypertextuality. Let us explore what Rafaeli says about each of these in turn.

## Packet-Switching

Rafaeli counts this technical aspect of the medium as one of its distinguishing features. As discussed earlier, the Internet was developed as a means for sending messages over multiple pathways rather than a single line like a telephone does. At one end of the transmission, a computer breaks down a message into packets of information. Each packet is then routed toward its destination where it is reassembled by another computer. Other media use packet-switching to some degree. For example, your telephone network may break your voice into packets. However, the telephone network creates a "pathway" of sorts to ensure that each packet arrives to its destination quickly—an important quality in voice communication. Packet-switching on a computer network works differently, by assigning each packet its own source and destination address—as if they are individual letters sent through the postal system.

Here's another example: Let us say that your younger sibling wants to view the Disney site on the World Wide Web. At your request, the collection of codes that tell your home computer how to display the Disney site are broken down into smaller units, or packets, and sent through a number of different paths along the computer network. The codes are then reassembled on arrival so that your sibling can view what is up on the Disney site. You may be somewhat confused by the fact that most households rely on a telephone connection to link to the network. Although it is true that the telephone connection between your home computer and your Internet service provider (ISP) does not operate on packet-switching itself, the ISP, in all likelihood, is connected to the network of networks that forms the Internet and thus receives information via packet-switching before passing it along to you.

## Multimedia

For now, this characteristic operates in only one form of Internet communication that is explored in more depth here, the World Wide Web. If you have explored the Web in some breadth, you are already aware that it facilitates messages in the forms of text, images, animation, and sound. In other words, the Web can communicate through multiple channels. Compare this to *USA Today*, which has the properties to convey text and images, but not sound, or the latest Garth Brooks compact disk, which has the properties to convey sound, but not text or images (excluding, of course, the colorful packaging it comes in). A quick peek at the Disney site, however, provides a multimedia experience. Here one can view trailers for Disney's upcoming theatrical releases or play recordings from its latest Broadway musical.

## Interactivity

It should be fairly self-evident that the Internet allows for interaction among its communicators. However, it is important to note that as far as different media go, interactivity occurs in various levels. Consider broadcast television, for instance. The meteorologist at the local TV station provides you a forecast for the next day's weather. Whether you are pleased that it will be sunny or disappointed that it will snow, you cannot express your reaction to the forecaster through the television. In fact, if you want to communicate with that person, you would probably have to choose another medium, perhaps the telephone, to communicate the message. The quality of interactivity is discussed in greater depth in chapter 3. For now, suffice it to say that people communicating over the Internet have some degree of interactivity. If you have exchanged e-mail messages with anyone, then you are already aware that two-way communication is possible, if somewhat delayed by the nature of the technology involved.

## Synchronicity

Messages exchanged over the Internet transverse not only space but also time (Strate, 1996). CMC allows for two different types of time to elapse in online communication. **Synchronous communication** occurs when two or more participants are interacting in real time. You have experienced synchronous communication if you've ever played with a set of walkie-talkies in real life or experimented with IRC. These messages tend to be more conversational in nature, being as they are composed off the cuff. In contrast, Internet messages can also be exchanged with lag time between them. **Asynchronous communication** occurs when participants interact with significant spans of time between their exchanges. You have experienced asynchronous communication if you have ever traded traditional letters with a pen pal or jokes with a friend over e-mail. Given that authors have time to think them through, asynchronous messages tend to be better planned than synchronous ones.

Interestingly, the time between when a message is sent and when it is responded to contributes to indications of relational cues. Although many nonverbal channels are filtered out of most CMC (i.e., gesture, facial expression, intonation), the management of **chronemics** can still present shared meaning between communication partners. We all know that in face-to-face conversations, a silent pause can "say" a lot about a person's reaction. The length of the pause in asynchronous exchange seems to hold meaning as well. Walther and Tidwell (1995) found that people based their perceptions of liking by the amount of lag time between asynchronously exchanged messages. When the messages exchanged between two people were task-oriented (i.e., "Do we have a system in place to keep track of this?"), the more prompt the reply was, the more intimate (and, by inference, respectful) the relationship between the conversants was perceived. On the other hand, when the messages were social in nature (i.e., "What is your schedule when you are here—any openings? We should make plans."), the slower (and presumably more thoughtful) replies were perceived as more the intimate expressions. Thus, the management of time is a consideration for the manner in which our messages are expressed on the Internet.

## Hypertextuality

Rafaeli's fifth and final distinguishing characteristic for Internet communication is hypertextuality. **Hypertext** is a type of nonsequential writing that challenges traditionally held notions about the way meaning is created through the experience of reading. As noted in chapter 1, Ong (1982) argues that writing was a technology that shaped how people think and ultimately how people interact with one another. Think of the ways in which the conventions of reading have shaped some of your perceptions. If you pick up a new book, you have been trained to start on the first page and read each page in turn rather than starting in the middle and jumping around the text. Likewise, you assume that words will flow in a left to right order across the page:

.arbitrarily reversed was order word the if frustrating be would It

Although such practices as page and word order seem normalized today, they are actually social conventions that evolved with the invention of writing and later print. Capitalization and punctuation are additional inventions used to make reading an easier task. That these conventions are invented rather than inherent characteristics of reading can be demonstrated by looking to other writing systems. For instance, the Chinese use not only a different alphabet but also a different word order, reading in a mirrorlike fashion to our own language with words flowing right to left across the page.

Writing in the days before a widely accessible source of hypertext was made manifest in the World Wide Web, Landow (1992) theorized that hypertext challenged several notions of our traditional reading of a text. He had been working with students of literature who were experimenting with the ways in which the relationships among the reader, writing, and text seemed altered in electronically linked (rather than printed) documents. In particular, he noted that the transition to hypertext represented a move from linearity to multilinearity, from centrality to a system of links, and from hierarchy to cooperation.

**From Linearity to Multilinearity.** As the examples of word order just cited indicate, the traditional practice of reading suggests that the reader proceed in linear, or sequential, manner. In this sense, readers are at the mercy of the author, who determines what topics will be addressed in what order. In contrast, some of that authorial control is yielded to the reader in a hypertext document. This control is facilitated by hyperlinks. **Hyperlinks** are selected words or images related to other sections of the same document or other documents. When one selects a hyperlink, typically by positioning one's cursor over it and clicking one's mouse, the computer program displays that other section or document for the reader. For example, as a reader of an electronic document on the history of writing, one might choose to select a hyperlink to Theodore Nelson and see an image of the man who first proposed hypertext.

In Landow's conception, every symbol in a hypertext document has the potential to be a hyperlink to another set of symbols, and yet in practice, a limited number of hyperlinks are available to readers, meaning that authorial control is still a determining factor in the presentation of hypertext in practice. Nonetheless, a reader has more choices of what hyperlinks to pursue or ignore in their own reading of the text and that in itself is a noteworthy transfer of power (see Table 2.1).

**From Centrality to Links.** Landow (1992) also argues that traditional texts create a fiction that they exist independent of the world of texts around them. Novels, in particular, seem to create self-contained universes, seemingly oblivious to the worlds of literature they inhabit or the influences that contributed to their creation. In this way, they seek to establish their own centrality to the experience of reading. A hypertext document, on the other hand, dispels this fiction and accepts a decentered position as one of many texts that contribute to a reading experience. In this way, a

**Table 2.1**

**Different Types of Hyperlinks (adapted from Shipley & Fish, 1996)**

| | |
|---|---|
| Target link | Connects one point in a given document to another point in the same document. |
| Relative link | Connects one page in a given site to a different page within the site. |
| External link | Connects one site to a distinct site. |

given hyperlink situated in a passage from the novel *Being There* might lead to a biographical essay on its author, Jerzy Kosinski. Documents thus exist in relationship rather than independent of one another. Landow calls each of these fragments **lexias**, and it is their relationship of one to another that moves the experience of reading away from centrality in hypertext. In the present practice of hypertext on the World Wide Web, a single page of any given Web site would function as a lexia.

**FROM HIERARCHY TO COOPERATION.** Finally, Landow sees hypertext marking a significant shift from an hierarchical to a networked relationship between author and reader. In the traditional conception, the author has long been valorized as the creator of meaning. Certainly, literary scholars have long hollowed names like Nathanial Hawthorne and Maya Angelo, to name but two canonized artists, for their creative gifts. Yet the hierarchy that places the creative genius of the author above the common intelligence of the reader is flattened in hypertext. Here author and reader must work together to make meaning out of the available symbols. Thus, the experience that comes from reading a given set of lexia flows from both the creative production of the author and the choices made by the reader. Such increased participation in constructing the reading experience is reminiscent of our earlier discussion of how online communication is facilitating a return to community. As experimentation with hypertext continues in forums like the World Wide Web, it will be interesting to see how the conventions of reading change for a new generation of meaning makers.

## HYPERLINK: THE DARK SIDE OF THE RAINBOW

The changing relationship between author and reader in a hypertextual environment understandably raises significant questions. Doesn't it *matter* whether the author intended that a particular text would communicate a specific meaning? Shouldn't we respect the author's wishes in reading a text in a certain way? The problem with this line of questioning is that we rarely can peer so clearly into the author's psyche that we can hardly presume to know for sure what she or he *really* meant. The worst part? Some authors aren't too sure either. Here's an example:

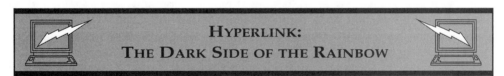

Over the last few years, various fans of the rock group Pink Floyd have turned to the Web to share their vision of what Roger Waters, Dave Gilmour, and band-mates *really* meant when they recorded their groundbreaking 1973 album, *Dark Side of the Moon*. Many careful students of this album claim that the band intended their album to follow the plot-line of the film, *The Wizard of Oz!* One researcher of the odd coincidences between these works, Charles Savage, points out:

- The Pink Floyd song "The Great Gig in the Sky" is closely matched to the film's tornado scene, rising and falling as the tornado spins across the screen.
- The album ends with the sounds of heartbeats—just as Dorothy listens to the Tin Woodsman's chest.
- "'Black . . . and blue' from 'Us and Them' is sung as the Wicked Witch of the West appears dressed in black. That is shortly followed by 'and who knows which is which' (witch is witch) as she and Glenda confront each other."

Did Pink Floyd intend for listeners of *Dark Side of the Moon* to start the album just as the MGM Lion roared? No one is sure. But it's fun to imagine that they did.

Ironically, *The Wizard of Oz* itself has invited a host of re-readings. Littlefield (1964) found that the original book could be interpreted as a response to the free silver movement of the 1890s. From this perspective, characters in this child's fantasy could be reconfigured to stand in for characters and symbols of the political struggle of that age: the yellow brick road representing the gold standard, the Scarecrow representing the farmers, and the Cowardly Lion representing political leader William Jennings Bryan.

Hypertext challenges us to think past the question of whether Pink Floyd *meant* to relate their music to *The Wizard of Oz*, or whether Lyman Frank Baum *meant* to write a subtle allegory of his time. Most fans of these works doubt whether either artist intended to create this strange set of connections. But that's not quite the point of our analysis. Hypertext allows us to imagine and interpret **synchronicities**—immediate but not necessarily intended connections and cross-references between people and ideas that unify public life and ground human experience.

Hypertextual analysis provides the reader a power to shape the meaning of a text by providing the means to establish meaning between and across texts. The World Wide Web provides an arena where various narrative interpretations are tested against common sense. Those that endure become part of our social fabric. Others remain as pages that people seldom visit. Either way, the texture of our communities becomes a lot more interesting.

- To learn more, visit Charles Savage's homepage: http://members.aol.com/rbsavage/floydwizard.html
- To read Henry Littlefield's essay on *The Wizard of Oz* visit: http://www.amphigory.com/oz.htm

## CHAPTER SUMMARY

In this chapter, we have explored the technology of CMC from historical and functional perspectives. We offered an abbreviated history of computer technology with particular emphasis on the role of cybernetics in the evolution of the Internet. Following this overview, we delved into five characteristics of online communication: packet-switching, multimedia, interactivity, synchronicity, and hypertextuality. At this point, we switch gears and head into the second major section of this text—a survey of issues related to online identity.

### Online Communication and the Law

The next time you are building a Web site, you might want to think twice about what hyperlinks you include. Linking to the Walt Disney Company or Coca-Cola probably won't get you into too much trouble, but linking to illegal software just might. Such a case came before a New York court in which the alleged engineer and some 72 Web masters who had linked to the software program were named as defendants (Kaplan, 2000). The suit was filed by the DVD Copy Control Association, acting on behalf of numerous entertainment industry companies that produce the Digital Versatile Disks. The association sought to restrict the engineer who created DeCSS, a program that allows one to decrypt and thus presumably pirate the increasingly popular home entertainment disks. They also sought damages from the engineer and from a number of people who posted or merely linked to the software program. In August 2000, a federal judge ruled in favor of the association, noting that web sites cannot provide links to illegal software. If restrictions against establishing hyperlinks continue to be upheld, we may find that in cyberspace a person can be guilty by association.

### Glossary

**Analytical engine**: A 19th-century concept that serves as the predecessor to the modern computer.

**ARPANET**: Early computer network designed for the U.S. Defense Department.

**Asynchronous communication**: The exchange of messages with significant lag time between them.

**Chronemics**: The use of time as a nonverbal channel for communicating qualities such as liking or dominance.

**Command and control**: The channeling of information to ensure that individuals act efficiently as a unit.

**Hyperlink**: Selected words or images that connect to other sections of a document or other documents in a hypertext environment like the World Wide Web.

**Hypertext**: A form of nonsequential writing that composes a text out of smaller bits of material that exist in relation to one another in a multilinear, decentralized network.

**Information**: An exchange of data necessary for one system to influence the behavior of another system.

**Internet**: A network of computers that allows for the transmission of data for multiple purposes through a common set of protocols according to a global address system.

**Jacquard Loom**: A device that allows a weaver to mass produce patterns of cloth by following the patterns of punch cards.

**Lexia**: A chunk of material in hypertext.

**Memex**: A theoretical machine for the storage and retrieval of information linked together by hypertext.

**Synchronicities**: Immediate but not necessarily intended connections and cross-references between people and ideas that unify public life and ground human experience.

**Synchronous communication**: The exchange of messages in real time.

**Technological determinism**: Perspective that our growing ability to alter or replace nature provides a central reason for most personal and social trends.

## Topics for Discussion

1. Select any one of the forms of CMC discussed in chapter 1 (e-mail, BBS, MUD, IRC, or the Web) and explain how Rafaeli's five qualities are or are not apparent. As part of your response, consider how communication practiced in that form is different from the other forms.

2. Spend some time exploring a site on the World Wide Web. When you are finished, consider how hypertext influenced your interpretation of the reading experience. Then write a brief explanation for each of the following qualities: How did you proceed in a nonsequential rather than linear fashion? How did the site de-center itself in relation to other sites through hyperlinks? In what way did you collaborate with the Web master in making meaning out of this site?

3. Conduct a Yahoo search for resources about the Internet. Select five Web sites that appear to offer timely and credible information about one or several of these topics: search engines, Web portals, e-mail, the role of Internet in education, the impact of CMC on business. Bookmark these online resources for your upcoming research efforts.

## REFERENCES


Apple's iMac led quarter computer sales. (1999, January 22). *The New York Times*, p. 20.

Bennahum, D. S. (1998). *Extra life: Coming of age in cyberspace*. New York: Basic Books.

Borenstein, D. (2000). Quoteland.com <http://ww.quoteland.com>.

Bush, V. (1945, July). As we may think. *Atlantic Monthly*, 176, 101–108.

Federal Networking Council. (1995, October 30). *FNC Resolution: Definition of "Internet."* <http://www.fnc.gov/Internet_res.html>.

Gibson, W., & Sterling, B. (1991). *The difference engine*. New York: Bantam Books.

Kaplan, C. S. (2000, January 7). DVD lawsuit questions legality of linking. *Cybertimes Cyber Law Journal* <http://www.nytimes.com/ library/tech/00/01/cyber /cyberlaw/07law.html>.

Kaye, B. K., & Medoff, N. J. (1999). *The World Wide Web: A mass communication perspective*. Mountain View, CA: Mayfield.

Landow, G. P. (1992). *Hypertext: The convergence of contemporary critical theory and technology*. Baltimore, MD: Johns Hopkins University Press.

Littlefield, H. M. (1964). The wizard of oz: Parable on populism. *American Quarterly, XVI*, 47–58.

Metz, J. M. (1994, April). Computer-mediated communication: Literature review of a new context. *Interpersonal Computing and Technology: An Electronic Journal for the 21st Century, 2*(2), 31–49.

Morris, M., & Ogan, C. (1996). The Internet as mass medium. *Journal of Communication, 46*(1), 39–50.

Moreau, R. (1984). *The computer comes of age: The people, the hardware, and the software* (J. Howlett, Trans.) Cambridge, MA: The MIT Press.

Newhagen, J. E., & Rafaeli, S. (1996, March). Why communication researchers should study the Internet: A dialogue. *Journal of Computer-Mediated Communication, 1*(4), <http://www.ascusc.org/jcmc/vol1/issue4/rafaeli.html>.

Ong, W. J. (1982). *Orality and literacy: The technologizing of the word*. New York: Routledge.

Shipley, C., & Fish, M. (1996). *How the World Wide Web works*. Emeryville, CA: Ziff-Davis.

Shurkin, J. (1984). *Engines of the mind: A history of the computer*. New York: Norton.

Strate, L. (1996). Cybertime. In L. Strate, R. Jacobson, & S. B. Gibson (Eds.), *Communication and cyberspace: Social interaction in an electronic environment* (pp. 351–377). Cresskill, NJ: Hampton Press.

Taylor, C. (1999, January). Apple's revolution in a box. *Time Digital*. <http://cgi.pathfinder.com/time/digital/feature/0,2955,18248–5,00.html>.

Walther, J. B., & Tidwell, L. C. (1995). Nonverbal cues in computer-mediated communication, and the effect of chronemics on relational communication. *Journal of Organizational Computing, 5*, 355–378.

Weiner, N. (1954). *The human use of human beings: Cybernetics and society*. Boston: Houghton Mifflin.

Zakon, R. H. (1998, December 31). *Hobbes' Internet timeline 4.0.* <http://info.isoc.org/guest/zakon/Internet/History/HIT.html>.

# PART II

# THE SELF AMONG OTHERS

A generation ago, a communication technology grabbed the nation's interest, and its enthusiasts eagerly incorporated the latest equipment for their systems, adopted quirky aliases for themselves, and spent hour after hour doing nothing more than talking to other enthusiasts. If this behavior seems a lot like the way people behaved when the Internet caught on in the 1990s, it is because there are some intriguing parallels between the previous popularity of Citizen's Band (CB) radio and the recent popularity of the Internet. Although amateur radio broadcasts had been evolving since the late 1940s, its popularity peaked in 1977 when an estimated 11 million Americans were taking to the airwaves broadcasting messages to one another (Drew, 1997). In fact, the recent film, *Frequency* (2000), nostalgically recalled the joys of this form of mediated communication. Although there are far fewer CB hobbyists today, people's interest in communicating with others who are not physically present has not diminished. Arguably, the introduction of e-mail into people's professional and personal lives has made such mediated communication an even more frequent occurrence.

Thus, today we can find people adding webcams to their computer systems, rechristening themselves with fanciful pseudonyms, and spending countless hours chatting with people they have never seen nor are likely to see. And yet despite the Internet's popularity, some people question the quality and effects of this latest form of mediated communication in our lives. This part of the book addresses both people's behavior in and the concerns about CMC. We consider behaviors like the creation of identities, the formation of relationships, and the maintenance of virtual communities. But we also address concerns like misrepresentation, hostile messages, and Internet addiction. In short, we discuss a host of issues that involve how individuals affect and are affected by the others they engage through communication.

## REFERENCES

Drew, K. (1997, March 20). Breaker, breaker: CB radio is back. *Christian Science Monitor*, p. 3.

Hoblit, G. (Producer/Director). (2000). *Frequency* [Film]. New York: New Line Cinema.

# CHAPTER 3

# FORMING ONLINE IDENTITIES

*Looking at the proliferation of personal Web pages on the Net, it looks like very soon everyone on Earth will have 15 megabytes of fame.*

—*MG Siriam (Borenstein, 2000)*

For 3 years, women who participated in a CompuServe discussion group grew closer and closer to a woman they knew as Julie Graham. During that time, Julie posted messages that disclosed increasingly intimate details of her life, including the fact that she was a mute, paraplegic victim of a car crash who had wrestled with suicidal depression. Her plight so moved her fellow participants that after a number of months of interacting with her online, one well-intentioned woman set out to find Julie and offer her face-to-face comfort and support. Much to this woman's surprise, "Julie Graham" turned out to be a fiction, and the facts behind the person creating her were quite contrary to what the woman and others had read. First of all, Julie wasn't a mute paraplegic at all. Second, she wasn't housebound, but a full-time professional psychologist. Third, she wasn't a she, but a man who had created the online persona of Julie to delve deeper into the female psyche by impersonating one. When the sleuthing woman reported her discovery to the rest of the bulletin board's participants, outraged contributors condemned the experiment, remarking that in impersonating one of them, the psychologist had violated their privacy (Stone, 1991).

Why were the women upset with "Julie's" deception? After all, how could these women feel betrayed by someone with whom they had never met face to face? Despite the intuitive conclusion of those outside the context that these were "just words," the self that this psychologist presented and the one that his conversation partners perceived seemed quite authentic. Computer-mediated communication contexts, like no other person-to-person media before them, offer communicators the ability to manipulate their personal identities in ways that call into question assumptions about what is possible and what is appropriate in the presentation of self.

This chapter explores several key issues dedicated to questions of identity in communicating through mediating technologies. An **identity** is a complex personal and social construct, consisting in part of who we think ourselves to be, how we wish others to perceive us, and how they actually perceives us. In particular, CMC research has looked at the second of these fragments: how we wish others to perceive us. The process of setting forth an image we want others to perceive is known as **self-presentation**.

In considering how people go about constructing their self-presentations online, we review research that considers several different channels for CMC. In particular this research has focused on human interaction in MUDs, IRC, and BBS although much of what has been suggested about the nature of these text-only media can be applied to e-mail and even the more graphically rich environment of Web sites. (A review of the tools just described can be found in chapter 1.) Social convention has dictated that most MUDs, many IRC channels, and several BBS serve a more playful than professional function. Thus, because their objectives tend to be social rather than task-oriented, they present especially rich opportunities for experimentation with self-presentation. As is seen here, these text-only media have introduced new forums for communicating one's identity. The lessons learned from people's use of them underscores how we construct our identities and points to ways we can more competently communicate about ourselves in the mediated environment.

In the following sections, this chapter introduces several concepts in understanding the communication of online identity. To begin, we consider the process of perceiving an audience through telepresence. Next, we review the construction of identity through a performance metaphor, examining how people construct online personas. After that, we examine the distinctions among nameless anonymity, inventive pseudonymity, and one's real-life identity. Finally, we conclude with some suggestions for protecting real-life identity in an era of enhanced technological access to potentially damaging personal information.

## Hyperlink: 15 Megabytes of Fame

Andy Warhol, the 20th-century artist who enjoyed a noteworthy reputation in art and popular culture circles, once said, "In the future everyone will be world-famous for fifteen minutes." Warhol was, of course, offering a sarcastic commentary on how society has grown obsessed with celebrity status. Today, more than ever, it seems there are figures who are famous simply for being famous, and people seem more likely to know the names of the entertainers who star in their favorite television shows than the names of their state's elected officials who legislate the laws that govern their lives. Some critics have noted that the Internet has only added to this dilemma, allowing more people than ever to engage in the pursuit for celebrity by allowing them to create mass-distributed images for themselves.

For instance, consider lam.com, a site that showcases the portfolios of aspiring actors, dancers, models, and musicians. On lam.com, these undiscovered entertainers can advertise their talents on the World Wide Web by displaying a multimedia portfolio including their resumes along with any combination of static images, video clips, or audio clips. "Be seen. Be heard" advocates the Web site, encouraging ambitious stars to join their database and thus seize an opportunity for "legitimate discovery." Inspired by promises of fame and fortune, numerous performers have posted information to the site, hoping that some well-placed publicity on the Web will bring them the notoriety they desire.

An alternative strategy toward gaining fame is to establish a presence using your own unique domain name, as was the approach of the DotComGuy. The former Mitch Maddox (he legally changed his name to DotComGuy) decided to live a year of his life online using products and services purchased exclusively through the Internet (Sheff, 2000). Beginning on January 1, 2000, DotComGuy moved into a house whose furnishings were limited to little more than the dozens of webcams used to broadcast his homebound activities day and night. In keeping with the promotional agreement that he made with his sponsors, DotComGuy never left his home and so bought everything from toilet paper to movie videos online. In making his exploits available to a worldwide audience, DotComGuy garnered the attention of numerous media outlets in addition to the fans who regularly chatted with him on his Web site, www.dotcomguy.com.

Of course, these examples are just the tip of the celebrity-seeking iceberg. From personal Web sites that function as electronic wedding albums to pay-per-view sites where amateur exhibitionists engage in all manner of revealing activities on live webcams, the Internet has seemingly put celebrity within everyone's grasp. Now instead of 15 minutes of fame, perhaps Warhol's prophecy could be revised to guarantee everyone 15 megabytes of fame as Siriam suggested in the opening quotation. Of course, in the rush to package, publish, and market themselves, those in pursuit of star status must compete with everyone else seeking the public's notice. What is an unknown to do in this competitive climate?

Perhaps another sarcasm taken from popular culture offers some perspective. A recent soft drink campaign mocked its competitor's use of celebrity endorsements to sell their products. "Image is nothing" quipped each ad in the series, attempting to remind us that the famous are not omniscient experts: Just because someone plays basketball well does not mean that he or she knows your tastes better than you do. As we encounter would-be Internet icons (or even consider becoming such icons ourselves) we should take the soft drink maker's advice under consideration. Is our own admiration of these stars based on legitimate contributions they have made to our lives or merely based on their own pursuit of fame?

## THE PRINCIPLE OF TELEPRESENCE: IS ANYONE OUT THERE?

One of the foundational issues in establishing a sense of online identity has to do with the degree to which people feel they are able to experience a connection to others through technology. Some people are able to look at a computer screen and declare, "Those are just words," whereas others report that they are able to perceive personal characteristics and relational content through text-only messages. As in many such cases where the same phenomenon can render different interpretations by different audiences, human perception functions to make the experience richer or poorer.

Whenever we interact in face-to-face contexts, we take our surroundings, and the multiple senses that are stimulated, for granted. When you take a walk in the park, you probably are aware, but don't deeply contemplate, all the sensations that make the experience real to you: the sight of oak trees, the sound of singing robins, the smell of spring blossoms, and the feel of the dirt path beneath your feet. These stimuli create a feeling of presence for you. In mediated contexts, such as reading a description of a walk through the virtual park of a MUD, requires that you perceive the same sensations as creating (or re-creating) the experience for you. This is **telepresence**, "the extent to which one feels present in the mediated environment, rather than in the immediate physical environment" (Steuer,

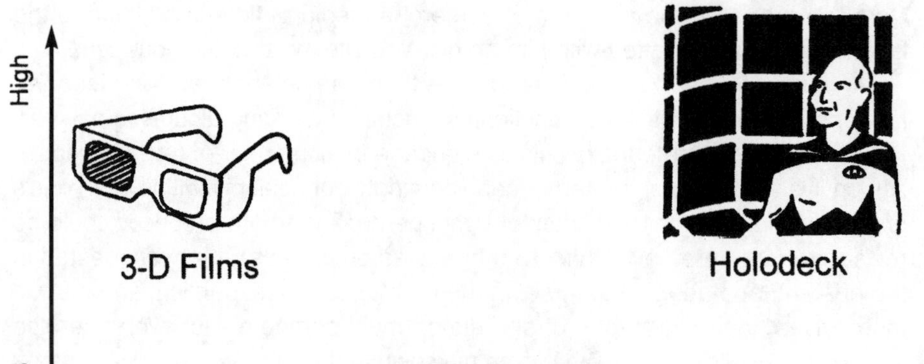

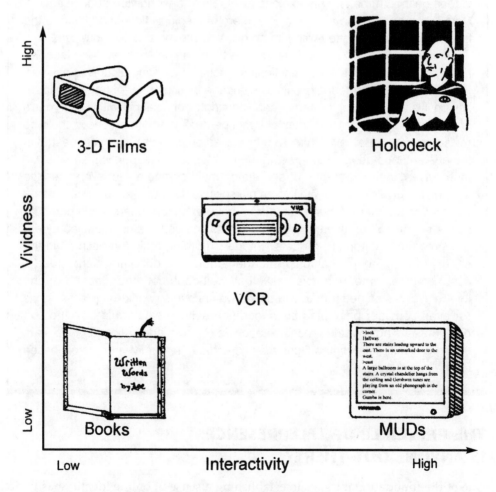

Fig. 3.1. Various media technologies classified by vividness and interactivity (adapted from Steuer, 1992).

1992, p. 76). Even slight distinctions among mediating technologies can vary the experience of telepresence. Consider, for example, the difference between an audio recording cut in the studio versus one made at a concert. A concert recording can seem more realistic because of the addition of background noises that recreate the experience of being a part of an audience for a listener.

According to Steuer (1992), the sense of "being there" that many report experiencing while engaged in the virtual realities communicated through cyberspace can be explained in terms of telepresence. His model (as depicted in Fig. 3.1) suggests that varying degrees of vividness and interactivity on the part of the medium indicate how realistic a person will perceive the limited stimuli offered.

The quality of **vividness** refers to the amount of sensory information the medium makes available to a person. According to Steuer, a sense of vividness is created by both the breadth of senses engaged and the depths to which any one of those senses are stimulated. If you compare media rated as "high" in vividness with those rated as "low," you will see a difference in both the breadth and depth of sensory information available. For instance, compare 3-D films, which rate relatively high on vividness, to books, which rate relatively low. A 3-D film, such as the Universal Pictures' classic *The Creature from the Black Lagoon,* is a more vivid depiction of an alternate reality than that available in the latest Tom Clancy novel. The film displays more breadth than the book because it makes use of both our senses of sight and hearing. The book would only engage our sight. The film also represents greater depth of vividness. Three-dimensional cinema uses technology to create an illusion of multiple layers to enhance our visual perceptions more than traditional filming or photography. Books lack such sensory depth, relying instead on our imaginations to add dimensions of meaning to the words we read in them.

The sense of realism that comes with telepresence is also enhanced by the degree of interactivity the medium presents to people. A measure of **interactivity** deals with the degree to which a person can manipulate the environment of a medium. A sense of interactivity is suggested by three factors. The first of these is *speed,* or how quickly a user can manipulate the environment. The second is *range,* or how much a user manipulates the environment, and the third deals with *mapping,* or how the actions of a user are related to reactions in the virtual environment. Let's return to the earlier example of books and compare them to another text-based communication medium, MUDs. With a few exceptions, books offer limited interactivity to readers. Readers can do little to change the content of books in any sort of timely fashion. Even if a typographical error is found in a textbook and it is reported to the publisher, a correction is unlikely to appear until a subsequent edition of the book is printed in 2 to 4 years. Thus, only limited control can be exerted over the speed or range of manipulation over this medium. One genre of book does allow some sense of mapping, the third quality of interactivity, and that is the "choose-your-own-adventure" books, popularized in the 1980s. These books allowed readers to determine the sequence of a story by choosing among limited choices of what page or chapter to read next. However, the vast majority of books are low in interactivity.

In contrast, MUDs are forums for greater participation. A MUD allows one to make contributions to the ongoing conversation and action in real time. Not only is one's contribution quickly transcribed onto the screen, it can alter the course of events or conversation indicating a much more significant degree of content manipulation than was possible with books. Finally, one's decision to move around objects or one's own position within the MUD is reacted to by the program governing its operations. Hence, when one directs one's character, <bud>, to "leave library," the program accommodates the directive and displays: "bud leaves library," providing a sense of mapping as one's actions appear to cause a reaction in the virtual world.

One of Steuer's (1992) more interesting selections for his comparison of various media includes one technology that only exists as fiction, the holodeck that originated on the television series, *Star Trek: The Next Generation* (1987–1994). The holodeck was a room aboard the Starship Enterprise that created recreational environments for the ship's crew during their long sojourns in space. Using holograms and force fields, the holodeck simulated everything from New Orleans' jazz clubs to alien landscapes with convincing detail. The holodeck not only provided a practical plot device to get the series' characters out of outer space from time to time, it also served as an idealized conception of the heights to which mediating technologies could aspire. The holodeck provided a forecast for an as-yet-unrealized medium that is exceptionally high in vividness and interactivity. Likewise, Steuer's dimensions determining telepresence help us appreciate just how complex a thing it is for the mind to interpret different mediated messages as realistic.

## PERFORMING IDENTITY ON THE INTERNET

People's perceptions of the amount of telepresence in a given medium suggest that they are likely to consider how the messages they fashion through media are reflections on them. Perhaps you have acquaintances who do not leave messages on telephone answering machines, declaring, "I don't like those machines." Such individuals are probably a bit self-conscious about what they say or how they sound on tape. This kind of self-awareness is but another manifestation of humanity's long struggle with identity. Again, an important aspect of **identity** is how we present ourselves to others. To some degree, we can control what others know of us by making some choices in life, and yet certain qualities of our identities are predetermined for us. In face-to-face interactions, people infer qualities of our identities based on our gender, race, clothing, and other nonverbal characteristics. Because many of these cues are invisible online, Internet technologies offer us the possibility of controlling more aspects of our identity for public consideration than has been possible before. As the following examples demonstrate, fashioning identity has been a perennial concern of human civilization.

Manipulating one's identity is nothing new to Western culture, and, indeed, neither are many of the insecurities associated with such a practice. Consider, for example, the ancient Greek myth of Oedipus, preserved for us in the works of Sophocles. According to the playwright's account, a prophet had declared that the king's newborn son was destined to kill his father. Hoping to avoid this fate, the king sent the infant off to be killed itself, but the soldier charged with the task instead left the baby to be raised by shepherds. Years later, the grown Oedipus, oblivious of his ancestry, unknowingly traveled back to the kingdom. Along his journey he got into an argument with a stranger, which culminated in the stranger's death. Unknown to Oedipus, he had just fulfilled the prophecy by slaying his own father, who was actually the king in disguise. Oedipus traveled on to the city of Thebes, where after solving the riddle of the monstrous Sphinx, he was proclaimed king and given the queen as his bride. That queen, as you might have guessed, turned out to be his own mother. Before the play is over, Oedipus discovers his true identity, and in anger for not recognizing the situation sooner, gouges out his own eyes with the pin of a broach. With such grisly repercussions, even for those ignorant of their circumstances, is it any wonder societies such as the Greek's, and the rest of Western cultures that followed them, have placed such a heavy emphasis on consistency in individual identity?

In addition to Greek tragedies, the problematic nature of personal identity has also been a theme for comedies. In fact, a source of humor in a number of William Shakespeare's timeless comedies is the misrepresented identity, and specifically the switching of identities that involve gender-swapping. Modern audiences were reminded of how complex and fun such manipulations of identity could be in 1998 Academy Award winner for best picture, *Shakespeare in Love*. In the film, noblewoman Viola de Lesseps (portrayed by Gwyneth Paltrow) wants to be an actor, but both her elevated social class and gender forbid her from mingling with common performers. It is only once she disguises herself as a boy that she is able to win a role on stage working with Shakespeare in his Globe Theatre. She traded her skirt for a pair of pants, tucked her long hair under a hat, and deepened her voice to perpetuate her disguise. According to the fictional movie, these events allegedly inspired Shakespeare to use gender-swapping as plot device in his comedies, including *As You Like It* and *All's Well that Ends Well*.

Although comparatively few of us elect to take on the characteristics typically associated with the opposite gender, most of us are adopting specific ornaments for our appearance and attitudes to suit the roles we find ourselves fulfilling during daily life. Consider the process you undergo in the morning when deciding what clothes to wear. Do you purposefully choose a professional outfit because you have to go to work or make a presentation for a class? Or do you throw on the first thing you trip over on your floor? If you know you have to work or make a presentation, would it be inappropriate to show up in baggy sweat pants and a T-shirt? Certainly. Just as it would be inappropriate to show up for a touch football game in a blazer, most of us are aware that costuming is an important aspect of the parts we play and the self we choose to present at one time or another.

## Casting Call: Performing Multiple Roles

Communication scholars have long pulled on the works of noted sociologist Erving Goffman, who wrote extensively on how people work to present themselves in everyday life. Goffman would have agreed with Shakespeare, who wrote:

> All the world's a stage,
> And all the men and women merely players.
> They have their exits and their entrances;
> And one man in his time plays many parts. (*As You Like It*, Act II, Sc. 7)

It was Goffman's (1959) contention that everyday life was a performance of sorts, and that our behaviors and attitudes could be explained in terms of a theatrical metaphor. Accordingly, Goffman wrote of how people adopted particular roles when they were in public view by putting on a face. The effort people invest in "staying in character," as it were, Goffman calls **face-work**, noting that people are persistently attending to the requirements of a particular face lest they break the image of their role. Over the years, Goffman's work has been instrumental in helping to understand how elements of performance contribute to what and how people communicate. More recent researchers have echoed Goffman's fascination with the theatrical metaphor and have invoked similar language in attempting to explain how people construct identities online.

Pulling on another theatrical term, Bruckman (1992) dubs text-based forums like MUDs as "identity workshops." A workshop, in theatrical training, presents an opportunity for actors to experiment with various roles. An actor in training might take on the role of a vocal football coach one moment and then change over to a portrayal of a sidewalk entertaining mime the next, all to practice the range of his or her acting ability. In like manner, then, an identity workshop presents people with a chance to display different manifestations of themselves. One could very well maintain an identity as a rough and tough sailor in one MUD but portray a sensitive artist in another chat room.

Turkle (1995) is a noted cybercultural expert who is especially interested in the computer's ability to enable users to explore multiple roles. Turkle says, "In . . .. computer-mediated worlds, the self is multiple, fluid and constituted in interaction with machine connections; it is made and transformed by language" (p. 15). This view of the self as multiple and fluid—subject to multiphrenia described in chapter 1—rather than singular and static is further explored in Turkle's writings by drawing a comparison to the multiple tasks one can accomplish in a windows-based environment. Current software allows users to change from using a word-processing program to author a research paper, to sending e-mail to one's boss, and to participating in a MUD, all by merely clicking from window to window. Thus, one can quite readily switch roles from student, to employee, to fantasy figure. Certainly, this is a manifestation of the concept of multiphrenia introduced in chapter 1. However, Turkle clearly suggested that people control the multiple roles rather than suffer from the burden of having to negotiate among them.

Why do people engage in such role-playing then? Turkle (1995) suggests one reason is that people can experience an identity they could not successfully portray in real life. A benefit of such role-playing is that individuals can gain a new perspective on their world and their place in it. Borrowing from anthropology, Turkle uses the term **dépaysement** to describe the experience of seeing the familiar through unfamiliar eyes. In interviews with people who adopted distinctly different identities from their own for their online personas, most notably those who changed their genders, Turkle found the experience of living a life unlike their own opened them up to the struggles and pleasures that come along with living with another gender, race, class, or other distinction.

Another reason might reside in the increased control people experience over their online identities. In real life, one can adopt a limited number of roles, given that one's gender, race, age, accent, and other nonverbal determinants influence people's perceptions of how well one functions in a given role. For instance, a middle-aged, Euro-American man might decide he wants to experiment with a female identity. With the appropriate costuming and mannerisms, he might be successful in appearing to be a female to someone he has not previously met. However, if he wants to know what it is like to be an African American, he is less likely to be able to pull off such a charade. However, in an online forum, he can more readily adopt and enact a change in his gender, race, or any other characteristic he chooses.

In whatever identity he selects, he can exert greater control over his identity in the online environment than in face-to-face interaction. In face-to-face interactions, we communicate not only through our words but also through our appearance. For example, in real life, someone might decide to discount your opinion because of your age, either because he or she perceives that you are too young or too old to know much about a topic. But in online forums, what people know about others is based on the disclosure of information that one wishes others to know (Cutler, 1996). If one's age is not relevant to the persona one wishes to have others perceive, then one needs merely not to reveal this information to prevent skewing others' perceptions one way or another.

## Learning One's Lines: Performing Through Language

In the presentation of self online, one is not recognized by one's physical appearance, but through one's textual behaviors. Obviously, one might offer a description of one's persona or disclose personal characteristics that contribute to others' impression formations. Yet according to Giese (1998), there is another way that people come to identify an individual as participants interact with one another. "In a sense I am 'recognized' by a host of personal markers that include my writing style, my .sig [signature attachment], the way I conduct myself with various members of the groups and my contributions to the cooperative narrative." In short, both what people say about themselves and how they behave with others contributes to a perception of personal identity online. The use of language is consequently of immense importance in cyberspace, for it is through the use of language that people construct their identities.

Language is thus the primary vehicle for establishing one's own and perceiving another's online persona. A term for such figures common among fantasy game-players and growing in usage among CMC practitioners is avatar. An **avatar** is a representation of oneself in a virtual environment, in other words, one's alter ego or persona.

The selection of a rather unusual term to express the relationships between identity and cyberspace is perhaps justified by the unusual nature of the medium itself. As with all mediated environments, one does not have a body in the non-space of cyberspace, only a representation of oneself, wholly constructed by individual choices. Even when in the case of writing a letter, which is seemingly devoid of so many nonverbal cues, people (like handwriting experts) infer qualities about the person on the other end based on something (loops in letters, dotting of letters) other than the content of what they have said. Only in cyberspace is the proverbial playing field leveled of such biasing cues, suggesting that a new type of representation is occurring in this context.

Of course, the practice of representing oneself through language and controlled cues (as in web pages that offer photographs or sound bites) is not above suspicion. People tend to mistrust what they cannot verify through other sources. We all know that lies are constructs of language. Even telling someone to "put it in writing" does not preclude deception. Socrates, whose philosophical treatises formed the foundations for Western thought, never committed a word to paper. (What we know of the insights attributed to him were set down by his pupil, Plato.) Socrates was suspicious of writing, fearing someone could just as easily misquote him as quote him. The persistent fear that language does not provide an accurate depiction of reality is revisited in the construction of avatars. How are we to know that what we read is what we get? Contributing to a lack of ease in dealing with people only though their online presentations is the much-touted practice of gender-swapping.

## Gender-Swapping: Performing in Virtual Drag

The opening vignette of this chapter illustrates one well-known case where gender-swapping was not favorably received. **Gender-swapping** occurs when an individual of one gender self-presents as a member of another gender. As you probably know, gender is a social construct that provides guidelines for how we expect people of a certain biological sex to behave. For example, men are expected to be masculine and thus strong and women to be feminine and thus compassionate. Such expectations are reinforced throughout our lives, and so when we encounter someone who seemingly violates these stereotypes, we can be frustrated by the inconsistency. Several years ago, *Saturday Night Live* featured a character called Pat, and the confusion over whether Pat's name and behaviors were indicative of a man or a woman revealed how obsessed we are with gender (Bruckman, 1996).

Research has indicated that when people gender-swap (and more typically than not it is men portraying women), they tend to adopt the same rigid gender roles that their culture has come to expect (Bornstein, 1994). As such, masculine avatars devote a great deal of attention to and will eagerly come to the aid of female avatars (Bruckman, 1996). The perpetuation of stereotypical responses to gender such as this suggests why when someone is exposed for gender-swapping, others can respond with disbelief, confusion, or anger.

Reports of gender-swapping, and the anxieties that accompany it and other forms of misrepresentation, may yet prove to be overly exaggerated. According to research reported by Schiano (1999), most people in online forums act as idealized versions of themselves (rather than markedly distinct individuals), and the majority of MUD participants maintain only one character. In fact, she found that participants experienced "an awareness of social pressure to maintain the authenticity and accountability afforded by a single primary identity." Such a finding corroborates survey results among people making presentations of self through personal Web sites. Approximately 67% of those responding to the survey reported that they did not feel it is appropriate for anyone to misrepresent themselves online (Buten, 1996). Interestingly, 91% agreed that they accurately represented themselves on their own homepages. Such research clearly suggests that although experimentation with identity is possible, it is neither encouraged nor the norm for the presentation of self.

### HYPERLINK: THE DOGGONED LOG ON

A perennial feature of *The New Yorker* magazine has been its whimsical cartoons. Over the years, they have provided witty commentary on social practices, including the one that appeared in the July 5, 1993, issue, featuring two dogs reflecting on the nature of personal identity on the Internet. As one dog sits poised in front of a computer screen, he turns to his companion and says, "On the Internet, nobody knows you're a dog." The cartoon, drawn by Peter Steiner, represents in stark brevity the point of much academic contemplation on the nature of self in online contexts (the contents of this chapter included). On the surface, the cartoon makes light of how easily online identity is manipulated, so much so that even an animal could successfully disguise itself. On a deeper level, it, like many other examples of humor, picks at the scabs of our collective insecurities. The dogs the cartoon depicts are almost conspiratorial in their misrepresentation of identity. Moreover, the label of *dog* is not only applied to a beloved household pet, but also used to describe an undesirable person (e.g., "That dog left me at the alter."). Perhaps without ever intending to, "On the Internet, nobody knows you're a dog" illustrates twin concerns associated with online identities: the playfulness they promote and the suspicions that surround them.

## ANONYMITY, PSEUDONYMITY, AND IDENTITY

When people enter chat rooms, contribute to bulletin boards, or participate in MUDs, they can exercise control over elements of their self-presentation. In choosing names, signature files, or personal descriptions, they make conscious decisions about how they wish to be perceived by others. The range of possible selves one might elect to present could be considered along a continuum (see Fig. 3.2) of identification (Marx, 1999). At one end of this continuum would be the nearly emp-

Fig. 3.2. A continuum of identity manipulation.

tied state of anonymity. Along the continuum would be differing levels of an invented self-representing pseudonymity. At the opposite end, then, would be the identity presented in real life (or as close as one could get to it through the limited stimuli of mediating technologies). In the section that follows, we look at the manipulation of identity along this continuum.

## Anonymity

Although most Americans would consider being "up front" with people to be a common value, the fact is that in many instances we value privacy even more than frankness. There are certain legitimate circumstances where our safety is protected by issuing our messages anonymously. In mediated contexts, **anonymity** is a state of communicating where the identity of the communicator is not readily apparent. People use anonymity to solicit dates in newspaper and magazine advertisements, to report knowledge of criminal activities on police tip lines, to engage in whistle blowing activities that draw media or legal attention to corporate misdoing, and to seek shelter when involved in abusive relationships (Wayner, 1999). In such circumstances, not being obliged to disclose one's true identity, and thus risk one's personal security, may well encourage important messages that might not otherwise be communicated.

The ability to communicate anonymously has been a particularly thorny issue in CMC. Although anonymity can function to protect people from reprisals it can also distance them from accountability, that is, taking responsibility for what they say. As we explain in the final section of this chapter, some people misuse the anonymity that online communication technologies afford to commit crimes. According to Lee (1996), the debates over online anonymity have centered on three key issues. The first issue has to do with the informative aspect of identity. Knowing the reputation of the person issuing a statement is a double-edged sword. On one hand, knowing who has said something suggests the credibility that person has to speak on that topic. For example, having information about a source's expertise on a given topic influences how much one will trust the source's position. On the other hand, knowing characteristics like the sender's gender, race, and social standing could lead to an unfair hearing based on a receiver's personal biases and stereotypes. A second issue of anonymity deals with group pressures. One side of this argument suggests that people who must be associated with their ideas will only express things they truly believe. Knowing that others will judge them by what they say serves to minimize blind attacks. The other side of this argument suggests that anonymity allows others to express unpopular opinions or question conventional wisdom. Such statements can function as agents of change when those who issue them are not suffocated by group pressures to remain silent. The third issue involves the enforcement of existing legal restrictions on speech. Without knowing who has issued them, it is impossible for law enforcement agents to prosecute those who commit libel, obscenity, or copyright infringement.

Although there are no quick fixes to these debates, scholars and legal experts have suggested that a compromise would be to enact "a principle of truth in the nature of naming" (Marx, 1999). As such, either the people issuing anonymous messages or the ISP facilitating them would indicate that their statements were anonymous. Such "visible anonymity" (Lee, 1996) would still protect the interests of the source while signaling to the receiver that the source has, for whatever reason, chosen not to associate with the message.

## Pseudonymity

If anonymity lies at one end of the identity continuum and one's real-life identity lies at the other, than pseudonymity covers a good deal of the area in between. **Pseudonym** comes from the Latin words for "false" and "name," and it provides an audience with the ability to attribute statements and actions to a common source. Like an anonym, a pseudonym provides its owner with some degree of protection. But unlike an anonym, a pseudonym allows one to contribute to the fashioning of one's own image. Authors and performers have long recognized such a virtue. In the 19th century, Samuel L. Clemens recognized that the river pilot's call, "Mark twain!" reflected his desire to be an author associated with life on the Mississippi River. A century later, would-be actor Bernard Schwartz realized that Tony Curtis was a much more glamorous name for earning recognition in Hollywood.

Although celebrities have popularized adopting pseudonyms, the practice of renaming oneself in different communication contexts is by no means inaccessible to common people. In fact, pseudonyms were quite popular among people who communicated on a medium that could be considered the predecessor to the Internet, CB radio. As we noted earlier, CB enthusiasts adopted "handles" to identify themselves when broadcasting messages over the airwaves. Because these messages were in the public arena, many people chose to participate in public discussions without giving up their real names (and some security) by using their handles instead. They also chose handles that allowed them to fashion some perception of their unique identities. As CB radio grew increasingly popular throughout the 1970s, participants adopted identities like "Stargazer" and "Midnight Delight," each of which conjures of up distinct images of what the person behind them might be like. One researcher found that women users in particular tended to adopt handles that suggested either the temptress imagery of an Eve figure or the loyalty and purity of a Mary figure, depending on what type of image they wanted to project (Kalcik, 1985). The precedent established by CB users to choose a pseudonym that reflects some aspect of their personal disposition was paralleled by Internet communicators in the decades that followed.

Bechar-Israeli (1995) investigated the function and personal importance of pseudonyms among IRC participants. Not surprisingly, Bechar-Israeli concluded that pseudonyms, or "nicks," as these nicknames are known among IRCers, served as attempts to present the self in a single line of text. Although he was able to categorize the nicks he discovered in a range of categories (as shown in Table 3.1), the most frequently selected pseudonyms were referential of some quality of one's identity. Nearly one-half of these participants choose to disclose something about their character <shydude>, profession <medoctor>, state <sleepless>, or appearance <handsom> through their nick. Though very few people choose to use their actual names in this setting, a clear majority tended to share qualities about their identities they wanted others to perceive through their choice of pseudonym.

**Table 3.1**
**Six Types of Nicks**

| Category | Examples | Percent |
|---|---|---|
| Self-related names | <shydude>, <handsom> | 45% |
| Names related to medium, technology, and their nature | <pentium>, <aixy> | 16.9% |
| Names of flora, fauna, objects | <tulip>, <froggy>, <cheese> | 15.6% |
| Play on words and sounds | <whatthehell>, <myTboy>, <uh-uh> | 11.3% |
| People using their real names | <Cortne>, <SusanLee> | 7.8% |
| Names related to figures in literature, films, fairytales, and famous people | <madhatter>, <rainman>, <elvis> | 6.1% |
| Names related to sex and provocation | <sexsee>, <sexpot>, <hitler> | 3.9% |
| Total[a] | | 106.6% |

*Note:* Adapted from Bechar-Israeli (1995).
[a]The total adds up to more than 100% because of the multiple coding method used by the researcher.

The ownership of one's pseudonym is something fiercely guarded in these contexts. As Bechar-Israeli observed, when a participant discovers his or her nick in use by another, the original owner reacts with hostility toward the perceived identity thief. Hence, even though play with identity is possible in such environments, consistency of presentation is practiced, even valued, among participants.

This same sense of perpetuated and consistent identity is found among personal Web sites. Unlike text-only channels like MUDs and chat rooms, Web sites allow the transmission of text, pictures, animation, and sounds to convey an online identity. However, the inclusion of any of these additional sources of information is still under the control of the author, allowing the individual to determine what identity will be presented. Chandler (1997) pointed out that the ubiquitous "Under Construction" signs found on so many personal Web sites is indicative of a process of creating identity. People are building a representation of themselves for the consideration and approval of others.

Certainly, electing pseudonymity can produce advantageous effect for those behind the false names, especially in opening channels to those who might be reticent to interact if their true names were known. In particular, research has indicated that working with pseudonyms can be a liberating experience for students.

Fig. 3.3. The "under construction" icon familiar to many web pages.

Chester and Gwynne (1998) conducted a class in which they and their students interacted exclusively online. Fully two thirds of their students later reported that they participated more in the online environment, where "there was no pressure to adhere to the scripts normally governing classroom behavior." The use of a pseudonym, one of the prerequisites for the course, allowed the participants to choose when and how they would disclose things like gender, race, and other social demographics.

The veneer of the Internet allows us to determine how much of an identity we wish to front in online presentations. These images can range from a vague silhouette to a detailed snapshot. Whatever the degree of identity presented, however, it appears that control and empowerment are benefits for users of these communication technologies.

## HYPERLINK: A RAPE IN CYBERSPACE

Few online characters are more infamous than Mr. Bungles, "a fat, oleaginous, Bisquick-faced clown dressed in cum-stained harlequin garb and girdled with a mistletoe-and-hemlock belt whose buckle bore the quaint inscription 'KISS ME UNDER THIS BITCH!'" (Dibbell, 1993, p. 37). The Mr. Bungles character is reviled not so much for his distasteful self-presentation as much as for his repulsive actions in LambdaMOO. In MOOs, those present not only exchange lines of dialogue, but can also offer descriptions of their actions.

On one fateful evening, Mr. Bungles joined one of the dialogues in LambdaMOO and proceeded to disrupt the normal conversational atmosphere with vulgar statements and vile actions at the hands of a voodoo doll. A voodoo doll is a program that allows its user to ascribe actions to another character and have them appear on the screen as though the owner of that character had issued them. Using his voodoo doll, Mr. Bungles directed a number of characters to perform sexual and sadomasochistic acts. As he proceeded to seize control of character after character, he ignored their protests and the objections of others present throughout his escapade. Eventually, a participant with a superior program was able to block Mr. Bungles' voodoo spell, silencing his mocking laughter and confining his tasteless activities.

In an ethnographic essay of the LambdaMOO experience, Dibbell (1993) recounts not only these events, but also the conversations among the participants that followed the Mr. Bungles episode. Despite the fact that Mr. Bungles' assault had taken place in an entirely symbolic rather than physical level, LambdaMOOers talked of the act as a rape because of the violation they felt as victims or perceived as witnesses. Although some participants found "rape" too strong a word to describe what had happened, those who had been victimized by Mr. Bungles insisted that the experience of having their virtual selves violated had the same impact on them as if they had been physically assaulted. In the months that followed, LambdaMOOers debated the actions and the fate of Mr. Bungles with great passion, demonstrating just how impacting words on a screen can be. Ultimately, Mr. Bungles was executed in the virtual world for his actions. In the real word, of course, this meant that his character name was retired, forbidden ever to log onto LambdaMOO again. However, the effects of his actions were far-reaching, leading LambdaMOOers to struggle with the difficult process of becoming a society. (This process is discussed further in a chapter 6 Hyperlink.) It is interesting, however, how our perceptions can lead to an interpretation of lines of text into a crime.

## PROTECTING IDENTITIES IN THE INFORMATION AGE

"A good reputation is more valuable than money," so said the Roman statesman Publius Syrus in 42 BC, noting the importance that a good name carried in his time. Today, people are discovering just how costly it can be to have a good name tarnished. Although criminals have found ways to uncover people's personal information in the past (most provocatively by routing through trash, looking for carelessly discarded personal documents) and malcontents have attacked people's reputations in many public forums, the introduction of information technologies has raised the profiles, and the stakes, involved in protecting one's identity online and off. In this section, we look at two identity-related threats of growing concern in the Information Age: identity fraud and shadow identities.

### Identity Fraud

Most of us spend a good deal of time, consciously or unconsciously, building a good reputation. We strive to make our credit card and automobile loan payments on time, we work hard to earn passing marks in our college courses, and we obey the laws to avoid marring our records. With all the hard work that we invest in building and maintaining our reputations, it seems almost inconceivable that someone could come along and wipe that out with as little information as our credit card or social security number. However, one's reputation can be grievously injured if a criminal targets one for identity fraud.

**Identity fraud** occurs when someone acquires personal information that allows that individual to impersonate you online or in real life and make purchases or commit crimes in your name. Armed with as little information as your name and nine-digit Social Security number, criminals can steal your identity and misrepresent you in online forums and in real life. It happened to Kenneth Morse of New York. After disclosing his name and Social Security number in an online forum, someone began purchasing sport utility vehicles in New Jersey in his name (Sandberg, 1999). Although the culprit was stopped as he attempted to make his third vehicle purchase, Morse had months of letter writing and phone calling ahead of him as he worked to convince creditors that he was not the "Kenneth Morse" who made the inappropriate purchases.

Although one's Social Security number is a particularly potent piece of personal information that criminals can use to impersonate you, it is by no means the only piece of information that they can use to their benefit and your detriment. Depending on what other information they might already have about you, the additional disclosure of your credit card number, its expiration date, your date of birth, or your mother's maiden name may be all they need to misrepresent you. Con artists were particularly active during the months prior to the end of 1999. Many would call pretending to represent banking institutions seeking account numbers that they needed to verify for Y2K compliance. The fraud was so pervasive that the U.S. Postal Service issued a warning post card to households to alert them not to disclose any personal information to callers. Passwords are also particularly vulnerable pieces of information in online settings. A criminal equipped with your password could use your Internet account to send messages you would never consider issuing.

A particularly chilling case of identity fraud occurred when a northern California woman who had never even logged on, discovered that she was the target of a stalker who was setting her up for disaster. Her alleged stalker, a man to whom she had been introduced by friends and who she then rebuffed when he became too intense about developing a relationship, had sent out alarming messages in her name. The stalker, masquerading as the woman, issued a number of state ments suggesting that she was interested in having a rape fantasy fulfilled. More than this, the impersonator provided contact information and a schedule of the woman's daily activities to help. After one of the recipients of this e-mail contacted her by telephone, the woman turned to the police and they began to investigate the source of her alter ego. Ultimately, the former acquaintance was arrested, but the fear that this individual caused through this intimidation complicated her life immeasurably (Foote & Van Boven, 1999).

If you suspect that you or someone you know is the victim of identity fraud, the Federal Trade Commission (FTC; 1998) recommends quick action. First contact one of the three major credit bureaus (listed in Table 3.2) and direct them to flag your file so that no one can open a new account in your name. Second, notify the creditors of any accounts that have been tampered with (e.g., Visa or JCPenny) by phone and then follow up by writing to them. Third, file a police report. The FTC offers more helpful hints on their Web site at www.ftc.gov. As increasingly more aspects of our lives become entwined with information technologies, we will find that we must be increasingly vigilant in how our personal information is distributed. As the case just presented indicates, not all instances of identity fraud are preventable, but Table 3.2 suggests steps that savvy consumers can take to safeguard their identities from such assaults.

## Shadow Identities

Another identity that is being further compromised by Internet technologies is the public identity of people, organizations, and their creations. Entities like manufacturers, film studios, and retailers go to considerable lengths to protect their images from misrepresentation (see the "Online Communication and the Law" section for another example of how corporations fight to safeguard their identities). Certainly, many of these entities have established a presence on the World Wide Web to promote their preferred image. For example, organizations ranging from

**Table 3.2**

**Steps for Protecting One's Digital Identity**

- Consumers should guard their personal identifying information. Before divulging it, they should find out how it will be used and whether it will be transferred to third parties. They should find out whether they have the choice of "opting out" of having the information shared with third parties [such as direct mail service].
- Consumers should ensure that items containing personal information—such as charge receipts, insurance forms and bank statements—are disposed of safely [preferably shredded].
- Consumers should disclose their Social Security numbers only when absolutely necessary. They should ask to use alternate numbers as identifiers whenever possible, including on motor vehicle licenses.
- Consumers should carry with them only the credit cards and identification they actually need. Consumers who lose credit cards should notify their creditors by phone and request that a "fraud alert" be placed in their file.
- Consumers should pay attention to billing cycles. Bills that do not arrive on time may have been misdirected by identity thieves.
- Consumers should periodically check their credit report by contacting one of the three major credit bureaus: Equifax (www.equifax.com), Experian (www.experian.com), or Trans Union (www.tuc.com).

*Note:* Adapted from David Medine with the Federal Trade Commission (1999).

the American Red Cross to Xerox sponsor sites that provide a positive perspective on their mission, growth, and services. In an increasing number of cases, some corporations may even conduct business *entirely* online (e.g., Amazon.com). Suffice it to say, such organizations would prefer not to have their reputations tarnished by anyone, and certainly not by an easily accessed competing Web site.

Wright (1996) explained that "shadow identities" can be created for virtually any site on the Web thanks to the way search engines work. When search engines are directed to look for a word or phrase on the Internet, they do not necessarily discriminate among the sites containing the indicated word or phrase. They merely report back the matches they have found online. Some of the matches they find might indeed be the **shadow pages** that Wright described, pages that can incriminate a reputation. Thus, in searching for information on a popular retail chain like K-Mart, the search results might also include a "K-Mart Sucks" page. Prior to the advent of the Internet, a disgruntled employee or dissatisfied customer had limited range and could only "bad mouth" an organization to personal acquaintances. Now that angry person can reach a global audience, casting doubt on the prestige and potency of an international reputation.

Although shadow pages may express legitimate concerns and issue relevant challenges to these entities, they do present some interesting hurdles for establishment and interpretation of identity. You may find your own name or that of the organization you are employed with in the cross hairs of one of these character assassins, and so find yourself in the position of having to cope with or offer rebuttal to the statements made on the shadow page. Yet, even if you do not find yourself or those you work for the targets of shadow pages, you as an information consumer are likely to have to consider what shadow pages have to say. For instance, if you go online to shop for a new car and find among your search results a shadow page labeled, "WARNING: Do not buy this model!", you might choose to ignore it entirely or on reading it, choose to forego purchasing the vehicle.

Clearly, shadow pages serve to remind us that we should not accept any message without some critical thought as to the motives of the producer. Many people and organizations active on the Web have something to sell you; likewise, many of those who author shadow pages have axes to grind. As information consumers, we have to consider critically what any information producer has to offer, be they the representatives of the original entity or its shadowy opposition.

## CHAPTER SUMMARY

As this chapter illustrates, establishing our own identities as well as determining the identities of others is surrounded by a host of issues, ranging from the metaphysical to the mundane. Although technology has introduced them into a new context, many of the questions that we confront about identity are as old as humanity's search for knowledge: Who am I? How can I get others to understand me? Can I accept that these people are who and what they claim to be? Certainly, we have not answered these enduring questions in this chapter, but we have reviewed concepts that have cast these queries into new light. By examining points about telepresence, performance, and pseudonymity, we have indicated directions that people are following in pursuit of answers to these questions in this electronic era. We have also noted identity vulnerabilities that technology exposes. Both identity fraud and shadow identities are problems that everyone, not just Internet users, must be prepared to confront.

### Online Communication and the Law

The law has long acknowledged the value of name recognition. That is why companies with distinctive names like Pepsi, McDonald's, and Michelin have sought the legal protection of trademark laws in order to exert control over the use of their names in public forums. And it was because name recognition is so popular in the world of marketing that corporations and entrepreneurs rushed to secure the domain names of well-known products and producers. Domain names are, of course, another term for the Uniform Resource Locator (URL), the address of a site on the World Wide Web.

In the mid-1990s, a number of enterprising "cybersquatters" laid claim to recognizable domain names, paying nominal fees to the Internet Assigned Numbers Authority (the official entity responsible for assigning domain names), and then turning around and leasing them to the corporations who owned them. A domain name is the cyberspace equivalent to a vanity plate on your automobile: It not only identifies you, it does so with distinction. In some cases, rather than agreeing to capitulate to a perceived extortion racket, some corporations took the cybersquatters to court . . . and won.

Yet the legal right to a domain name just because someone owns a trademark blurred in the case of Hasbro v. Clue Computing, Inc. Hasbro is a toy manufacturer who owns the copyright to the popular board game "Clue." In 1996, Hasbro discovered that Clue Computing, Inc., a small Colorado-based consulting firm, already held the domain name "clue.com." Lawyers for Hasbro argued that by claiming the domain name first, the consultants were engaged in dilution of the trademark; in other words, it weakened the recognition of the trademark ("clue") with the product (the board game).

The Massachusetts judge hearing the case, however, did not agree. He ruled that although extorting money from a trademark holder was illegal, a company that used a domain name for its own legitimate purposes did not dilute trademark. Furthermore, *clue* itself is such a common word that Hasbro was unable to establish that every use of the word suggested the product (Kaplan, 1999).

The legalities of domain names are far from solved, however. The introduction of the ".net," ".xxx," and ".fan" domains open new avenues for competing presences on the Internet. How much time and labor will trademark holders have to invest in the future to protect their images? "Whitehouse.net," for instance, is a well-known parody site mirroring "Whitehouse.gov" but what happens when the next "dot.domain" opens up? What kind of regulations, if any, should be placed upon who gets and keeps a domain name?

## Glossary

**Anonymity**: Communicating without one's identity being apparent.

**Avatar**: An incarnation of oneself in a virtual environment.

**Cybersquatter**: An entrepreneur who registers for a domain name and then sells the rights to use that domain name to another person or corporate entity for a profit.

**Dépaysement**: Process of seeing the familiar through different eyes.

**Domain name**: A recognizable URL, or address on the World Wide Web, typically used by corporations and individuals to distinguish themselves through a popular term or trademark (e.g., www.mcdonalds.com).

**Face-work**: Effort invest in maintaining a role.

**Gender-swapping**: The adopting of a gender other than one's own in presenting oneself in mediated contexts.

**Handle**: A pseudonym in CB radio.

**Identity**: A construct formed by the interaction of the self with the social environment.

**Identity fraud**: A criminal's misuse of another individual's personal information (e.g., credit card number) to make unauthorized purchases or commit crimes using the victim's name.
**Interactivity**: The quality of telepresence that measures a person's ability to manipulate the content of the medium.
**Nicks**: A pseudonym in an IRC.
**Pseudonym**: An alias, or "false name," a person adopts to identify him or herself.
**Self-presentation**: The process of creating a perception of oneself for others.
**Shadow page**: A page on the Web established to attack the reputation of person, corporation, or another site.
**Telepresence**: Experiencing an environment through a communication medium.
**Vividness**: The quality of telepresence that measures the breadth and depth of sensory stimulation a medium presents.
**Voodoo doll**: A computer program used in synchronous conversation forums like MOOs that allows its user to enter lines of text describing another's dialogue or activity.

## Topics for Discussion

1. Review Steuer's classification of various media technologies in Fig. 3.1, then select one medium and think of an example for it (i.e., *The Little Mermaid* as an example of a videocassette recording). Write a brief essay in which you explain the amount of telepresence the medium possess by comparing how high or low it is in terms of vividness and in terms of interactivity.
2. Consider how unified your own self is by listing five different roles you fulfill in your daily life. Along with each role, note what steps you take to be perceived as competent in that role.
3. Log on to a chat room or MUD as a participant-observer for a few hours. As you observe the contributions of various participants, see if you can identify any "stars." Summarize a significant exchange you witnessed during your tenure and provide a brief explanation of the participants' behavior in terms of the theatrical metaphor.
4. Create an avatar of your own. In addition to dubbing your persona with a nick, provide a description of the qualities you would want to communicate to others. Once you have done so, consider how closely or distinctly your avatar compares to your presentation of identity in real life. What elements have you added to or omitted from the description?
5. Draw a reproduction of the continuum of identity manipulation presented in Fig. 3.2. and indicate where your pseudonym would rest (more anonymous or closer to your real life). Write an explanation for why you situated your pseudonym the way that you did. What factors contribute to

your perception that you are more or less "true" to real life through this presentation?

## REFERENCES

Bechar-Israeli, H. (1995). From <Bonehead> to <cLoNehEAd>: Nicknames, play, and identity on Internet relay chat. *Journal of Computer-Mediated Communication, 1*(2) <http:www.ascusc.org/jcmc/vol1/issue2/bechar.html>.

Borenstein, D. (2000). *Quoteland.com.* <http://www.quoteland.com>.

Bornstein, K. (1994). *Gender outlaw: On men, women, and the rest of us.* New York: Vintage Books.

Bruckman, A. (1992). *Identity workshop: Emergent social and psychological phenomena in text-based virtual reality.* <ftp://ftp.lambda.moo.mud.org/pub/MOO/papers>.

Bruckman, A. S. (1996). Gender-swapping on the Internet. In P. Ludlow (Ed.), *High noon on the electronic frontier: Conceptual issues in cyberspace* (pp. 317–325). Cambridge, MA: MIT Press.

Buten, J. (1996). *The personal home page institute.* <http://www.asc.upenn.edu/usr/sbuten/survey.htm#top>.

Chandler, D. (1997). *Writing oneself in cyberspace.* <http://www.aber.ac.uk/~dgc/hompgid.html> (1998, January 22).

Chester, A., & Gwynne, G. (1998). Online teaching: Encouraging collaboration through anonymity. *Journal of Computer-Mediated Communication, 4*(2) <http://www.ascusc.org/jcmc/vol4/issue2/chester.html>.

Cutler, R. H. (1996). Technologies, relations, and selves. In L. Strate, R. Jacobson, & S. B. Gibson (Eds.), *Communication and cyberspace: Social interaction in an electronic environment* (pp. 317–333). Cresskill, NJ: Hampton Press.

Dibbell, J. (1993, December 21). A rape in cyberspace: Or, how an evil clown, a Haitian trickster spirit, two wizards, and a cast of dozens turned a database into a society. *Village Voice,* pp. 36–42.

Federal Trade Commission. (1998, May 20). *Legislation could help protect consumers from credit identity fraud.* <http://www.ftc.gov/opa/1998/9805/ identity.htm>.

Federal Trade Commission. (1999, April). *Identity crisis: What to do if your identity is stolen.* <http://www.ftc.gov/bcp/conline/pubs/alerts/idenalrt.htm>.

Foote, D., & Van Boven, S. (1999, February 8). You could get raped. *Newsweek,* pp. 64–65.

Giese, M. (1998). Self without body: Textual self-presentation in an electronic community. *First Monday,* 3 <http://www.firstmonday.dk/issues/issue3_4/giese/index.html>.

Gigliotti, D., Weinstein, H., Zwick, E., Norman, M., Parfitt, D. (Producers), Madden, J., & Greatrex, R. (Directors). (1998). *Shakespeare in love* [film]. Miramax Films.

Goffman, E. (1959). *The presentation of self in everyday life*. Garden City, NY: Anchor.

Kalcik, S. J. (1985). Women's handles and the performance of identity in the CB community. In R. A. Jordan & S. J. Kalcik (Eds.), *Women's folklore, women's culture* (pp. 99–108). Philadelphia: University of Pennsylvania Press.

Kaplan, C. S. (1999, September 17). Judges pick David over Goliath in domain name suits. *Cyber Law Journal* <http://www.nytimes.com/library/tech/99/09/cyber/cyberlaw/17law.html>.

Lee, G. B. (1996). Addressing anonymous messages in cyberspace. *Journal of Computer-Mediated Communication, 2*(1) <http://www.ascusc.org/jcmc/vol2/issue1/anon.html>.

Marx, G. T. (1999). What's in a name? Some reflections on the sociology of anonymity. *Information Society*, 15, 99–112.

Sandberg, J. (1999, September 20). Losing your good name online. *Newsweek*, pp. 56–57.

Schiano, D. J. (1999). Lessons from LambdaMOO: A social, text-based virtual environment. *Presence: Teleoperators & Virtual Environments, 8*(2), 127–140.

Sheff, D. (2000). Net nut in a shell. *Yahoo! Internet Life, 6*(6), 100, 102–104.

Steuer, J. (1992). Defining virtual reality: Dimensions determining telepresence. *Journal of Communication, 42*(4), 73–93.

Stone, A. R. (1991). Will the real body please stand up? Boundary stories about virtual cultures. In M. Benedikt (Ed.), *Cyberspace: First steps* (pp. 81–118). Cambridge, MA: MIT Press.

Steiner, P. (1993, July 5). On the Internet, nobody knows you're a dog. *The New Yorker*, p. 61.

Turkle, S. (1995). *Life on the screen: Identity in the age of the Internet*. New York: Simon & Schuster.

Wayner, P. (1999). Technology for anonymity: Names by other nyms. *The Information Society, 15*, 91–97.

Wright, R. (1996, July 8). The cybersmear. *Time*, p. 46.

# CHAPTER 4

# RELATING ONLINE

*Those strangers, who had no arms to put around my shoulders, no eyes to weep with mine, nevertheless saw me through. As neighbors do.*
—*John Perry Barlow (Borenstein, 2000)*

> Molly Perkins, a student at Wake Forest University in North Carolina, was on the Internet checking on some friends at the University of Rochester in New York. But it was an unknown user name, one that included the name Arwen in it, that caught Mollie's attention.
>
> After all, her roommate was named Arwen Blayney, and Mollie knew it was the name of a character in the J.R.R. Tolkien book, *Lord of the Rings*, which is one of Arwen's favorites. So Mollie contacted the user in New York.
>
> She wanted to ask if he or she also liked the book and if the book was the reason he or she was using the name. She also made it known that her roommate was, in fact, Arwen.
>
> The person on the other end was my son Scott, who responded and ended up corresponding through e-mail with Arwen. When she made plans to come to South Bend over Thanksgiving to visit an old friend . . . Arwen discovered that her e-mail pal at the University of Rochester was from nearby Niles.
>
> Arwen and Scott, accompanied by friends, met for the first time at University Park Mall . . . just two months after her e-mail correspondence with Scott had begun at the start of the 1993-1994 school year. . . .
>
> In time their relationship deepened and, on June 25 [1999] at Calvary Baptist Church in South Bend, they married. (Lietz, 1999, p. 3)

Like Linda Lietz, some of you might also know the story of someone who has initiated a personal relationship over the Internet. Others may well have struck up a friendship or experimented with some romantic relating of your own with someone you have never physically encountered. The distance-transcending technologies of the electronic age have enabled people like Arwen and Scott to initiate, escalate, and maintain interpersonal relationships to degrees that were once considered only possible when two parties shared common physical space.

Whether or not CMC can be an effective context for building relationships has been an issue of contention among scholars since the formal study of networked interaction began. Early research concluded that computer usage focused people on more task-oriented messages and precluded the development of social relationships among users. However, a growing body of literature argues that people not only use networked technologies for social purposes, in some cases, people prefer the medium for interpersonal relating. Albert Bressand, a respected French economist, has even said that systems we presently refer to as information technologies are more aptly named relationship technologies, "the new machines of today are between man and man, rather than between man and nature. And relations rather than material products are what is processed in these machines" (Schwartz, 1996, n.p. ).

This chapter reviews the arguments against and for the growth of interpersonal relationships through CMC. In tracing the development of these arguments, we borrow a pattern from Walther (1996), who suggested that CMC has been characterized as impersonal by some, interpersonal by others, and potentially "hyperpersonal" in his view. After reviewing the theories relevant to each of these levels of interactivity, we consider some of the implications of conflict and attachment that persons relating online should consider. By the end of this chapter, we hope you have a firmer understanding of why the prospect of relating online might mean to some less than they imagine and to others more than they hope.

## IMPERSONAL COMMUNICATION: DEFINING LIMITS TO CMC

Can you recall the last time you flirted with someone you were interested in? What behaviors did you engage in? Chances are you might have found yourself smiling a lot, leaning in that person's direction, and looking directly into that person's eyes. Certainly, you might have carried on a conversation with the person, but your interest was probably signaled more by what you did than by what you said. You were likely to use a lot of **nonverbal cues** to indicate your interest. Facial expressions, posture and movement, and eye contact are all channels through which we can share meaning without using language. As you probably already know, nonverbal communication constitutes a major portion of our face-to-face messages, with specialists estimating that anywhere from 65% to 93% of the social meaning in communication comes through these channels (Birdwhistle, 1970; Mehrabian, 1972).

Until recently, the character of most forms of CMC has meant that limited amounts of nonverbal information could be exchanged between people over computer networks. From its inception and continuing through contemporary practice, the Internet primarily has been a vehicle for sharing verbal messages. Of course, the advent of technologies like webcams, photographic devices that upload television-like images to Web sites, certainly present a challenge to this common conception, but in many network channels, including e-mail, messages are still comprised mainly of textual information. Early research into communication using computers, then, was dealing with media characterized by displays of words and symbols without the apparent benefit of other cues. Accordingly, this led to a reference for computer-mediated being a **cues-filtered-out** approach to communication (Culnan & Markus, 1987). Because there is less information exchanged between people, then, it is not surprising why some would find this media more impersonal when compared to the richness of face-to-face interaction.

## Social Presence Theory

Initial research into interaction using computer networks seemed to confirm that this cues-filtered-out quality led to an impersonal perception of CMC. Much of this work was laid on the foundation established by **social presence theory** (Short, Williams, & Christie, 1976). Social presence is the degree to which we as individuals perceive another as a real person and any interaction between the two of us as a relationship. Social presence theory suggests that different media convey different degrees of perceived substance to an interaction. The degree of the connection is based on the amount of nonverbal information available to the receiver through any particular channel.

Thus, you might feel a certain degree of social presence while listening to your favorite morning radio personality. The nonverbal qualities of his voice might suggest to you that this person is fun, sharp-witted, and engaging. You might even faithfully tune into his show, and only his show, because you want to maintain loyalty to him. Even though the two of you have never met, and he is certainly not physically present, you still have a sense that in listening to him, he is "there" with you. Consider how much more nonverbal information is available about your favorite television personality. Is it any wonder people begin to feel that they know the actors they watch on a weekly basis? In contrast, think of how much social presence you feel when reading your local newspaper. Few of us identify with our local journalists as strongly as we do with radio and television personalities, and according to social presence theory, that is because we lack sufficient cues to prompt us to perceive the reporters as "real" as we do the broadcasters.

In comparison to other media for interpersonal interaction, then, computer-mediated channels would provide less presence than other channels. In different situations this could be more or less desirable. This is what Rice (1987) discovered in one of the early examinations of how people in organizations were using CMC systems. Rice found that people perceived the appropriateness of using a channel such as e-mail corresponded to the amount of social presence required for successful completion of the task. Hence, users rated tasks like exchanging information and asking questions as a highly appropriate use of the computer network. Such tasks require less social presence than some others. On the other hand, users rated tasks like resolving disagreements and persuading others as inappropriate to communicate online. Because the participants apparently believed that these tasks require more of a perception of social presence in order to be effective, they would be more likely to choose another medium for exchanging these messages.

More recent research corroborates the assertion that the quality of social presence factors into people's choices among communication media. In a survey of college students, Flaherty, Pearce, and Rubin (1998) conclude that people do not necessarily use computer-mediated channels for the same purposes as they do the face-to-face channel. Hence, they assert that the Internet and face-to-face communication are not **functional alternatives**. In the process of constructing their survey, they identified six commonly accepted motivations for human interaction: inclusion, affection, control, pleasure, relaxation, and escape. What they found was that there were statistically significant differences for people's motivations when it came to choosing channels. Only the motivation of pleasure was rated as comparably high between the Internet and face-to-face communication, meaning that people turned to both of them for the enjoyment they derived from interacting with other people.

For the remaining motives, however, people chose one channel over another to fulfill specific needs, and generally people preferred face-to-face interaction to meet their other needs. For example, their research would suggest that a lonely worker is more likely to join his or her co-workers in the lunch room than to log onto a chat room in order to fulfill his or her need for inclusion. The results of this study suggest that the Internet and face-to-face communication are **specialized channels**, meaning, quite simply, that people choose them to fulfill particular needs. Consequently, a person might turn to the Internet if he or she wants to enjoy some conversation, but the same individual would seek out a physical presence for affection.

Social presence theory offers one possible explanation for why some people may find online communication impersonal. Because many computer-mediated channels provide fewer nonverbal cues to interpret the meaning of messages, the relatively "lean" messages they deliver can be perceived as less personal. People who prefer the nods, smiles, and touches that can accompany a face-to-face interaction would probably find little warmth in the phosphorescent glow of the computer screen. However, social presence is not the only theory that sides with an impersonal perspective on CMC.

## Social Context Cues Theory

Whether we are consciously aware of it or not, we all tailor our communication behaviors to the settings around us. Both what we say and to whom we say it are influenced by our social environment. Consider how you adapt your own messages to the settings around you. As a competent communicator, you are unlikely to shout in a library or in a place of worship. Yet there are places, like at a football stadium or rock concert, where shouting is acceptable, if not necessary. How is it that you know where it is and is not appropriate to shout?

According to Sproull and Kiesler (1986), **social context cues** serve as indicators of appropriate behavior. They govern both contact, telling us who we should and should not communicate with, and content, regulating what kinds of information we should and should not disclose. Some social context cues include geographic, organizational, and situational variables. Thus, in the example just given, the geographic location suggested the appropriate level of volume. Of course, a combination of these variables could work together to suggest the appropriate social context. Let us say that you and your co-workers stop by the local diner for a bite to eat after work. Away from the office at last and surrounded by your peers, you feel comfortable enough to express some discontent with your mutual supervisor. Suddenly, your boss walks into the restaurant and sits down within ear-shot of your table, and you change the subject. The arrival of the supervisor suggests a new situation in which you discontinue talking about her in order to comply with the social norm of not talking about a person who can hear you without including them in the conversation. In response to strong cues, then, we focus on others, make subtle differentiations among stimuli, and exert greater control over ourselves in order to meet social expectations.

As you might have surmised, many social context cues are conveyed through nonverbal channels, and, as previously established, computer-mediated channels lack as many nonverbal cues as we are familiar with in face-to-face contexts. Accordingly, Sproull and Kiesler (1986) found that the short supply of social context cues has an effect on the nature of human behavior in mediated contexts. In a survey of e-mails exchanged among employees of a Fortune 500 company, they found that communicators were more likely to exhibit self-absorbed behavior, to display little differentiation among people of different status, and to act more uninhibited. In fact, evidence from their survey suggests that this last quality was particularly pronounced in the newer context. Scores indicated that people within this organization encountered uninhibited message an average of 4 times a month in face-to-face conversations but 33 times a month over e-mail. One example message from the research demonstrates the degree of this uninhibited behavior. As you read the following message, imagine saying this to 100 of your co-workers:

> It's great to worry about fine points, but I think we should concentrate on getting rid of those aspects of [product] which are TRULY MONSTROUS to the native users (such as yours truly). I had to ask about three people to figure out how to get the @#$%*ing insertion point beyond a graphics frame. the answer, it appears, is some *incredibly arcane* nonsense about show structure, select after anchor, and repaginate. WHY CAN'T I JUST POINT THE *BLOODY* MOUSE BELOW A GRAPHICS FRAME AND GET AN INSERTION POINT? (Sproull & Kiesler, 1986, p. 1506)

Such inhibitions seem to flourish under conditions with weak social context cues. The e-mails that the respondents in this survey exchanged tended to lack information about a sender's location, department, position, job, age, or gender, qualities that serve as social context cues. Kiesler, Siegel, and McGuire (1984) argue that the lack of social context cues leads to feelings of anonymity, reduced self-regulation, and reduced self-awareness. From one perspective, this state can foster greater personal independence, getting one out from under the thumb of social control. On the other hand, it can foster the flouting of social standards, leading one to utter things that are later regretted. In short, the short supply of social context cues can create perceptions of impersonal replies and impersonal interpretations of messages.

## The Impersonal Perspective Reconsidered

As the initial work from both the social presence and social context cues theories exemplifies, many of the early studies in CMC were conducted in organizations. According to Metz (1994a), this resulted in a bias of conceiving of computer networking as a task-oriented rather than socially oriented media. Moreover, Metz points out that these efforts may have overlooked the presence of nonverbals within text-based messages. In citing one of the earliest ethnographies of MUDding (Reid, 1991), Metz points out that people interacting in those environments have innovated methods for implying emotional content as part of their messages through **emoticons**. These emotional icons take on four different forms as outlined in Table 4.1. Although these emoticons arguably are but echoes of traditional nonverbal cues, they do, nonetheless, serve the same function as their face-to-face counterparts in that they provide more communicative information to the receiver. The innovation of emoticons suggests that new norms for communicating social presence and social context are likely to emerge over time, not because they have to, but because people want them to.

**Table 4.1**
**Forms of Emoticons**

| Form | Description | Examples |
|---|---|---|
| Verbalizing | Textual representations of vocal rather than verbal utterances | <snort> ha ha ha |
| Descriptions of physical actions | A narration of the speaker's activities, usually set off by asterisks or brackets | *I raised my glass.* <smugly turning to go> |
| Stress | Emphasizing key words or phrases by using all capital letters | Please bring the car by on the NEXT day. |
| Smileys | Arrangements of keyboard characters read side-on and used to suggest a message's emotional intent | :-) grinning happily<br>;-) winking reassurance<br>:-P sticking out one's tongue in jest |

*Note:* Adapted from Reid (1991).

Despite such compensations for the character of the medium, relating in cyberspace may yet be handicapped by one crucial factor: time. According to Walther (1992), social relationships in cyberspace simply take longer to develop than those in face-to-face interaction. People who meet in person have multiple channels in order to process information about a potential partner. People who meet in cyberspace may have only one, the text that they exchange. Given a more limited source of input, it takes longer for a bond to emerge between people. This **social information-processing** perspective would also explain the lack of relational development in early studies of CMC. Groups that met briefly and for an experiment would not have had sufficient interaction time to develop a relationship.

Although we now turn to an examination of how CMC can be interpersonal, we cannot simply dismiss those who find the experience impersonal. Interacting in any given context is a subjective experience. As Walther and others argue, it is not inherent characteristics of the media that make the experience impersonal or not, it is our own perception that helps make it so.

## INTERPERSONAL COMMUNICATION: OPENING CHANNELS THROUGH CMC

The research just discussed establishes support for why individuals perceive networked interaction unfavorably. Yet despite its evidence, this body of research seems to fall short of an explanation for why some people feel they have found satisfying relationships with persons they have never met. Remember Arwen and Scott from the beginning of this chapter? How can we explain the connections people like them find in their mediated conversations?

Lea and Spears (1998), two researchers who have investigated online interaction, submit that we have a great deal yet to learn about the complex nature of human relationships in mediated contexts. Specifically, they say that research to this point has been guided by several assumptions and biases that have proven to be unfair to online relationships. Lea and Spears count dispositions toward physical attraction and physical cues as governing relational development and an emphasis on the oral exchanges among people in intimate relationships among these biases. Clearly, if the nonverbal qualities of physical presence and orality are unquestionable criteria for what can and cannot be defined as a relationship, than those initiated online clearly fall short. However, if in opening our explanation of what constitutes relating is broadened to move beyond these biases, it may well be that theories for defending the legitimacy of online relationships are possible.

Not surprisingly, then, Lea and Spears offer one such theory that helps explain why genuinely felt relationship bonds seem to emerge online. Postumes, Spears, and Lea (1998) assert that they can predict the conditions under which relationships will emerge through their **social identification/deindividuation (SIDE) model**.

## The SIDE Model

In order to understand the SIDE model, we must first review our understanding of identity. As we suggested in chapter 3, our identities are defined by the tensions between our culture's desire to have us conform to particular roles and our own desire to resist this pressure and establish a unique sense of self. Noting the lack of nonverbal markers that could serve to pigeon hole any one of us, many argue that Internet is the ultimate liberating channel, freeing us to be the persons we always wanted without the stifling restrictions that culture enforces because of our gender, race, physical attractiveness, and so on. However, the SIDE model suggests just the opposite is true. People online seem to rely even more on group-based discriminators.

According to Postumes et al. (1998), it is exactly because there are so few nonverbals cues to process in online environments that people more actively seek out norms of behavior in order to find acceptance among the other participants. A **norm**, as you might know, is an accepted social behavior. Using a fork to eat a salad is a norm, and people who comply with norms generally tend to find acceptance among others who practice the same. Let us say you enter a chat room in which you observe the other contributors using a lot of abbreviations in their messages, such as BTW for "by the way" or LOL for "laugh out loud." The SIDE model predicts that you are likely to pick up this norm for yourself. In doing so, you are likely to appear more attractive to those around you and thus have a better chance of initiating relationships.

As you can tell, the SIDE model asserts that you are more likely to comply with a social role than worry about asserting your individual identity. This is not to say that people become cardboard cut-outs in the process. Instead, it is to say that people learn to play by the rules, as it were, and in doing so increase their attractiveness to other players in this social game.

Interestingly, the foundations of the SIDE model are built on psychological investigations into mob mentality. If you have ever seen news footage of a crowd in the midst of a riot, you may have questioned how people could ever behave so outrageously, smashing windows, setting fires, and looting stores. Clearly, these are all antisocial behaviors, and yet they are committed in a very social moment. Psychologists call this process **deindividuation** because personal identity is decreased in favor of one's social identity. This social identity reacts to the situation and correspondingly takes its cues for appropriate behavior from others in the same situation. Thus, although looting a television set from a store window display might seem like an outrageous act to commit in the context of an everyday stroll down Main Street, in the midst of a riot where others are making off with all kinds of home electronics, taking the TV appears to be the appropriate thing to do.

Of course, Internet communicators are not engaged in a crime, but the same psychological conditions seem to govern interaction and attraction online. In text-based interaction, there is less individuating information available to communicators. In lieu of relying on distinctions to mark us as attractive, the SIDE model argues that it is our similarities that foster attachment among people online.

Over the last decade, Postumes et al. have conducted a series of experiments with group interaction to establish the power of the SIDE model to predict human behavior. These studies have suggested two important qualities to this processes. First, visual anonymity among participants in a group seems to foster stronger SIDE effects toward conformity and group norms than in groups where participants saw one another face to face. Second, anonymity also seems to encourage stronger self-categorization among users. In one experiment where the participants were made aware of one another's gender, the communicators tended to behave along the lines of their gender roles more so than those to whom this information was not disclosed.

In summary, the SIDE model predicts that people will set aside personal identity and adopt the appropriate social identity in order to find acceptance among others. We can observe this same subversion of the personal self in favor of social self on a typical playground. Imagine a child, Pat, arrives at the park only to find all the other children playing basketball. Pat might have no particular knowledge of basketball but wants to find social acceptance among these peers. Provided that Pat picks up the rules of the game and makes the effort to dribble, pass, and shoot like the others, the rest of the children are likely to accept Pat as one of their own. Likewise, when one enters an online social setting, one must put forth an effort to play along with one's peers.

The other side of the SIDE model is, of course, that of the receivers. Even as the individual must struggle to figure out the norms of a group, the group must struggle to figure out whether or not the individual has the qualities to be "one of the gang." This results in a reliance on stereotyping in order to define who this other is. One individual actively attributes a great deal of meaning to the evident behaviors of the other during their interactions. Quite often then, one will turn to stereotypes to help decode this behavior. Stereotyping is one way we try to make sense of the world by focusing in on what we might believe to be certain patterns of behavior exhibited by members of a group. Thus, if an individual introduces him or herself as a hacker, your stereotype of hackers might lead you to conclude that the person is technically proficient with programming and prompt in you a favorable evaluation of the individual.

Perceived similarity has long been held to be a strong predictor of individual attraction (Trenholm & Jensen, 2000), and it seems to be a key in explaining the

SIDE model's effects in cyberspace. From this perspective, people who meet online must communicate enough common ground with one another that the parties involved are interested in sustaining relational ties. How commonly and effectively this is accomplished is the focus of the next section.

## Frequency of Interpersonal Relationships

In further support of the notion that interpersonal communication can, and does, take place in online media, Parks and Floyd (1996) conducted survey research among users of various Usenet BBS to see to what degree personal relationships are formed online. Almost two thirds of the people responding reported that they had initiated a personal relationship with someone they had met online. The people who tended to have personal relationships seemed to be those who used the newsgroups with more frequency and with greater duration in contrast to those who did not feel any personal attachment achieved through this channel. In looking at relational qualities such as interdependence, breadth and depth of information exchanged, and commitment, Parks and Floyd found that relational partners reported statistically moderate levels of these qualities, indicating that despite the boundaries between them, these people shared a connection to one another.

Furthermore, one half of those with personal relationships (about 30% of the survey) had high enough scores in these areas that they could be considered to be in highly developed relationships. As such, they are likely to migrate to other channels as well. In this survey, a majority of those with some kind of personal relationship followed up with their online interaction by contacting their partner through some other channel, be that telephone, snail mail, or face-to-face meetings. Even if this extension into other channels hints at a shortfall in maintaining relationships through only one channel, it still provides support for the ability of people to initiate relationships in cyberspace.

Despite the earlier reservations expressed by those favoring the impersonal perspective, research suggests there is enough information for some people to find that they can connect with others in personally meaningful ways even without as much information as one would find face to face. In fact, the lack of nonverbal cues might be more helpful to some than harmful in helping them to connect with others. As is seen in the next section, characteristics of this context could make communication more conducive to communication.

### Hyperlink: Task and Social Function of E-Mail among Undergraduates

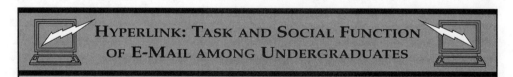

When instructors ask students in their classes to communicate with one another using e-mail, they expect that the students will use the network to discuss course topics or perhaps collaborate on assignments. According to the research findings of McCormick and McCormick (1992), students will indeed use e-mail to exchange a lot of task-related comments, but they will exchange a lot more social messages throughout the term. In a study aimed at discovering what undergraduates in a computer science course wrote about in their e-mail, McCormick and McCormick found that a good deal of the communication was work-related (41.1%), but a majority of the messages served social functions (51.7 %).

Of the messages they categorized as fulfilling social functions, 50% displayed less intimate content and the rest more intimate content. The less intimate content consisted of salutations ("Helllllllooooooo"), crude flirtations ("I'm looking forward to your slobbering kisses!"), humor ("Old Geologists never die, they just weather away."), and put-downs ("You are trully [*sic*] the scum of the earth . . . "). Although we might think of put-downs as being more antisocial than social, McCormick and McCormick explain that "Rather than being a sign of dislike or alienation, such threats and put-downs may be an adolescent sign of affection and trust among some male, undergraduate, computer users" (p. 390).

Although such superficial communication might be expected among the messages of people interacting in a public forum, it surprised the researchers to find that almost one quarter of the messages collected in their survey displayed deeper relational sentiments. More intimate content was expressed in messages that functioned as sharing ("I wish that I was [*sic*] graduating this year though!"), refined flirtation and relationship establishing ("I realize that we don't know each other, but how does dinner and a movies [*sic*] sound to remedy that situation?"), work on relationships and love messages ("I just wanted to say I had a great weekend and I Love You very Very Much."), and making social plans ("I will bring your notes on Wed. Se [*sic*] you then!!"). Overall, sharing was the second most popular type of message (21.2 %) right after work comments (26.4%).

Other findings in their survey suggest that students seemed more likely to write messages to one another at times when their academic demands were less, that they sent more flirting and relationship establishment messages early on in the semester when people do not know one another as well, and that "C" students were more likely to use the system than "A" and "B" students were.

McCormick and McCormick conclude that students use e-mail to support one another through both task and social messages. Although it might be preemptive to consider closing down the traditional student center just yet, it does appear that e-mail opens another channel for students to accomplish the important tasks of being a college student, from exchanging assignments to exchanging phone numbers.

## HYPERPERSONAL COMMUNICATION: TRANSCENDING RELATIONAL LIMITS THROUGH CMC

Different people shine in different conditions. Consider Jose, a junior whose soulful poetry has won him numerous awards. And yet when people meet Jose, they are often surprised by how quiet he is. Because he has such a powerful way with words in his writing, people expect him to show equal skill in his speaking. We all know someone like Jose, individuals who find their voice in one channel rather than another. Those who find their voices through CMC engage in **hyperpersonal communication**. In short, hyperpersonal communication occurs when individuals find they are better able to express themselves in mediated environments than they are in face-to-face interaction.

According to Walther (1996), author of this theory, hyperpersonal communication can be attributed to four interdependent factors: the sender, the receiver, the channel, and feedback. Let us take a look at how each of these four elements contribute to a potentially hyperpersonal experience. As an example, let us imagine Ling, a first-year student at a small, state-run college who is having difficulty relating with the other women in her dorm, and has begun to frequent a chat room seeking support.

The first factor that can contribute to a hyperpersonal experience is the *sender*, who possesses greater control of self-presentation to others. Thus, one can be highly selective in what one chooses to reveal about oneself. Because one is not handicapped by many nonverbal characteristics outside one's control, one is able to create an even more idealized self-image. For example, Ling has always been very self-conscious about a large mole on her right cheek. When talking with friends in face-to-face situations, she swears that she can sense their eyes wandering over to this disfiguring "beauty mark." Needless to say, she has chosen not to mention this feature in her dialogues with online contacts. Instead, she has described herself as musically gifted, a talent she is most proud of, but something, unlike the mole, that people wouldn't immediately notice about her in real life. Having her musical talent forefronted as a distinguishing quality, rather than her blemish, boosts Ling's confidence in her online interactions.

Second, the *receiver* can overestimate the qualities of a conversation partner in a hyperpersonal experience. The previously discussed SIDE model supports the notion that people can overattribute qualities to the people on the other end of a message. In her online conversations, Ling has been interacting with Scooby-Snak, a self-professed sophomore at a Big Ten institution. From early on in their interactions, Ling feels a kinship with Scooby-Snak because they both report having received some verbal abuse from seniors in their schools. Even though she doesn't know that much about Scooby-Snak, she begins to infer certain similarities between them and decides that this is a likeable person.

Third, characteristics of the *channel* itself, most notably its asynchronous aspects, factor into the hyperpersonal experience. As noted previously, asynchronicity means that communication is occurring nonsimultaneously. In face-to-face interaction, not only must partners be physically co-present, they are expected to exchange messages back and forth in a process akin to a tennis match. Asynchronous communication allows individuals to overcome the limitations of co-presence and to construct messages in a more deliberative manner. Case in point, Ling returns from her 10 a.m. class to find an e-mail from Scooby-Snak asking her the latest question in a music trivia contest the two have initiated between them. Ling is stumped by the question, so she walks across campus to the music library, finds the answer, and then returns to write back to her partner. In a face-to-face interaction, Ling would have been at a disadvantage. The nature of their asynchronous exchange, however, allowed her the freedom to construct a suitable reply, one that no doubt made her feel more confident about herself and thusly the relationship.

And finally, *feedback* between the partners can intensify the experience. According to Walther (1996), feedback within CMC can lead to "an intensification loop" where the confirming messages of each partner reinforce the behavior of the other. Feedback is, of course, an important part of many communication interactions. Without feedback, we would be left to wonder whether or not our messages made any impact on our audience. The contributions of feedback in an electronic encounter seem to reduce the uncertainty about whether or not the message was received and interpreted in the way it was intended. Replies would seem to be particularly important sources of feedback in such instances because information gathered by nonverbal channels (say, a confirming smile, for instance) are not immediately accessible.

In Ling's case, she and Scooby-Snak continue to exchange messages pertaining to their musical trivia contest for some time. Each time Scooby-Snak issues another question, Ling is encouraged to respond with an answer, issue her own question, and keep the process flowing. Ling perceives Scooby-Snak's continued feedback as a confirming sign for the continuation of the relationship, especially because this partner's demonstrated interest in the topic is more attention than has been shown to her interests from those people who share her dorm.

The hyperpersonal perspective is a provocative explanation for why some people are intensely attracted to networked conversations. The promise of greater control over the nonverbal elements of your self-presentation, of interacting with someone predisposed to reading a favorable impression of you, of more time to create more thoughtful and articulate messages, and of affirming feedback creates a situation that many cannot experience in real life. For Ling, and others like her, online interaction may provide a forum to find a voice that might otherwise remain silent.

Whether communication via networked channels is found to be impersonal, interpersonal, or hyperpersonal, the research discussed here collectively suggests that it is not so much the nature of the technology that determines the evaluation of the communication experience as much as it is one's perception of that experience. Thus, this body of research suggests a counter point to the technological determinism discussed in previous chapters. Accordingly, individual perception, rather than the qualities of the medium itself, once again reasserts its dominance in human interaction in this context as in all others. Our interpretive lenses lead us to look on network interaction as distant, immediate, or extraordinary. All three perspectives view interaction as relevant but the quality as divergent. As you think about your own opinion on this debate, we turn now to a consideration of issues that have emerged in the wake of online relationships.

## Hyperlink: The Love Beeper

With so many stories about people meeting the love of their life online, you might be tempted to think that using technology to mediate romance is something unusual. The unorthodox meetings of couples because of chat rooms, MUDs, and Web sites may make it seem like technology introduces something unnatural to a relationship. However, people have used various communication technologies throughout this century to find a mate.

For example, take the consistent popularity of newspaper personal ads. As an aid to relationship initiation, they not only allow one to advertise one's best attributes, but because they specify qualities sought in a partner, they help to reduce the uncertainty and awkwardness of face-to-face interaction (Parrott, Lemieux, Harris, & Foreman, 1997). An even more "scientific" approach was popular in the middle of the century. Computer dating services had singles fill out questionnaires that then electronically matched them with persons with highly consistent answers. The success of this method can be attested to by one of the authors of this book. His parents met and married thanks to computer dating. Arguably, every technological development of the electronic era, from the telephone to the television, has played a role in courtship.

Of course, the recent marriage of personal ad and computer in the form of electronic bulletin boards does not mean that people will stop innovating ways to have technology enrich their love lives. Take the Japanese "Lovegety," or Love Beeper, for instance (Associated Press, 1998). The pocket-sized device can be set to broadcast one of three different signals for you: "karaoke" for those in the mood for singing, "chat" for talkers, and "friends" for those up for something more intimate. When one comes within 5 meters of a Lovegety of the opposite sex, it flashes a signal to the owner. If the beepers are on the same setting, the flash is green, and if they are on different settings, the flash is red. The little "love get" device can break the ice while at the same time it can weeding out those with dissimilar relational goals.

Finding a romantic partner can be a difficult process, one that many find is best not left up to chance. In due course, it seems that many people are turning to technology in order to narrow the odds in their favor. And yet there is a persistent doubt in the minds of those who question the authenticity of such tactics, preferring human intervention to technological intervention. Ultimately, the question comes around to what difference does it make if your matchmaker is breathing or beeping?

# MANAGING ONLINE RELATIONSHIPS

Just as we experience different kinds of relationships in our real lives, we are likely to develop different kinds of relationships online as well. If you have not already experienced them, you may well develop some working relationships, and perhaps even some friendships or romances in cyberspace. In order to manage these relationships effectively, competent communicators need to attend to some issues that are even more salient in online relationships than in real-life relationships. In particular, we think you should pay close attention to the challenges of depersonalization in working relationships and emotional detachment in romantic relationships.

## Working Relationships

In 2000, it is estimated that nearly 18 million Americans were telecommuting to work, spending at least part of the normal business hours working for an outside employer from their homes ("Telecommuting," 1999). Engineers, artists, designers, programmers, sales people, and writers are just some of the career fields that are moving toward telecommuting. As you might imagine, the nature of telecommuting requires that employers communicate their directives and that employees submit their products over electronic communication systems. Even if you don't find yourself engaged in a telecommuting job, you are still likely to find yourself interacting with employers and clients through e-mail and other communication systems. (More is discussed about telecommuting and the role computer technologies play in professional life in chapter 7.)

As these systems become increasingly more common as part of the working experience, it becomes easier to take for granted the effect they have on human communication. As the impersonal perspective suggests, however, there is a temptation to forget many of the rules that govern civil face-to-face interaction. Although sufficient evidence exists that CMC is not inherently depersonalizing, people can still behave in manners that are injurious to others.

This is most obvious in the act of **flaming**. A message can be considered a flame when it is intended and/or interpreted to be hostile in nature. Take a look at the following hypothetical exchange:

```
  ArchEE: I think that the client really appreciates my
          contribution.
 JuggHed: ALL the clients at Riverdale appreciate you.
  ArchEE: What's THAT supposed to mean?!?!
```

JuggHed might have intended to compliment ArchEE (if he really does think he's that well liked), or he might have intended to mock him. It is difficult to tell what his comment intended to communicate without the accompanying vocal qualities that distinguish awe from sarcasm. However, ArchEE's heated reply suggests that he perceived it to be an attack.

Thompsen (1996) claims that the confrontational nature of flaming can best be understood by a **social influence model** on technology use (originating in the work of Fulk, Steinfield, Schmitz, & Power, 1987). Accordingly, "a social influence perspective on flaming thus considers both the behavior of flaming and the social negotiation of what that behavior means . . . flaming is both a media use and a media evaluation—a [CMC] behavior and an interpretation of that behavior" (pp. 303–304). Several components contribute to a deeper understand of flaming.

Thompsen lists direct statements, vicarious learning, group behavioral norms, social definitions of reality, media experience and skills, media evaluations, task evaluations, situational factors, media features, and prior use of other media as potential contributors to the creation and interpretation of flames. From the user's perspective, social influence and media experience seem to be the key factors in leading to flaming. Social influence comes in many forms, including vicarious learning. If JuggHed has observed others flaming in the chat room where he and ArchEE meet, then he is more likely to know how to flame but also to infer that it is okay to flame. As for media experience, if JuggHed is new to the online experience, he might have inadvertently flamed without intending to. His novice status might have led him to make an online faux pas.

From an evaluator's perspective, social influence and media experience continue to affect our perceptions of a message. Here again, our perceptions of what is appropriate in the setting and our own familiarity with the conventions of the technology will lead to an interpretation of a given message. ArchEE's heavily punctuated response certainly suggests that he has negatively interpreted JuggHed's message. His own perception of the online environment might suggest that JuggHed has issued a personal innuendo inappropriate to this context. As such, he sees a flame where his partner might or might not have intended one to be.

Intentionally or unintentionally, flames can cause turmoil in a relationship. The challenge for communicators is twofold, as well. From the message creation side, one must know the norms of a given setting and practice reading a message from the other person's point of view. Asking yourself, "In what ways could ArchEE misread this message?" before you send it could lead you to make some subtle, yet meaningful revisions to the text. Had JuggHed intended his comment as a compliment, he might have elaborated further, adding, "ALL the people I have spoken with at Riverdale have told me just how much they appreciate you."

On the other end, receivers could benefit from an accounting of their own interpretation and bracket that within the realm of possible interpretations. Had ArchEE been open to the possibility of multiple meanings, he might have replied with a question that engaged in more perception-checking than inquisition, "Do you mean to say that you've heard a positive response?" Although it is entirely possible that people will be intentionally caustic at times, it is a shame when unintended interpretations lead to a series of hurtful messages, a "flame war" in the online vernacular, when there are ways to quench the sparks. We now turn our attention to another kind of spark, the romantic kind, and challenges communicators face in these online relationships.

## Romantic Relationships

When it comes to romantic relationships, many people like to think that they are mutually beneficial. Ideally, both parties have their needs for affection, inclusion, and control met through the arrangement (Schutz, 1958). Yet, experience has taught most of us that romantic relationships are rarely ideal. For one reason or another, most of them are complicated by shortfalls. When it comes to relating online, relationships can be no less perfect. In particular, research centered on romantic relationships has been characterized by some degree of emotional detachment between partners. As the following two cases demonstrate, this detachment suggests a game-playing type of love displayed and results in a lack of commitment to the online relationship.

In the first case, Clark (1995) found that dating in online contexts is more likely an exercise in self-fulfillment than in building relational bonds. She studied teens who participate in chat rooms to determine the character of their dating relationships. What she found was a degree of emotional detachment that seemed sharply contrasted to that of face-to-face interactions. Summarizing the teens' responses, Clark asserts that the primary motivation for dating online is to have "fun" rather than to establish strong emotional ties or lasting commitments. In fact, although the relationships practiced in cyberspace offered each participant a strong sense of emotional gratification, participants often failed to follow up these relationships in offline contexts.

Removed from the constraints imposed by physical appearance and one's social groups, teens, most especially girls, reported a stronger sense of emancipation and power in online dating than they had encountered in real-life dating. Girls said that they described themselves as meeting the imagined "ideal" of the desirable female, thus garnering more attention from boys and competing with other girls on the basis of their personality and wit rather than their physical attributes. Other reasons girls reported finding the medium emancipatory included the option to avoid unwanted sexual advances (seeing as how it is much easier to avoid a pursuer who inhabits a chat room than one who is seated in a classroom) and to express themselves verbally. As one of Clark's respondents explained, "I act a lot more aggressive on the Internet. I just express my feelings a lot more in the chat rooms and stuff, so if somebody talks about something that I don't like, then I'll say it. And I would probably never do that in class, in school and everything" (p. 165).

As such, the disembodied relationships that can emerge in teen dating scenarios in chat rooms offer their participants fewer "emotional hazards" than face-to-face interactions. With the resulting decreased emotional attachment, one might wonder why teens bother to engage in such "dating" encounters at all. In Clark's (1995) estimation, the answer can be found in self-gratification. Experimenting with others in an exercise of imagined intimacy contributes to the development of one's own self-concept. Finding acceptance from a suitor who is not a threat to one's physical well-being or one's social standing (which can be risked by dating beneath one's socioeconomic group under the watchful eyes of one's socially sensitive peers) can be rewarding, especially to persons who might be less competent in other social settings. But, as they lack the consequences that romantic relationships with personal contact introduce, these relationships should be assessed with some caution. Although they might serve as strong contributors to the construction of self-identity, they seem to fall short in equipping teens to deal with people in more enduring, more immediate interactions.

Consequently, our real-life relationships seem to involve greater emotional attachment than those thus far documented online. This would explain why one party in a real-life relationship like a marriage can be harmed if another turns to the computer rather than to the spouse to meet needs for identity affirmation and sexual gratification.

Although researchers have yet to conclude that there is anything inherently harmful with establishing ties via the Internet, there is evidence that online channels can help manifest problems in an existing real-world relationship. For example, the Internet may provide an avenue that enables one or more parties to retreat from a real-life relationship and seek emotional support from their online relationships. Young (1998), a clinical psychologist, shares accounts of couples who have suffered strain and undergone divorce because of one partner's "online addiction." (This is discussed in greater depth in chapter 5.)

Certainly at the extreme of this type of behavior is a so-called **cyberaffair**, where one partner in a relationship carries on an interpersonally, but not necessarily physically, intimate relationship with someone online. Some have doubted the viability of a cyberaffair, likening it to the reading of a romance novel. However, the key distinction of interactivity seems to suggest infidelity in the perception of a partner (Sullivan, 1997). The root of cyberaffairs, however, might rest outside the medium. According to one physician's commentary:

> This is a marital-dysfunction problem, not an Internet problem. The Internet has simply made the problem manifest. It can't be very flattering to be replaced by a machine, and the natural response is to blame the machine instead of examining the relationship and the part that you are playing—or not playing—in it. (Sullivan, 1997, p. 1618)

In both the case of flaming and emotional detachment, it seems like a common theme threads these implications together. The evidence presented here points to people behaving in ways that are more self-centered than not. Expressing one's anger or fulfilling one's own emotional gratification are, after all, self-rather than other-centered activities. As illustrated in Table 4.2, each of the three perspectives explained earlier in this chapter might view the inclination of these behaviors differently.

## CHAPTER SUMMARY

This chapter reviewed several perspectives and implications of online relationships. Research has suggested that there are three relevant perspectives in examining online relationships: the impersonal, the interpersonal, and the hyperpersonal. Early work in the field of CMC suggested that interaction there was task-oriented and, consequently, impersonal in nature. It was argued that the lack of nonverbal and social cues handicapped communicators interacting in this context. However, it might be that relating online simply takes longer to deepen than in face-to-face settings. Indeed, evidence suggests that people do form interpersonal bonds. The SIDE model argues that there are enough cues for individuals to adopt social roles for them to fit into these relationships. Moreover, some find the reduction of cues enabling, leading them to perceive it as hyperpersonal in nature. Certainly, there are some implications for building relationships online, whether they are working, friendly, or romantic in nature. Competent communicators need to be weary of the potential self-serving bias that comes from disregarding the implications of flaming and emotional detachment.

**Table 4.2**
**Three Perspectives on Working and Romantic Relational Issues**

| Perspective | Depersonalization Through Flaming | Emotional Detachment Through Self-Gratification |
|---|---|---|
| Impersonal | Limited cues encourage disinhibited behavior such as letting one's temper flare | Because the other is unknown, it is easy not to think of this conversation partner as a feeling individual |
| Interpersonal | Conflict is a natural part of interpersonal relationships | Both parties know what they want to get out of this relationship |
| Hyperpersonal | The freedom that comes with expressing yourself sometimes means people express themselves in negative ways | These folks aren't constrained by convention; they're able to experiment with their own identities and relationships |

In the future, scholars have much to learn about the nature of online relationships. There are a number of questions that still need to be answered. For instance, communication scholars theorize that interpersonal relationships develop in stages. Do online relationships develop in a parallel or unique fashion? We also know that people involved in face-to-face relationships use a number of compliance-gaining strategies in order to persuade their partners to do things for them. Are there now unique strategies that have emerged among the online communicators? Finally, how and why do these relationships terminate? Although there are certain processes that are quite similar across contexts, we cannot take for granted that what we know about face-to-face interaction is necessarily the case in cyberspace. Although there are many unanswered questions about online relationships, there are many people whose curiosity about these issues will propel the search for understanding them forward.

## Online Communication and the Law

Flaming behavior is not limited to interaction between individuals. As the following two cases demonstrate, people have used online communication to voice their displeasure with organizations with legal implications.

In the first case, issuing a potentially antagonistic message worked to the people's advantage. After the packing, traveling, and unpacking in a cross-country move, George Musser, Jr., and Talia Schaffer were frustrated at finding that their moving company damaged or lost some of their belongings. When the couple complained to the company, Bekins Van Lines, their cries fell on deaf ears. That is until they posted their own complaint site on the World Wide Web, www.bekinsbeware.org. With the accessibility of the complaint magnified by its presence online, lawyers for Bekins offered to settle the couples $1,734 claim if they would agree to remove the offending site (Kaplan, 1999a).

However, you might think twice before expressing just any opinion you might have about a corporation or its representatives. Flaming comments could open you to charges of libel if the statements prove to be untrue. Case in point, Wade Cook Financial Corporation sued for Yahoo! to release the real names of 10 people who posted disparaging comments about its president (Kaplan, 1999b). The message board posts implicated the executive in fraudulent activities. Lawyers for the firm argued that such messages defamed not only the individual but also damaged the credibility of the company, as well. Anonymity does not excuse one from responsibility.

What role do you believe the courts should play in policing online conflict? Should people be allowed to use the media at their discretion or should the rule of law provide some mediation in such conflict situations?

## Glossary

**Cyberaffair**: A perceived infidelity that occurs when one partner in a real-life relationship maintains a romantic relationship with another partner online.

**Deindividuation**: A psychological process of surrendering personal identity in favor of the dominant social identity; the so-called mob mentality.

**Emoticons**: Text-based cues designed to reveal the emotional intent of a message.

**Flaming**: The practice of sending intended or perceived hostile messages in mediated contexts.

**Functional alternatives**: A perception that one channel accomplishes the same task just as well as another.

**Hyperpersonal communication**: A perspective on mediated communication suggesting that greater control over self-presentation by the sender, overestimations by the receiver, the asynchronicity of the channel, and confirming messages offered through feedback allow some people to better express themselves in mediated rather than in face-to-face interactions.

**Nonverbal cues**: All the nonlanguage elements to communication, including vocal qualities, facial expressions, posture, movement, and eye contact.

**Norms**: Behaviors accepted among members of a social group.

**Social context cues**: A perspective on human behavior suggesting that actions are governed by subtle indicators in the social environment.

**Social identification/deindividuated (SIDE) model**: A perspective on mediated communication suggesting that interpersonal attraction and acceptance come from identification with group norms.

**Social influence model**: A perspective on mediated communication suggesting that a media use results from a negotiation between the features of the medium and the social conditions.

**Social information processing**: A perspective on mediated communication suggesting that mediated interaction takes more time to develop relationships than face-to-face interactions given the presence of fewer nonverbal cues.
**Social presence theory**: A perspective on mediated communication suggesting that people perceive differing degrees of substance to others they interact with over mediated channels and to their relationship to them.
**Specialized channels**: A perception that each medium is particularly well suited to accomplishing a particular task.

## Topics for Discussion

1. In addition to those mentioned in the text, make a list of five other nonverbal cues on which you interpret meaning during your face-to-face interactions. In what ways do you see these cues compensated for in online interactions? Does the absence of any of them make communicating easier or more difficult in the online environment?
2. According to the SIDE model, people are willing to give up their personal identities and assume social identities in order to find acceptance online. Write a paragraph in which you identify situations, online and in real life, where there are advantages to choosing one over the other. How can one avoid being swept up by deindividuation in these situations?
3. In the explanation of hyperpersonal communication, we focus on an example of how it could explain a positive encounter. Explain how a negative encounter could be accentuated by the hyperpersonal factors of sender, receiver, channel, and feedback?
4. Cite five criteria you use to determine if a message is a flame. Print out a message that you have interpreted as flaming in nature. What response would you typically follow up with? How is your interpretation and response affected by social influence and media experience?
5. Make a list of the qualities that you think lead people to seek out romantic relationships online. Is it fair to judge the standards for relating in face-to-face relationships with those in mediated relationships?

## REFERENCES

Associated Press. (1998, June 1). Lonely Japanese seek mates with love beeper. *CNN Interactive.* <http://cnn.com/WORLD/asiapcf/9806/01/japan.love.machine.ap/ index.html>.
Birdwhistle, R. L. (1970). *Kinesics in context*. Philadelphia: University of Pennsylvania Press.
Borenstein, D. (2000). *Quoteland.com.* <http://www.quoteland.com>.

Clark, L. S. (1995). Dating on the net: Teens and the rise of "pure" relationships. In J. T. Wood & S. Duck (Eds.), *Under-studied relationships: Off the beaten track* (pp. 159– 183). Thousand Oaks, CA: Sage.

Culnan, M. J., & Markus, M. L. (1987). Information technologies. In F. M. Jablin, L. L. Putnam, K. H. Roberts, & L. W. Porter (Eds.), *Handbook of organizational communication: An interdisciplinary perspective* (pp. 420–443). Newbury Park, CA: Sage.

Flaherty, L. M., Pearce, K. J., & Rubin, R. R. (1998). Internet and face-to-face communication: Not functional alternatives. *Communication Quarterly, 46,* 250–268.

Fulk, J., Steinfield, C. W., Schmitz, J., & Power, J. G. (1987). A social information processing model of media use in organizations. *Communication Research, 14,* 529–552.

Kaplan, C. S. (1999, January 8). Unhappy customers find a complaint site pays off. *Cyber Law Journal* <http://www.nytimes.com/library/tech/99/01/cyber/cyberlaw/08law.html>.

Kaplan, C. S. (1999a, May 12). Companies fight anonymous critics with lawsuits. *Cyber Law Journal* <http://www.nytimes.com/library/tech/99/03/cyber/cyberlaw/12law.html>.

Kiesler, S., Siegel, J., & McGuire, T. W. (1984). Social psychological aspects of CMC. *American Psychologist, 39,* 1123–1134.

Lea, M., & Spears, R. (1998). Love at first byte? Building personal relationships over computer networks. In S. G. Jones (Ed.), *Cybersociety 2.0: Revisiting CMC and community* (pp. 197–233). Thousand Oaks, CA: Sage.

Leitz, L. (1999, September 26). Couple clicks on romance. *South Bend Tribune: Vows,* p. 3.

McCormick, N. B., & McCormick, J. W. (1992). Computer friends and foes: Content of undergraduates' electronic mail. *Computers in Human Behavior, 8,* 379–405.

Mehrabian, A. (1972). *Nonverbal communication.* Chicago: Aldine.

Metz, J. M. (1994a). Computer-mediated communication: Literature review of a new context. *Interpersonal Computing and Technology: An Electronic Journal for the 21st Century.* <http://www.helsinki.fi/science/optek/1994/n2/metz.txt>.

Metz, J. M. (1994b, November). *Computer-mediated communication cultures: An ethnographic examination.* Paper presented at the annual Speech Communication Association conference, New Orleans, LA.

Parks, M. R., & Floyd, K. (1996). Making friends in cyberspace. *Journal of Communication, 46*(1), 80–97.

Parrott, R., Lemieux, R., Harris, T., Foreman, L. (1997). Interfacing interpersonal and mediated communication: Use of active and strategic self-disclosure in personal ads. *Southern Communication Journal, 62,* 319–332.

Postumes, T., Spears, R., & Lea, M. (1998). Breaching or building social boundaries? Side-effects of CMC. *Communication Research, 25,* 689–716.

Reid, E. (1991). *Electropolis: Communication and community on Internet Relay Chat.* Unpublished master's thesis, University of Melbourne, Australia. <http://www.ee.mu.oz.au/papers/emr/electropolis.html>.

Rice, R. E. (1987). CMC and organizational innovation. *Journal of Communication, 37*, 65–94.
Schutz, W. C. (1958). *FIRO: A three-dimensional theory of interpersonal behavior*. New York: Holt, Rinehart & Winston.
Schwartz, P. (1996, June). R-tech. *Wired, 4.06*. <http://www.wired.com/wired/archive/4.06/rtech.html> .
Short, J., Williams, E., & Christie, B. (1976). *The social psychology of telecommunication*. London: Wiley.
Sproull, L., & Kiesler, S. (1986). Reducing social context cues: Electronic mail in organizational communication. *Management Science, 32*, 1492–1512.
Sullivan, P. (1997). Physicians debate Internet-related marital problems on CMA's online service. *Canadian Medical Association Journal, 156*, 1617–1618.
Telecommuting boosted in 1998 by Internet and economy. (1999). *Working moms refuge*. <http://www.momsrefuge.com/telecommute/survey.html>.
Thompsen, P. A. (1996). What's fueling the flames of cyberspace? A social influence model. In L. Strate, R. Jacobson, & S. B. Gibson (Eds.), *Communication and cyberspace: Social interaction in an electronic environment* (pp. 297–315). Cresskill, NJ: Hampton Press.
Trenholm, S., & Jensen, A. (2000). *Interpersonal communication* (4th ed.). Belmont, CA: Wadsworth.
Walther, J. B. (1992). Interpersonal effects in computer-mediated interaction: A relational perspective. *Communication Research, 19*, 52–90.
Walther, J. B. (1996). CMC: Impersonal, interpersonal, and hyperpersonal interaction. *Communication Research, 23*(1), 3–43.
Young, K. (1998). *Caught in the net: How to recognize the signs of Internet addiction and a winning strategy for recovering*. New York: Wiley.

# CHAPTER 5

# SEEKING THERAPY ONLINE

*The internet is so big, so powerful and pointless that for some people it is a complete substitute for life.*

—*Andrew Brown (Borenstein, 2000)*

One evening in December 1999, aspiring actor Michael Campbell of Cape Coral, Florida, found himself in a chat room, exchanging messages with Erin Walton of Littleton, Colorado. Walton was a survivor of the Columbine High School massacre earlier that year. Campbell, using the pseudonym "Soup81," wrote to Walton, alias "Gingerhrts," warning her not to attend school the following day.

```
     Soup81:  Listen, I can't tell you who I am because
              you know me. . . . Do me a favor, don't go
              to school tomorrow.
Gingerhrts:   Why?
     Soup81:  Please, I trust in you and confide in you.
Gingerhrts:   I have to go. I can't miss school.
     Soup81:  I need to finish what begun and if you go I
              don't want blood on your hands.
Gingerhrts:   Please don't do this. You are really scaring
              me.
     Soup81:  There is nothing to be scared about, just
              don't go to school and don't tell anyone.
              If anyone finds out, you'll be the first
              to go.
```

Horrified by the exchange, Walton reported the threat to Columbine's principal and the authorities. Columbine closed its door 2 days early for the winter break, Walton decided to switch schools after this incident, and the FBI tracked Soup81 back to Campbell. They then arrested him for making a threat across state lines. Campbell would later profess regret for the seriousness with which Walton reacted to his statements but maintained that he had never intended to hurt anyone. Rather, he claimed to be caught up in the role he perceived himself as playing within the chat room. His lawyer, Ellis Rubin, subsequently attempted to capitalize on this notion, offering a defense of "Internet addiction" on his client's behalf (Janofsky, 2000).

Although Campbell later changed his plea to guilty, the attempt to displace responsibility for his statements using addiction to the Internet as an excuse was a legal first. Campbell's case is just one example of how people can jeopardize everything from their jobs, their families, their health, to the well-being of others and blame it on too much use of the Internet. Whether or not Campbell's criminal actions can, at least in part, be attributed to the communication context rather than solely his own poor judgment is certainly an issue for debate. Although various scholars and therapists have dismissed the notion that the Internet can lure people into a dependency on CMC, others argue that case studies and surveys support their claims that for some people, over-reliance on online interaction can have detrimental effects, little different than if one were suffering from any other behavioral disorder. One large study claimed that as many as 6% of Internet users suffer from some form of online addiction (Donn, 1999).

This chapter examines the effects that online communication can have on users' well-being, both negatively and positively. We begin by examining the alleged problem itself by reviewing the symptoms of online addiction. In the course of examining the effects of this phenomenon, we focus particular attention on human sexuality as a contributor to this life-altering behavior. However, we also want to acknowledge that although some people suffer detrimental effects because of their online affiliations, others can reap rewards. Thus, we conclude this chapter with a look at the ways in which people benefit from online therapy sessions and support groups.

## INTERNET ADDICTION DISORDER

The results of one of the most widely cited studies of Internet usage suggests that greater use of the Internet has a detrimental effect on one's well-being. According to a research team from Carnegie Mellon University, the more that participants used the Internet, the less likely they were to communicate with members of their household; moreover, their social circles were likely to grow smaller, and they experienced increases in depression and loneliness (Kraut, Patterson et al., 1998).

In February 2000, the Stanford Institute for the Quantitative Study of Society reported findings that the Internet has detrimental effects upon people's lives (Stanford, 2000). The poll indicated that 13% of the respondents reported spending less time with family and friends, 26% talked less with family and friends on the telephone, and 8% attended fewer social events. According to Norman Nie, a Stanford University political scientist, "The Internet could be the ultimate isolating technology that further reduces our participation in communities even more than television did before it" (Associated Press, 2000). Although evidence we present later in this chapter contests these findings, such conclusions lend support to the notion that the Internet indirectly reduces the quality of life enjoyed by some users, leading in some cases to an extreme condition that psychiatrist Ivan Goldberg dubbed "Internet Addiction Disorder."

Like other psychological disorders, **Internet Addiction Disorder** (IAD), has distressing implications for one's psychological, physical, and social well-being. For some people, the addiction is to the applications made available through the Internet, and they find themselves caught up in the lure of online gambling, competitive auctions, and stock trading (Young, 1998b). For others, however, the appeal is interpersonal. The case of Sandra Hacker received national attention when she was discovered neglecting the care of her children because she was preoccupied with the Internet. Her obsession with online interaction allegedly led her to lock her children in a filthy room for up to 12 hours a day (Bricking, 1997). Cases like Hacker's demonstrate that communication can be just as addictive as any other behavior. Affirming this notion is Pavel Curtis, creator of the social MUD, LambdaMOO, who noted a warning in the following statement:

> I am concerned about the degree to which people find virtual communities enchanting. We have people who use LambdaMOO who are not in control of their usage who are, I believe, seriously and clinically addicted. . . . These people aren't addicted to playing video games. It wouldn't be the same for them. They're communication addicted. They're addicted to being able to go out and find people twenty-four hours a day and have interesting conversations with them. We're talking about people who spend up to seventy hours a week connected and active on a MUD. (cited in Rheingold, 1993, pp. 151–152)

Certainly, one of the presumptions held about online addicts is that they are repressed, socially awkward, inwardly focused individuals. However, Curtis counters that presumption by arguing, "if someone is spending a large portion of their time being social with people who live thousands of miles away, you can't say that they've turned inward. They aren't shunning society. They're actively seeking it. They're probably doing it more actively than anyone around them" (p. 152). Thus, it is the interpersonal connection made through communication, rather than the novelty of the technology itself, that contributes to the Internet's allure.

## Symptoms of IAD

Having a problem and recognizing that one has a problem are often two different things. In order to help people identify when their behavior has changed from casual to addictive levels, the American Psychiatric Association has recommended attending to the following indications (Ferris, 1997). If people suffer three or more of the following symptoms within a 12-month period, they may be experiencing IAD.

1. They build a **tolerance** for the Internet. That is, if they feel the need for more exposure to the Internet in order to feel the same amount of satisfaction as with previous amounts of exposure.
2. They experience **withdrawal** symptoms after they stop using the Internet. Withdrawal symptoms can include feelings of anxiety or obsessive thinking about what they are missing online.
3. They find themselves accessing the Internet more than they intend to or they access it for longer periods of time than they intend to.
4. They have a desire to reduce or have been unsuccessful in reducing Internet use.
5. They spend a good deal of time with activities related to the Internet (e.g., buying Internet-related books).
6. They neglect to attend to social, occupational, or recreational activities because of the Internet.

7. They continue to use the Internet despite an obvious problem with their health, relationships, job, or mental health because of their Internet use (e.g., insomnia, marital conflict, neglect of occupational duties, or anxiety).

In short, these criteria imply that use of the Internet becomes a problem when it comes to occupy a disproportionate amount of one's life. But what attracts people to the Internet, per se?

According to Young (1998a, 1998b), founder of the Center for Online Addiction and author of *Caught in the Net*, one explanation for the attraction to the Internet is found in her **ACE model**. This acronym stands for *accessibility, control,* and *excitement*. In Young's view, these qualities of the communication context make it particularly attractive to some people. For many, the Internet is readily accessible. If they have a connection at home or work (or both!), they can log on many times a day and seek the personal gratification that comes with indulging in conversation, gambling, or whatever particular reward one is seeking. Control is also a major attractor. People like to feel that they have control over what they will do, when they will do it, and how they will do so. Finally, excitement contributes to the attraction. There is a mental "high" that is associated with good conversation, winning a bet, or discovering something one does not know or has never seen before. The ACE model thus suggests that the rewards one perceives from interaction with the Internet is, at least initially, a strong lure for people getting caught up in addictive behaviors.

Interestingly, Young also suggests that the reasons leading people to addiction may be gender-based. In her research, Young found that men tend to gravitate toward online interaction because it offers them the opportunity to exercise power and dominance. In particular, MUDs are known for both their creative and combative characteristics. One exercises control over the creation of identities, tools, and stories in these forums. Men also seem to enjoy the domination they can exercise in sexually explicit chat (which is discussed in greater depth later). Young also found that women, on the other hand, seem attracted to the absence of judgment on their physical appearance and the company of others that the context provides. Thus, even though women will participate in romantic dialogue, for them it is a matter of being appreciated for their personalities rather than for their bodies. Given that human sexuality contributes to the attraction of IAD, we focus some attention in the next section on a particular form of the disorder and one that has certainly garnered much attention in the popular media, the type based on sexuality.

## HYPERLINK: OBSCENITY IN CYBERSPACE

If you have ever made the error of typing in www.whitehouse.*com* instead of www.whitehouse.*gov* (as a senior colleague of ours once did while trying to show his mother how to find information on the presidency), then you are probably aware, at least in part, of the vast repository of pornographic material available online. Whitehouse.com is just one of the countless sites featuring sexually explicit materials that many people consume on a regular basis. In fact, about one third of the Internet's users regularly visit some sort of sexual Web site *(San Francisco Examiner*, 1999).

The proliferation of erotica online has been one of the thornier issues over which legislators and Internet advocates have tussled. On one hand, authorities have sought to protect children from literature and images of an adult nature. On the other hand, cyberculture enthusiasts have vehemently objected to any kind of government regulation over online speech. The problem of regulating obscene material and protecting free speech is not a new one, and the Supreme Court established some guidelines for what materials would fall into the category of the "obscene" and thus within the bounds of regulation. In its 1973 decision on Miller v. California, the court established a three-part test, each part of which must be met in order for material to be considered obscene:

1. the material, taken as a whole appeals to prurient interests, that
2. the work depicts or describes, in a patently offensive way, sexual conduct, and that
3. the material lacks serious literary, artistic, political, or scientific value (cited in Birsch, 1996).

As you can tell, even these guidelines themselves are somewhat ambiguous. However, when Congress attempted to reduce that uncertainty by prohibiting "indecency" on the Internet in the Communication Decency Act of 1996, its tight restrictions on free speech met with the disapproval of the courts (Bilstad & Godward, 1996).

Given the difficulty that government has had with regulating the morality of certain messages within this new medium, a better solution to coping with obscenity online might rest with private entities rather than legislative agencies. One possible solution would be to have local service providers censor materials that fail to meet community standards (Birsch, 1996). For years, CompuServe monitored and blocked the flow of objectionable material through its commercial system. Another possible solution is for households to control this material through the use of software programs like Surfwatch, Cyber Patrol, or NatNanny, each of which filter out obscene sites on the Web (Bilstad & Godward, 1996). Although such alternatives are not foolproof, they do provide a less constitutionally questionable solution to coping with the bounty of obscene material online.

## Addiction to Sexual Content

According to their testimony in the *Columbus Dispatch*, one Franklin County, Ohio couple had a healthy and happy relationship until the husband logged onto the Internet. Shortly after buying a home computer in 1995, the husband began to explore the darker side of the Internet, visiting pornographic Web sites, exchanging pornographic images with other users, and participating in more risky chat rooms. Gradually, his compulsion led him to spend increasing amounts of time online, at home and on the job, until as much as 75% of his work day would be spent chatting. Eventually, he connected with a woman who lived in Philadelphia and began exchanging increasingly flirtatious messages with her, culminating in a weekend drive to meet her face to face. Shortly after that trip, the husband could bear the guilt no longer and confessed his unfaithfulness to his wife. Coincidentally, his employers discovered that he had embezzled $300 to finance his weekend in Philadelphia. They fired him. Within just 6 months, this man had gone from being upright to down-trodden (Fiely, 1999).

This midwestern fellow is not alone. A recent study concluded that more than 9 million people visit erotic Web sites daily, send suggestive e-mail, or join sexual chat rooms (*San Francisco Examiner*, 1999). Throughout the Internet's rapid growth, people have found numerous ways to experiment with sexuality online. Beyond the presentation of graphic material on the World Wide Web, the Internet is also home to a library of erotic literature as well as a forum for the posting of bulletin board messages and real-time exchanges in which conversants describe sexual activity to one another. Called "cybersex chat," "hot chat," or "tiny sex," among other things, such interactive messages seem attractive for three reasons. According to Dr. Alvin Cooper, director of the San Jose Marital and Sexuality Centre, online sexual content owes its popularity to the affordability, accessibility, and anonymity of the Internet (*San Francisco Examiner*, 1999).

Because of these factors, consuming sexual content on the Internet is a lot different than visiting the local adult bookstore. Beyond the expenses charged by one's ISP, a great deal of this material is free to the consumer. Moreover, wherever one has an Internet connection, at work or at home, one can easily access this material. There is no store one has to drive to in order to consume it. And, of course, one is less likely to have one's pseudonym recognized during a visit to an adult chat room than one's face recognized when walking out of the adult bookstore on a busy city street. Thus, the conditions of affordability, accessibility, and anonymity suggest logical explanations based on convenience and security for why sexual content is so popular online.

However, a healthy curiosity about human sexuality does not indicate abnormality. As Cooper explains:

> We have this myth that people go online in an uncontrolled way and cybersex takes over their lives. But those who use the Internet as a recreational tool rather than in a sexual way demonstrate no significant problems. It's like watching *Baywatch* or looking at Victoria's Secret catalogs. (n.p.)

Problems arise, of course, when one's interest in cybersex interferes with the rest of one's life, leading to the neglect of one's professional responsibilities and personal relationships, as was the case with the Ohio man.

Recognizing the implications of such behaviors posed to one's professional and personal reputation, Witmer (1997) sought to understand why people would engage in such risky CMC. After all, electronic forums are certainly not secure channels for interacting. Although the Electronic Communications Privacy Act of 1986 makes breaking into someone's account a criminal offense akin to wiretapping, the fact is that most people are more vulnerable to intrusions on their privacy than they may think. For instance, a system's administrator, such as a university's director of computer services, has access to the accounts in a given organization. E-mail messages with potentially embarrassing or inflamatory content ("Our boss is a cheesehead!") can easily be forwarded to any number of recipients with a mere click of the mouse by the recipient. And certainly, a skillful hacker can break through security measures and access a person's files. Given that anything they say or forward on an electronic platform is stored somewhere and can be recalled and made public, why would people risk making contributions to discussion groups such as alt.sex, alt.sex.bestiality, or alt.sex.bondage?

Interestingly, the results of Witmer's (1997) survey found that a majority of respondents perceived that their participation had little bearing on their reputations. In fact, 57.7% said that their privacy was unimportant or extremely unimportant and an additional 25% reported neutral feelings about privacy. As Witmer notes, "respondents tended to feel personally and technically secure in their CMC, and felt that they had little or nothing to lose if their activities were discovered by unintended others" (n.p.). Thus, even though a number of cases testify to the negative impact that such participation can have on one's life, this survey's results demonstrate how many people do not perceive the detrimental possibilities until they are made manifest in their lives.

Mental health professionals have spoken to the need for people to cope with addictions like those who are engaged in compulsive cybersexual behaviors. The first step, as with any problem, is to recognize that one has a dependency on the Internet. Once this basic premise is acknowledged, one can begin to explore the underlying problems that have led to the addiction. Thereafter, one can construct and enact a plan to cope, rather than escape, from the addiction (Ferris, 1997). Young (1998b) points out that one need not go "cold turkey" to overcome Internet addiction. The Internet is, after all, a useful tool, and one should learn to use it wisely, not recklessly. The key to healthy Internet use, as seemingly with all things in life, is moderation.

## Is IAD Real?

Cases of people whose lives have been negatively affected by the presence of the Internet—including the recent Carnegie Mellon and Stanford studies—can serve as evidence for why society should be aware of IAD. However, a study by the UCLA Center for Communication Policy contradicts these conclusions. "According to respondents' reports, concerns that the Internet reduces household time together appear to be nearly groundless. Nearly all users (91.8 percent) say that since being connected to the Internet at home, members of the household spend about the same amount of time together or more time together" (Cole et al., 2000, p. 29). Given that the medium itself might not be inherently capable of inducing a disorder, we might ask if problemmatic behaviors are indicative of a bona fide mental disorder or merely instances where people with larger problems found an outlet or excuse through the Internet? Some critics have stepped forward to question the validity of claims suggesting IAD as a distinct affliction.

In particular, Walther and Reid (2000) point out the scant amount of research that supports the notion that these cases are indicative of a psychological disorder. They would like to see more scrutiny on people's activities on the Internet. The presumption that seems to support a number of the present arguments "is that offline activities are better—healthier, or more natural—than online behavior, but we haven't examined whether that is so" (p. B4). Also, at present no evidence exists that people engaged in compulsive online behaviors would not engage in the same activities offline. Moreover, the increased amounts of time people seem to spend online may not necessarily stem from an addiction so much as a characteristic of the medium. Because most people type much slower than they can talk, a conversation that takes 1 hour offline could run 4 hours online.

Walther and Reid (2000) also note that research exists to suggest that increased amounts of time online is nothing unusual for participants to experience and is not necessarily indicative of an addiction. They point to work being done by Lynn Roberts in Australia. Roberts has studied how chat room participants seem to go through phases during their online tenure. A participant's initial exploration is typically followed by "obsessive enchantment," but that in turn is followed by a disillusionment phase and decreased usage thereafter.

Other critics have argued that attention focused on addictive behaviors is exaggerated. Szalavitz (1999), who has experienced substance addictions in the past, is suspicious of IAD, noting, "People can and do use everything from methamphetamine to mountaineering to avoid doing what they should. If you can't face the world, you'll always find somewhere to hide" (p. 11). Moreover, she wonders if the hype over IAD has been publicized by a bunch of pundits who may well be promoting the disorder in order to lay claim to the profits and notoriety that come along with the media attention.

Such opposition suggests that the introduction of the Internet has caused some discomfort and suspicion about the technology. A natural reaction to dealing with new technology is to use it as a scapegoat when it appears to be the cause of life's problems. Indeed, history has shown that the introduction of any new communication medium into society has met with some suspicion. Alarmists have objected to the influence of everything from the printed book to the television. Even comic books, despite their conservative avocation of American values, were once accused of contributing to juvenile delinquency (Wertham, 1954). With the widespread influence of the Internet in recent years, Jim Clark, president of Netscape, reminds us that all new media are attacked as something dangerous at first (cited in Doyle, 1996). Thus, discussions about IAD, whether the disorder itself is real or not, may well be indicative of society's suspicion about this complex, new factor being introduced into our lives.

Despite indictments against the Internet's viability as a beneficial communication tool, there are a number of scholars, and far more practitioners, who see personal and social benefits to CMC. In contrast to the view that the Internet is detrimental to personal well-being, the next section examines ways in which people have used the networks of the Electronic Age to promote their mental health through various forms of online therapy.

## Hyperlink: Computer-Assisted Therapy Programs

As you know from your experience with various software packages, computer programs can be highly interactive tools. You may have experience turning to Quicken to order your finances, to GroupWise to consult your daily calendar, and to the latest version of Sonic the Hedgehog for entertainment. But would you turn to your computer for mental health advice?

Engineer Joseph Weizenbaum stressed that computer programs were good for a number of tasks, but he did not advocate that they be used for human counseling. In order to make his point, he wrote ELIZA, a program that could recognize and respond to natural language. An exchange with ELIZA could go something like this:

User: Men are all alike.
ELIZA: IN WHAT WAY
User: They're always bugging us about something or other.
ELIZA: CAN YOU THINK OF A SPECIFIC EXAMPLE
User: Well, my boyfriend made me come here.
ELIZA: YOUR BOYFRIEND MADE YOU COME HERE
User: He says I'm depressed much of the time.
ELIZA: I AM SORRY TO HEAR YOU ARE DEPRESSED
(Weizenbaum, 1976, p. 3)

Counter to Weizenbaum's intent, ELIZA turned out to be the first in a generation of Computer-Assisted Therapy (CAT) programs. Today, there are programs available to help people deal with depression, dilemma, and lifestyle problems. Although Weizenbaum intended to use ELIZA as a demonstration of the limits of the computer's ability to interact successfully with people, many responded favorably to the program (Mainville & Valerius, 1999). His collaborator, Kenneth Colby, a psychiatrist, contended that the ELIZA's positive reception rested in the fact that a human being had written the original codes that ELIZA used and thus the program still conveyed a human ethos (Turkle, 1995). Nonetheless, Weizenbaum argued that successful psychotherapy depended on the relationship between the patient and the therapist, and many in the psychology field have agreed, viewing ELIZA and her progeny with a suspicious eye.

## ONLINE THERAPY

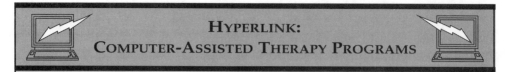

Despite the potential for self-destructive behavior, many people turn to the Internet for support and guidance in coping with life's problems. Several studies have demonstrated the possible benefits to mental health that people can gain through the use of CMC. For example, in a study of senior citizens, McConatha found that after 6 months of Internet use, the participants in the study improved scores on the Geriatric Depression Scale by 14% (Sorenson, 1997). On the other end of the age spectrum, a separate study found that severely disturbed adolescents were more comfortable expressing their thoughts and feelings in computer-mediated rather than face-to-face settings (Zimmerman, 1987). Such findings suggest that mental health can benefit from the presence of mediating technologies in people's lives. In fact, research has shown that people actively seek out online interaction to improve their psychological well-being. In this section, we review some of that research, tracing the emergence of online therapy, its methods of support, and its potential shortfalls.

## Coming to Online Therapy

Many people who go online in search of help are searching for some kind of therapy. To mental health professionals, **therapy** is "a series of contacts between a professionally trained person and someone seeking help for problems that interfere with his or her emotional well-being" (Binik, Cantor, Ochs, & Meana, 1997, pp. 71–72). Thus, traditional therapy consists of a meeting between a trained therapist and a client or group of clients. In recent years, a precedent for more distant contact has been established by so-called "self-help" books and cassette tapes that purported to provide the same content that a therapy session would. However, such products clearly lack the crucial relationship between therapist and client that many mental health professionals would insist is crucial to the process. Because this connection is perceived as fundamental to the success of any treatment program, a common concern is expressed among scholars considering the implications of online therapy. Even those who celebrate the potential benefits of online therapy note that it should function as a complement, rather than a replacement, for personal interaction with a trained therapist.

Another move away from traditional therapy has emerged in the form of social support groups, also called "self-help groups," such as Alcoholics Anonymous. The key feature of these therapy programs is that people suffering from the same concern provide guidance and support to one another. In this way, they not only help themselves, but one another at the same time (King & Moreggi, 1998). The popularity of this type of therapeutic interaction has gained considerable momentum, and now includes programs to help people coping with other addictions, including gambling and sex, among others. Estimates place between 8 and 10 million Americans in some sort of face-to-face social support group (Kessler, Mickelson, & Zhao, 1997).

Both forms of nontraditional therapy can be found online. On one hand, a number of psychotherapists offer their services through mediated channels by providing their clients with e-mail, chat, or telephone consultations. On the other hand, **virtual support groups** have been founded on topics ranging from anorexia to cancer to help people who have these conditions communicate with one another. Several factors contribute to the attraction of seeking therapy online.

The first of these factors is *anonymity*. There is, unfortunately, a good deal of social stigma still attached to seeking professional help when it comes to mental health. E-mailing a concern to an online psychologist or visiting an electronic bulletin board discussing a particular concern allows people to seek out the help they may need without exposing themselves to the potential embarrassment that comes with visiting a mental health facility or attending a social support group meeting. Coincidentally, participants in online exchanges have been found to disclose more about their conditions, probably because they do not sense being as readily judged by any recipients of their messages, given the lack of nonverbal cues to indicate disapproval or disappointment. Fewer status cues (such as dress and jewelry) also seem to level the playing field for participants who may be from different socioeconomic groups. For these reasons, online therapy might be especially helpful in treating people who experience apprehension in social settings (King & Moreggi, 1998).

A second attractive quality to online therapy has to do with its ability to *transcend distance*. People who live in rural areas, the physically disabled, and those with no transportation have difficulty getting access to mental health care through traditional means. Thus, forms of online therapy have the potential to reach people who otherwise might not be able to get access to this kind of help. Additionally, the comfort of being able to experience therapy in the security of one's own home was highly rated by participants in one survey (Dublin, Simon, & Orem, 1997).

In the case of virtual support groups more so than in one-on-one therapy sessions, a third attractor is in the *opportunity to find others* who share one's same concern. Mickelson (1997) followed Usenet groups like alt.education.disabled in order to better understand the reasons why parents with mentally challenged children went online. In her research, she found that parents turned to the virtual support groups because they felt misunderstood by traditional support networks like their spouses, parents, and casual friends. They needed to talk with others who were experiencing the same reactions. Finding others who share their experience is particularly relevant for those who suffer an uncommon problem and may not be able to identify and associate with any social support group in their area.

## Communicating Support in Online Therapy

People are attracted to online therapy for a number of reasons, then (see Table 5.1 for a sampling of some virtual support groups). Once involved in some form of therapy, the process relies on interpersonal communication. A number of scholarly investigations has examined the kinds of communication that goes on in the public setting of virtual support groups. The findings of these studies indicate that the two most common types of communication occurring in virtual support groups are statements of support and self-disclosures.

Miller and Gergen (1998) found that the participants in an electronic bulletin board focused on suicide survivors demonstrated a great deal of support for one another. In fact, statements of empathetic understanding were the most frequently used during the 11 months they followed messages. An example statement of this type would include, "I really do feel and share your pain. I understand where you are coming from" (p. 196). Such statements were complemented by expressions of gratitude, including the following:

> Thank you for your support . . . . I really appreciate your notes and e-mail. As I've said before, this is the group therapy I've been looking for. One can count on the caring and trust and, most of all, understanding and belief that is found here. (p. 197)

**Table 5.1**
Selected Usenet Newsgroups

| Newsgroup | Topic |
|---|---|
| alt.support.depression.seasonal | Seasonal Affectiveness Disorder |
| alt.support.schizophrenia | Schizophrenia |
| alt.support.big-folks | Fat-acceptance |
| alt.abuse.recovery | Abuse recovery |
| alt.support.eating-disorder | Eating disorders |

In addition to statements of support, people who posted to the BBS also engaged in frequent self-disclosures. In these statements, participants would share their experiences with the topic. Intimate details and emotional energy were frequently incorporated into such disclosures, which unto themselves have therapeutic value. As Binik and colleagues (1997) points out, "The energy and time a person takes in the very act of formulating and expressing his or her distress may provide at least some release from tension and anxiety" (p. 89).

Given these qualities, virtual support groups seem to assist people in coping with their problem, but as Miller and Gergen (1998) point out, they may be less successful in helping people move beyond their problems. In their review of messages, they found very few statements directed at growth or transformation. In traditional therapy, the therapist might suggest alternative interpretations of events or offer new plans of action for the client to adopt. With a substantial lack of such suggestions, Miller and Gergen indicate one limitation of online therapy, although other scholars have suggested more.

## Shortfalls in Online Therapy

In addition to the shortfalls in helping people grow beyond the problems cited by Miller and Gergen, several other criticisms have been issued by concerned professionals. In particular, Lebow (1998) worries that virtual support groups might make some conditions worse rather than better:

> Take, for example, ideas about helplessness in relation to depression. Learned helplessness is often integral to depression, and most therapy for depression today is aimed in some way at reducing the client's sense of helplessness. What happens when people with the same difficulty merely share their feelings? Might one person's helplessness reinforce another's? (p. 204)

Other critics have objected to the very premise that effective therapy can occur online. These observers worry that the lack of nonverbal cues diminishes a therapist's ability to read and ultimately relate to a client. As such, they harbor doubts about the ethics of some commercial, Internet-based therapists (Hamilton, 1999; Nakazawa, 1999).

Despite these objections, people are still turning to online therapists and virtual support groups for aid. Given that trend, perhaps a more practical warning is more imperative for those who elect to seek help in the forums. People who use the Internet for therapy should be cautious consumers of the information and advice they receive. According to statistics documented by the U.S. Health and Human Services Department, as many as 43% of all Internet users have looked for medical advice online (cited in McDermott, 1998). Although many reputable agencies and practitioners post authentic information, there is always the possibility that inaccurate information could be downloaded. The BBS used by many virtual support groups seem especially vulnerable to misinformation, given that someone with inaccurate or even harmful information could post a message to the board just as easily as anyone else. Even a well-meaning poster could communicate some erroneous facts. For these reasons, McDermott (1998) warns that one could use newsgroups for expressing frustration, asking questions, or offering support, but one should never rely on them as sources for factual information without confirming that information with a doctor. Clearly, even in times of pain, grief, and suffering, we must still be critical consumers of information. McDermott's remedy is readily agreed on by many health care professionals: Online therapy works best when used as a complement to professionally supervised care.

## CHAPTER SUMMARY

This chapter examined how CMC plays a role in one's well-being. For some people, the combination of accessibility, convenience, and excitement creates a trap with serious ramifications on their lives. In some cases, the trap is made all the more alluring by the sexual "bait" within. Whether or not the deleterious use of the Internet constitutes a distinct psychological disorder seems open to debate, but it is clear that there are negative effects associated with people who use the Internet disproportionately. On the other hand, people are also discovering ways to improve their well-being through use of the Internet. Online therapy and virtual support groups evidence positive contributions to the lives of those who might otherwise not receive the advice and recognition that they need. At present, however, experts contend that any use of online therapy works best when used in conjunction with qualified professional interaction.

### Online Communication and the Law

Engaging in a little online flirtation may be a harmless exercise in sexual experimentation, but when it comes to soliciting a physical sexual encounter, using the Internet can put one behind bars. That's a lesson learned by Patrick Naughton, an executive vice president for Infoseek and one of the developers of the Java programming language. In September 1999, Naughton was arrested for soliciting sex with a minor whom he had met in a chat room (Houston, 1999). The minor, "KrisLA," claimed to be 13 years old, but turned out to be an undercover FBI agent patrolling the teen chat room for sexual predators. Following several months of exchanges between "KrisLA" and "hotseattle," Naughton's alias, a meeting between the two conversants was arranged on a Santa Monica pier. When Naughton showed up for the rendezvous, he was promptly arrested.

In his defense, Naughton claimed that his comments were directed by the fantasy world he perceived himself in while participating online. Moreover, he argued that he did not believe that "KrisLA" was actually a 13-year-old, given that many people invent fictitious identities in these forums. Apparently, some members of the jury agreed, for they were ultimately deadlocked on the charge of intent to have sex with a minor. However, they did convict Naughton of a lesser charge, possession of child pornography. While searching his hard drive for evidence, FBI agents came across a number of files with images of nude, underage models. Thus, although there was no proof that Naughton ever touched, much less harmed, another person, he now faces up to 10 years in prison for his interest in cybersexuality.

## Glossary

**ACE model**: A theoretical explanation for the allure of the Internet that suggests the qualities of accessibility, control, and excitement lead to IAD.

**Cybersex**: Textual descriptions of sexual behavior exchanged between two partners in an online encounter.

**Internet Addiction Disorder (IAD)**: A psychological condition associated with Internet use that leads to adverse effects with one's psychological, physical, or social well-being.

**Therapy**: Traditionally, a series of contacts between a trained professional and a client seeking emotional well-being; also broadly taken to include similar interactions with a group of people.

**Tolerance**: The condition of being able to endure the effects of a stimulus; in particular, being able to endure increasing amounts of exposure to the Internet with decreasing effect or satisfaction.

**Virtual support groups**: A type of social support group that meets online and provides participants to give and receive positive feedback from one another.

**Withdrawal**: The moving back from a stimulus that typically results in adverse mental or physical effects.

## Topics for Discussion

1. The individuals indicted in this chapter's first anecdote (Michael Campbell) and its final one (Patrick Naughton) claimed to be "under the influence" of the Internet when they said the things that they did. Write a paragraph in

which you analyze these defenses from the perspective of those who believe IAD is a legitimate disorder. Then write a second paragraph about these cases from the perspective of those who say this is not a disorder. Which side do you believe offers a more credible explanation?

2. In reflecting on the material covered in the Hyperlink "Obscenity in Cyberspace," what role would you prescribe for government intervention in the future of the Internet? Adopt a position in which you call for either national regulation or limited/no regulation of content. In your response, consider how you will answer critics from the other extreme.
3. The results of Witmer's research in risky CMC suggest that people hold a perception that it is harmless to engage in disreputable behavior. Is this symptomatic of a larger social belief that it is okay to do anything unless you get caught? Write a response in which you provide three reasons in support of the majority's position in that study or three reasons the people should reconsider their position.
4. Visit a Usenet newsgroup focused on a particular ailment and read through several dozen postings. In what ways can you see a virtual support group functioning on this electronic bulletin board? In your response, record examples of supportive and self-disclosive statements. How do you think these statements may have helped or hindered the well-being of visitors to the BBS?
5. McDermott, among others, advises users to be wary about the factual information they find about medical conditions while online. Why is this a wise recommendation? In your response, recall a situation in which you received allegedly factual information (online or in real life) that proved to be untrue. How can people avoid falling prey to misleading information?

## REFERENCES


Associated Press. (2000, February 17). *Internet survey criticized.* (2000, February 18).

Bilstad, B. T., & Godward, C. (1996, September). Obscenity and indecency on the Usenet: The legal and political future of alt.sex.stories. *Journal of Computer-Mediated Communication, 2*(2) <http://www.ascusc.org/jcmc/vol2/issue2/bilstad.html>.

Binik, Y. M., Cantor, J., Ochs, E., & Meana, M. (1997). From the couch to the keyboard: Psychotherapy in cyberspace. In S. Kiesler (Ed.), *Culture of the Internet* (pp. 71–100). Mahwah, NJ: Lawrence Erlbaum Associates.

Birsch, D. (1996, January). Sexually explicit materials and the Internet. *CMC Magazine* <http://www.december.com/cmc/mag/1996/jan/birsem.html>.

Borenstein, D. (2000). *Quoteland.com.* <http://www.quoteland.com>.

Bricking, T. (1997, June 16). Internet blamed for neglect. *The Cincinnati Enquirer* <http://enquirer.com/editions/1997/06/16/loc_hacker.html>.

Cole, J. I., Suman, M., Schramm, P., van Bel, D., Lunn, B., Maguire, P., Hanson, K., Singh, R., Aquino, J., & Lebo, H. (2000). *The UCLA Internet report: Surveying the digital future.* <http://www.ccp.ucla.edu/newsite/pages/internet-report.asp>.

Donn, J. (1999, August 23). Can't resist the online pull. *ABC News.* <http://www.abcnews.go.com/sections/tech/DailyNews/netaddiction990823.html>.

Doyle, M. W. (Producer). (1996). *Cyberspace: Virtual unreality?* [Videocassette]. Princeton, NJ: Films for the Humanities and Sciences.

Dublin, J., Simon, V., & Orem, J. (1997). *Analysis of survey results.* Paper presented for New York University School of Social Work, New York.

Ferris, J. R. (1997). *Internet addiction disorders: Causes, symptoms, and consequences.* <http://www.chem.vt.edu/chemdept/dessy/honors/papers/ferris.html>.

Fiely, D. (1999, February 28). Web junkie. *The Columbus Dispatch,* pp. 1G–2G.

Hamilton, A. (1999). On the virtual couch. *Time, 153* (20), 71.

Houston, P. (1999, September 18). Executive VP Patrick Naughton arrested for allegedly using chat and e-mail to solicit undercover agent posing as a 13-year-old girl. *ZDNN* <http://www.zdnet.com>.

Janofsky, M. (2000, January 13). Defense sites an addiction to the Internet in threat case. *The New York Times on the Web.* <http://www.nytimes.com/library/tech/00/01/biztech/articles/13colo-school-threat.html>.

Kessler, R. C., Mickelson, K. D., Zhao, S. (1997). Patterns and correlates of self-help group membership in the United States. *Social Policy, 27*(3), 27–47.

King, S. A., & Moreggi, D. (1998). Internet therapy and self-help groups—the pros and cons. In J. Gackenbach (Ed.), *Psychology and the Internet: Intrapersonal, interpersonal, and transpersonal implications* (pp. 77–109). San Diego, CA: Academic Press.

Kraut, R., Patterson, M., Lundmark, V., Kiesler, S., Mukopadhyay, T., & Scherlis, W. (1998, September). Internet paradox: A social technology that reduces social involvement and psychological well-being? *American Psychologist, 53*(9), 1017–1031.

Lebow, J. (1998). Not just talk, maybe some risk: The therapeutic potentials and pitfalls of computer-mediated conversation. *Journal of Marital & Family Therapy, 24*(2), 203–207.

Mainville, S., & Valerius, L. (1999, May). Nothing but Net: Therapeutic recreation and the Web. *Parks & Recreation, 34*(5), 86–93.

McDermott, I. E. (1998, June). Informed consent: Disease and ailment information on the Web. *Searcher, 6*(6), 50–55.

Mickelson, K. D. (1997). Seeking social support: Parents in electronic support groups. In S. Kiesler (Ed.), *Culture of the Internet* (pp. 157–178). Mahwah, NJ: Lawrence Erlbaum Associates.

Miller, J. K., & Gergen, K. J. (1998). Life on the line: The therapeutic potentials of computer-mediated conversation. *Journal of Marital & Family Therapy, 24*(2), 189–202.

Nakazawa, L. (1999). Virtual therapy. *Psychology Today, 32*(2), 11.

Rheingold, H. (1993). *The virtual community: Homesteading on the electronic frontier.* New York: HarperPerrenial.

*San Francisco Examiner*. (1999, April 14). 4.6 million could become addicted, cybersex study says. <http://dispatches.azstarnet.com/joe/1999/cybersex.htm>.

Sorenson, J. (1997). *Seniors in cyberspace*. <http://192.211.16.13/individuals/sorensoj.home.htm>.

Stanford Institute for the Quantitative Study of Society. (2000). *SIQSS Internet Study* <http://www.stanford.edu/group/siqss/Press_Release/Internet Study.html>.

Szalavitz, M. (1999, December 6). Can we become caught in the Web? *Newsweek, 134*(23), 11.

Turkle, S. (1995). *Life on the screen: Identity in the age of the Internet*. New York: Simon & Shuster.

Walther, J. B., & Reid, L. D. (2000, February 4). Understanding the allure of the Internet. *Chronicle of Higher Education, 46*(22), B4–B5.

Weizenbaum, J. (1976). *Computer power and human reason: From judgment to calculation*. San Francisco: Freeman.

Wertham, F. (1954). *Seduction of the innocent*. New York: Rinehart.

Witmer, D. F. (1997, March). Risky business: Why people feel safe in sexually explicit on-line communication. *Journal of Computer-Mediated Communication, 2*(4) <http://www.ascusc.org/jcmc/vol2/issue4/witmer2.html>.

Young. K. S. (1998a). *Caught in the Net: How to recognize the signs of Internet addiction and a winning strategy for recovery*. New York: Wiley.

Young, K. S. (1998b). *The Center for Online Addiction* <http://www.netaddiction.com/>.

Zimmerman, D. P. (1987). A psychological comparison of computer-mediated and face-to-face language use among severely disturbed adolescents. *Adolescence, 22*, 827–840.

# CHAPTER 6

# Communicating in Virtual Communities

*Without a sense of caring, there can be no sense of community.*
—*Anthony J. D'Angelo (Borenstein, 2000)*

Once upon a time, when people spent their evenings chatting on their front porches, folks knew what made a community. The romanticized community consisted of tree-lined roads like "Main Street," buildings like "McNamara's Drug Store," and most importantly, people like your next door neighbors, the "Daileys."

In more recent times, chatting is still a popular pastime, but many people's conception of what makes a community has changed. A community might now consist of a data-laden Information Superhighway; pharmaceutical advice is dispensed on an electronic bulletin board; and the neighbor you feel closest to could be half a world away in Australia.

Despite the distances that can separate them, people have an intrinsic need for community. Consider the invention of the Walt Disney Company's idealized community of Celebration in central Florida or a film such as 1998's *Pleasantville*. Both of these nostalgic recreations are reminiscent of a simpler time, when community was easier to define. Yet the introduction of computer-mediating technologies has challenged many of the concepts and definitions people have long taken for granted, including that of community. As such, people who use CMC technologies and people who study them are increasingly aware that the Internet is fostering relationships not just between two individuals, but among many, many more people.

## DEFINING VIRTUAL COMMUNITIES

Take for example the community of fans that found one another online based on their common interest in the television series, *Lois and Clark: The New Adventures of Superman* (1993–1997). The *Lois and Clark* series was based on the Superman mythos, but took a unique perspective in focusing on the romantic "triangle" among Lois Lane, Clark Kent, and his alter ego, Superman. In various online forums, including the "Lois and Clark Krypton Club" and the "L&C Metropolis Club," these fans of Lois and Clark, or FoLCs as they refer to themselves, united to share their common interest in the series despite the geographic distances that separated them. For some, this distance was considerable, because their membership counted fans from the United Kingdom, Australia, Sweden, Israel, Germany, and people scattered across the United States. The FoLCs would regularly exchange their reviews of the series' episodes, notify one another of their favorite stars' guest appearances on talk shows, and announce one another's birthdays. In short, they fostered a sense of community through their communication.

The quality of their commitment was best demonstrated when the FoLCs united to react to a perceived threat. By its fourth season, *Lois and Clark* had begun to lag behind in the ratings and there were rumors that this would be the series last season on the air. Working together, the FoLCs raised $7,000 to buy an ad in *USA Today*, hoping to draw the readers' attention to their favorite show (Graham, 1997). Although ABC ultimately ended the show that season, the series cancellation did not diminish what the FoLCs were able to accomplish by working together online nor did it mark the end of the FoLCs interaction. They simply followed the series to syndication on TNT and kept the conversation going.

Self-identified communities, such as that created by the FoLCs, are examples of how CMC interaction questions the assumption that a community is geographically bound and that the people who share a community must interact face-to-face. After all, the FoLC relationships began in cyberspace, without the benefit of any face to face initial meetings. Unlike cities in the United Kingdom, Germany, or the United States, their community is not a physical place you can pack up your belongings and move to. The FoLCs, like many other communities we discuss in this chapter, exists not as a physical presence but as a shared understanding of interrelatedness among its participants.

Scholars have taken to calling these communal constructs **virtual communities**. In *The Virtual Community: Homesteading on the Electronic Frontier*, Rheingold (1993) introduced his often quoted definition of this phenomenon. "Virtual communities are social aggregations that emerge from the Net when enough people carry on those public discussions long enough, with sufficient human feeling, to form webs of personal relationship in cyberspace" (p. 5). Note that Rheingold's definition does not account for the need for structures or the proximity of participants to one another or even the necessity for face-to-face interaction, all features long associated with traditional communities. Instead, his definition asserts that community is based in ongoing communication.

Unlike many traditional communities, virtual communities are not bound together by economics or the need for mutual protection. Why then do people join them? As psychologist William Schutz (1966) explained, all people have a need for inclusion, a desire for the company of others. Virtual communities provide individuals with a means for acquiring that feeling of inclusion, especially among those individuals who seek the company of like-minded people. At the heart of the concept of community, then, is the quality of commonality (Fernback, 1999). After all, you might be the only person in your small town who collects Pez candy dispensers, but there are many such collectors located across the country that you can meet online. Virtual communities thus allow people to transcend geographic boundaries and unite with others who share their common interests, whether that's watching a particular television series or buying plastic figures of Charlie Brown and Bugs Bunny.

This chapter explores the concept of the virtual community in greater detail. As a prominent metaphor in both people's experiences with the Internet and within the study of CMC, we felt it deserved your attention. What follows then is an examination of some historical precedents for contemporary virtual communities, the common features they share, the ways in which members are regulated through norms, and some objections to the viability of the virtual communities themselves.

### HYPERLINK: WHAT A DIvI'!

One of the many virtual communities that have thrived on the Internet is the one existing among practitioners of invented language Klingon. Originally developed by linguist Marc Okrand for use in Paramount Pictures' *Star Trek* franchise, Klingon, or HolQeD, as it is called in its own language, became even more popular among fans after Okrand published *The Klingon Dictionary* in 1985. Linguists and other academics interested in this phenomenon formed the Klingon Language Institute (KLI) to study it in 1992.

Now with more than 1,000 members in more than 30 countries, the KLI perpetuates its work through an academic journal (catalogued by the Modern Language Association), its Web site (http://www.kli.org/), and its online mailing list (Schoen & Shoulson, 1999). KLI serves as a good example of an organization that transpires geographic-bound definitions of community. With members all over the world, it took their common interest to unite them, and it seems evident that CMC is playing a significant role in helping to expand their membership and sustain their mission to share their love of language play with like-minded individuals.

(Oh, and just in case your Klingon is a bit rusty, *DIvI'* translates loosely into "community.")

## PRECEDENTS FOR VIRTUAL COMMUNITIES

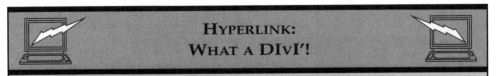

Although the Internet represents the latest medium to facilitate the construction of community, it is certainly not the first. Anderson (1983) supposes that newspapers were an earlier medium used to help establish what he termed **imagined communities**. Like virtual communities, Benedict explains that imagined communities emerged because of the intervention of mediated communication. As he elaborated, the national identity that led the British colonies to form the United States was due, in part, to the communication fostered by colonial newspapers. Given the strength of the union today, it is hard to imagine the differences that separated the colonies in the 18th century, but the differences among the 13 separate colonies made unity a problem that had to be addressed if any of them were to free themselves from British rule. The newspapers, with their messages of uniting against a common foe, helped create an imagined community of Americans and fostered ideals that could be adopted by people whether they lived in such geographically disparate places as Maine or Georgia. Today, we recognize this once imagined community as a nation, and newspapers—such as *USA Today*—continue to serve as a medium for uniting an even more geographically dispersed population by fostering a common identity among them.

Another example of media's ability to unite people in communal bonds can be found earlier this century, when print media gave rise to other imagined communities whose participants used self-publication and networking innovations to come together. Fan magazines, which eventually became known as "fanzines" and still later as simply "**zines**," were at the root of modern day fan cultures. Beginning with the printing of the first fan letter to the editor in a 1926 edition of the science-fiction magazine *Amazing Stories*, publications have served as vehicles for fans to build "communities based upon the exchange of ideas and recounting of events instead of immediately shared experience and pressing of the flesh" (Moskowitz, 1994, p. 27). In following the precedent established by *Amazing Stories*, fans began to self-publish their commentaries and original works in their own homespun periodicals. Historically, zines have had small press runs, limiting the number of fellow fans one could reach. However, fans attempted to improve the diffusion of their publications by establishing networks called amateur press associations (**apa**). In an apa, one member receives and then redistributes a collection of fanzines to each contributing member across the country (Bosky, 1994). The continuation and variety of apas over the years, covering everything from monster movies to soap operas, testified to their ability to unite and sustain another breed of imagined community. Once again, a participant's sense of belonging to such a community was based on mediated communication and not immediate interaction.

Certainly, the emergence of community on the Internet goes hand in hand with the development of the medium itself. As discussed earlier in this text, the Internet began as a network of computers linked for military communication but increasingly used by academics to share research information. Although much of the early messaging was carried out in a one-to-one fashion, much like an individual sending a postcard to a colleague, eventually the number of channels expanded to include the one-to-many communication of BBS. Your campus is likely to have any number of bulletin boards filled with flyers posted by various people trying to get rides home, to sell old computers, or to encourage you to attend a campus event such as a speaker or club meeting. Anyone can read such messages and get a sense of what is going on around the campus community. In like manner, the sharing of these messages among the early research scientists helped to foster the sense that these contributors were a part of some communal experience. As different discussion groups began to break off and form new bulletin boards around specific areas of interest, new communities arose.

Initiatives like the Cleveland Freenet have continued to increase both the diversity of and access to virtual communities. The Freenet, introduced by Case Western Reserve University in the mid-1980s, provides people living in the Cleveland area with free access to an interactive computer system. It offers bulletin boards for messages of local interest (such as the city schools) and e-mail for messaging capabilities to the rest of the world. With tens of thousands of subscribers, Freenets, subsequently replicated in a number of cities, offer people the opportunity to discover a community beyond that of their immediate face-to-face experience.

## HYPERLINK: SOCIETY COMES TO LAMBDAMOO

In chapter 3, we presented a Hyperlink about a "virtual rape" committed by a lewd character named Mr. Bungles. However, when we were discussing that incident and the meaningful impact it had on a number of people, we only told you half the story. Dibbell's (1993) ethnography of the MUD known as LambdaMOO tells an interesting tale not only of how individuals are affected by online communication but also of how societies are formed through their interactions.

According to Dibbell's account, after Mr. Bungles had used a "voodoo doll" program to force a number of characters to commit demeaning sexual acts, a number of his victims, several eyewitnesses, and various interested parties who participate in the LambdaMOO forum began to discuss punitive actions against Mr. Bungles. Several people proposed that Mr. Bungles be "toaded" for his actions. In the Dungeons and Dragons forebearers to more contemporary MUDs, a wizard could change a character into a toad, divesting that character's on-screen description of all individual markers and replacing them with those of a common toad (green complexion, warts, etc.). In LambdaMOO and other MUDs, toading had evolved into a process that resulted in the characters being barred from entering the database and thus being forbidden from participating henceforth in the online discussion. Some participants perceived this to be the equivalent of banishment from the tribe, whereas others contended that it was so severe that it could be likened unto a death sentence.

Dibbell recounted how participants of various opinions and various political persuasions first exchanged bulletin board messages and then met in a LambdaMOO chat room to decide what kind of action should be taken. Amidst these debates, no clear consensus emerged as to what punishment Mr. Bungles should suffer nor, perhaps more importantly, how that punishment should be decided. Some argued that it was time for LambdaMOO to develop a judicial system to hear and try cases such as this. Others suggested that the wizards, those master programmers who had originally written the codes to create the MUD, should take a more active role in policing their creation. Still others, including, interestingly enough, Mr. Bungles himself, said that no action at all should be taken.

Ultimately, Mr. Bungles' fate was unilaterally decided by a lone wizard named JoeFeedback, who toaded Mr. Bungles right out of the system. But that's not the end of the story, for when the founder of LambaMOO, another wizard named Haakon, discovered the whole messy affair, he decreed that a system of petitions and voting be put in place to handle any future sanctions against objectionable behavior.

The Mr. Bungles incident served as a catalyst to hasten LambdaMOO's development as a community. Although it clearly was possible for LambdaMOO to function without formalized social rules until this incident, it became clear that an "anything goes" attitude wasn't going to work as increasing numbers of participants demanded a reprisal for Mr. Bungles' behavior. Sustaining bonds that unite people, that make a community, seem to call for some amount of formal regulation.

## QUALITIES OF VIRTUAL COMMUNITIES

Being part of a virtual community means more than merely having a group of people communicating online. Even in the tangible world, it is understood that the quality of community takes more than mere presence. Consider sharing a crowded elevator ride with a group of strangers. Although everyone on board shares a common experience in a common space, few would label this assembly a community. Elevator rides are all too brief and all too impersonal. (In fact, the norms of American culture dictate that passengers do not look at one another and rarely speak in an elevator.) What then makes a group of people into a community?

At the heart of it, community is based on a sense of belonging. Individuals rarely feel as if they belong with a group of strangers on an elevator in the same way they belong with their classmates in school or with their co-workers on the job. The German social theorist, Ferdinand Tönnies (1887/1957), makes this distinction clear in his classic comparison between society and community. The detached, happenstance gathering of people he called *gesellschaft*, but the sense of belonging, a sense of "we-ness" he called *gemeinschaft*. The distinction is a subtle, but important one, for it helps define the virtual communities forming online. Therein, the feeling of belonging to a fellowship reflects the bonds experienced in a state of *gemeinschaft*.

Jones (1997), writing in the *Journal of Computer-Mediated Communication*, establishes four qualities that he feels characterizes these virtual communities. Interestingly, these qualities could just as easily define a geographically bound community, as well. According to Jones, virtual communities distinguish themselves from a simple online gathering when they feature:

1. A minimum level of interactivity.
2. A variety of communicators.
3. Common public space.
4. A minimum level of sustained membership.

Let's explore each of these qualities by matching them with an existing virtual community.

Fan communities seem to be among the strongest represented among virtual communities and so we discuss Jones' criteria in regards to one such group: fans of *Star Wars*. The anticipation that surrounded the 1999 release of *Episode I: The Phantom Menace*, drew the attention of the national media on this virtual community, including a feature story in *Newsweek* about its participants and their online activities (Hamilton & Gordon, 1999). Although most of the residents of this virtual community have never met in person, their fulfillment of Jones' (1997) criteria testifies to their communal identity.

## Minimum Level of Interactivity

In order for a virtual community to exist, there must be a flow of messages among the participants. If one individual were to post a Web site and no one were to comment on it, there would be no basis for a virtual community. However, when a poster gets a comment and then responds to it, and then the original sender responds again, we have the interactivity among participants. A visit to the *Countdown to Star Wars* Web site (http://countingdown.com/starwars/) shows the coordination resulting from such interaction occurring among fans. Prior to the release of the film, these fans worked together to plan month-long vigils outside major movie theaters in anticipation of the film's release. In order to make this a nationwide effort, they had to exchange a lot of messages over these distances.

## Variety of Communicators

Of course, interactions among two individuals can establish a relationship, but more contributors need to join the conversation for a virtual community to arise. The richness of different virtual communities is enhanced by the variety of people who participate and the contributions they make. When the trailer for *Episode 1* was recorded with a video camcorder and downloaded to the Internet in the months before the film's release, it did not take long for the contribution to surface across the Internet on multiple Web pages. More than 60 other sites had the trailer within hours of its online appearance (Hamilton & Gordon, 1999).

## Common Public Space

Although they are not situated in a physical location, virtual communities still need to identify with a cyberplace. Jones (1997) suggests that these are the forums in which the community participants most regularly engage in communication. In the early days of CMC, BBS were the "place" where individuals went to post and read messages. Today, chat rooms serve the same purpose, but allow people to interact in real time rather in delayed messages. A number of these touchstones exist for *Star Wars* fans, including *Jedinet* (http://www.jedinet.com/), which features its own chat room for community participants to engage one another in conversation.

## A Minimum Level of Sustained Membership

Finally, the virtual community exists for those who have some ongoing relationship with the other participants. In other words, one visit or a simple exchange does not constitute membership in a virtual community. Rather, those who form the virtual community have relationships to one another that are perpetuated through time. Some of the main contributors to *theForce.Net* provide a biography section (http://www.theforcenet.net/) recounting their involvement with the virtual community of online fans going back to 1995.

These four qualities, interactivity, variety, common space, and sustained participation, establish virtual communities as forums for communicating and relating to multiple people in ways that their contributors find meaningful. Although there are some obvious difference between virtual and immediate communities, there are several significant similarities. In the next section, we look at one such parallel, the question of citizenship, and examine what it means to be a valued participants in the social setting of an electronic village.

## Hyperlink: GeoCities—Your Nearest Neighbor is Just a Click Away

One company has gone to great lengths to appeal to people's desire to feel like they are part of a community when online. GeoCities (http://www.geocities.com/), who provides subscribers with free computer storage space for their personal web pages in exchange for displaying advertising banners, uses the community metaphor in both its language and imagery.

When registering for space to post their pages, "homesteaders," as they are called, are asked to choose from over forty "neighborhoods" designed to match people with similar interests. Thus, those interested in science fiction and fantasy reside in Area 51, those tempting fate with extreme sports move to Pipeline, and gay, lesbian, bisexual, and transgendered people find a home in WestHollywood. In its early years, GeoCities attempted to perpetuate its illusion of proximity among it clients visually as well. While choosing an address to register one's site, one would tour a virtual suburb along a two-lane street, looking for images of homes marked "vacant."

Like other communities, GeoCities has its rules to help people live alongside one another peaceably and consequently maintains these rules through a "community watch" of sorts. With more than 2 million pages on its servers, the officials at GeoCities have turned to the community members themselves as guardians of their content guidelines. Using "GeoCities Content Violation Reporting Form" as a type of 911 call, members are encouraged to report instances of pornography, piracy, and profanity, as well as other violations, so that the offending sites can be disciplined and, if necessary, shut down.

Of course, simply forwarding the metaphor or sharing similar URLs does not make a group of people into a community, a fact GeoCities has been sensitive to. Accordingly, they have appointed certain individuals to serve as community leaders who are responsible for assisting newcomers in the production of their pages, organizing get-togethers, and acknowledging outstanding design skills with awards. The involvement of such community leaders testifies that some people do see themselves as active participants in a shared experience.

GeoCities, and other service providers, go to considerable trouble to encourage the metaphor of community. Why do you suppose such commercial entities work hard to make people feel "at home"?

## NETIZENSHIP: RESPONSIBILITY AND REGULATION IN THE VIRTUAL COMMUNITY

Although being a member of a virtual community suggests a number of privileges, it also seems to imply a number of responsibilities. People who self-identify with a virtual community are referred to as **netizens**, and these "Internet citizens" are presumed to shoulder responsibilities to the larger community. Writing about the nature of netizenship in *CMC Magazine*, Hauben (1997) qualifies that true netizens distinguish themselves through active contributions to the development of a sustained community:

> Netizens are the people who actively contribute online towards the development of the Net. These people understand the value of collective work and the communal aspects of public communications. These are the people who actively discuss and debate topics in a constructive manner, who e-mail answers to people and provide help to new-comers, who maintain FAQ [frequently asked questions] files and other public information repositories, who maintain mailing lists and so on. These are people who discuss the nature and role of this new communications medium. . . . Netizens are people who decide to make the Net a regenerative and vibrant community and resource. (n.p.)

Although Hauben praises the selfless contributions of many participants, he argues that not everyone visiting a virtual community is necessarily a netizen. He sites some specific terminology to designate nonparticipants, including the **surfer** (an infrequent and detached visitor), **lurkers** (who are present but offer no comment or contribution), and **privateers** (people using the net for profit), who do not qualify as netizens in his conception of the term because of their selfish, rather than selfless, use of the technology. Accordingly, netizens help to build the virtual community, not with brick and mortar per se, but with contributions of ideas and information.

Like other cultures, those emerging online need new members to perpetuate their ideals. Among the functions of good netizens, Hauben notes the importance of maintaining Frequently Asked Questions (FAQ) files. FAQ files serve to explain the culture of any given virtual community by providing the basic information a newcomer, or **newbie**, would need to function competently within the virtual environment. They might answer questions associated with accessing the technology at use in the environment, observing norms of engagement among members, or learning the history of the organization. Certainly not every virtual community has created such a code to govern itself, but even in the well-intentioned social worlds shared by netizens, it sometimes helps to know what rules everyone has agreed to follow.

Certainly, there are those who do not play by the rules. In fact, when participants have behaved in ways that are unacceptable to the virtual community's standards, others have enforced certain regulations to counter, curb, or eliminate the offender. Maltz (1996) catalogues the mechanisms used to sanction offenders in Table 6.1. As you might expect, the distance and anonymity associated with CMC make it difficult to punish an offender in customary ways, such as levying fines or imprisonment. The community's remaining recourse, then, is to sanction the individual through communication. They can do so by chiding the offender through harassing responses, obstructing the offender's access to information, or by interfering with that person's ability to use the medium effectively.

As you can see, participation in a virtual community is not unlike participation in a physical community. Despite the lack of physical contact, such communities can thrive. The key to making them work, as the theories discussed here have suggested, lies in the reliance of these communities to define and to regulate themselves through communication.

Clearly, any competent communicator will want to learn and then operate within the social norms established by a given community. Like any other society, virtual communities establish rules that they expect their members to observe. Any number of these rules governing accepted behavior have been codified as Internet etiquette, or **netiquette**. Although advice varies among the sources recording just what netiquette one should follow, we have abstracted some general principles that help govern other users' expectations. Like many other forms of etiquette, these guidelines can be summarized with one simple rule, "Do unto others as you would have them do unto you."

**Table 6.1**
**Methods of Sanctioning Online Offenders**

| Mechanism | Meaning | Examples |
|---|---|---|
| Harassment (reception) | • Forced reception of unwanted information | • Flaming |
| Silencing (transmission) | • Interfering with either the current or future transmission of information or destroying past archives of transmissions | • Canceling current messages. Deleting stored messages from public database |
| Capture (transmission) | • Controlling transmission | • Posting offensive messages under other user's name |
| Interference (reception) | • Obstructing ability to receive information | • Mail-bombs and mass flaming<br>• The controller of a MUD denies a user access to a MUD, or to a part of the MUD |

1. Assume publicity. Although you might intend for any message you send over the Internet to be between you and another user exclusively, you should realize that electronic messages can be stored for later retrieval and easily forwarded to other addresses. An often repeated rule of thumb is to avoid writing anything that you would be embarrassed to see printed in the newspaper.
2. Avoid spamming. People find it rude when others clutter their in-boxes with countless messages. **Spamming** is the term used to describe the act of forwarding unsolicited (and ultimately unwanted) e-mail. Common netiquette further dictates that it is unacceptable to send people chain mail that demands their participation or reply.
3. Flame off. A flame is a message that is perceived to be hostile. Before you respond with a flame of your own (and thereby contribute to a flame war), pause, consider the effects of your response, and remember that common courtesy is expected of all netizens. (For more on flaming behavior, see chapter 4.)
4. Be brief. Messages are expected to be brief and to the point in CMC. Long diatribes are viewed as bothersome.
5. Observe good form. Some writers have abandoned standards of grammar, spelling, style, and document form in moving into mediated communication. Netiquette requires that you apply the same courtesies to the reader of an electronic message as you would to the reader of a printed message (including the standard use of capitalized letters, spaces between paragraphs, and spell-checking one's document).

It should come as little surprise that such rules may seem comparable to those of good behavior that people are expected to observe in other contexts, especially face-to-face interaction. In fact, Sutton (1996) suggests that netiquette, true to its name, is a reworking of the classic rules of common etiquette, such as that espoused by Emily Post or Miss Manners. Consider the following comparison offered by Sutton:

> Etiquette: Those with vivid imaginations are often unreliable in their statements. (Post, 1922/1955, p. 46)
>
> Netiquette: Make yourself look good online: Know what you're talking about and make sense. (Shea, 1994, p. 33)

Although the words have clearly changed between 1922 and 1994, the intent of the advice still holds true: Know something before you speak.

Again, the netiquette we suggest here may not be the only rules one needs to learn in order to function effectively within a given virtual community. In fact, there may even be communities where one or more of the above suggestions are contradicted in common practice. However, if you are first and foremost attentive to the practices of those already a part of the community, you will probably adapt to their standards given sufficient observation.

## Hyperlink: Group Decision Support Systems

Not all group interaction using computer-mediated technology is necessarily as socially oriented as the examples in this chapter suggest. In fact, as you enter the professional world you may find yourself directed to use communication technology in certain task-oriented situations as well. Small-group and organizational communication scholars have been intrigued by the introduction of computer systems to enhance workplace communication. Poole (1995) provides a description of one of these Group Decision Support Systems (GDSS) called SAMM:

> Developed at the University of Minnesota, SAMM is intended to promote participative, democratic decision-making in 3- to 16-person groups. Designed to be operated by the group itself, SAMM provides public and private messaging and a number of decision tools such as problem definition, idea or solution evaluation, stakeholder analysis, and nominal group technique. The group assembles at a horseshoe-shaped conference table with a terminal and keyboard for each group member. . . . At the front of the room is a large screen for display of group information (such as vote tallies or idea lists). Any member of the group may call and use any procedure in SAMM and it is up to the group to manage usage. (p. 91)

Teams working with GDSS like SAMM have demonstrated a number of improvements in group processes. Research indicates that groups equipped with GDSS can process more information, more quickly, with greater participation among its members than in traditional meetings (Poole, 1995).

It is that third quality that is among the most intriguing, for in traditional group processes, members seem to gravitate toward dominant and subordinate roles. Recall the student council, fraternal, or any other brainstorming meeting you have attended, and you probably can remember various people who contributed more than their fair share and those from whom you never heard an utterance. Nonverbal status cues help to explain why this occurs: A person who stands up and shouts during a meeting is difficult to challenge. However, GDSS do not allow interactants to shout over one another (unless, we suppose, they do so in ALL CAPS!). Studies have shown that GDSS promote a greater degree of equity among participants using the systems than they experienced before they were introduced (Scott & Easton, 1996). Such findings certainly promote the notion that people can improve aspects of goal-directed behaviors like decision making using new technologies.

## CRITIQUES OF THE COMMUNITY METAPHOR

Despite the fact that a number of people have embraced the metaphor of community as an explanation for their online networks, others object to this analogy, suggesting that the label inflates what is actually occurring online.

One line of argument questions whether or not the exchange of information is enough to establish a community. Some researchers, like Weinreich (1997), insist that community can only exist where face-to-face interaction can occur. As evidence, Weinreich followed the progress of a number of BBS systems. In one survey he conducted with several hundred participants, 62% of the respondents reported that they had met other users. These face-to-face follow-up meetings, Weinreich suggests, are indicative of the claim that mediating communication is simply not enough to establish meaningful relationships among individuals. Indeed, participants often can and do seek one another out for face-to-face interaction (Rheingold, 1993), lending some support to Weinreich's indictment.

Another line of argument questions the suitability of the community metaphor in a world where access is still limited to a privileged few. Although access to the Internet continues to grow at a steady rate, economically depressed people in the United States and across the globe do not have access to the technology and thus cannot become contributors to this online community. The ideals of community cannot be achieved as long as this inequity persists. (We explore these inequalities in greater detail in chapter 8.) Moreover, a new threat to this cyberdemocracy is encroaching on the metaphor. The increasing commercialization of the Web, for instance, may supplant the metaphor of a community with that of colonization as the dominant images and ideals of corporate culture supersede the home-spun values of the original virtual homesteaders (Riley, Keough, Meilich, & Pierson, 1998).

Certainly, like any other metaphor, that of the virtual community can be useful in explaining part, if not the whole, of what it seeks to compare itself to. As these criticisms suggest, we must continue to refine our understanding of what this online experience will yet emerge to be without being bound by previous conceptions of what community has heretofore meant to be.

## CHAPTER SUMMARY

Virtual communities have challenged our conception of what a community can be. The Internet has allowed people to relate to groups of people who live beyond the borders of their small towns or outside the wall of their tenement apartments. For those who chose to involve themselves in the lives of others through mediating technologies rather than in face-to-face encounters, the virtual communities they inhabit represent a widespread movement into a manner of relating that defies the limitations of physical space.

Certainly, such distance transcending communities have been constructed before, among the American colonialists, among science fiction fans earlier last century, and among the developers of the early Internet. Such communities share some similar characteristics, including interactivity, variety of participants, common space, and sustained membership. As we saw with the *Star Wars* fans, such characteristics are evident in virtual communities. As responsible netizens, participants are expected to make contributions to the community and respect others in it. When they fail to do so, virtual communities regulate their members through sanctions. Although the metaphor can help to explain some aspects of online behavior, it is not immune from criticism. Face-to-face follow-ups and unequal distribution of resources suggest some limitations to the metaphor that we should weigh along with its virtues.

Virtual communities remain fascinating arenas for further exploration. People seem to be attracted to these outlets for three reasons. Like other CMC venues, they allow people to experiment with, and in many cases transcend identity. Second, they provide interaction for those who might not otherwise be able to do so. Third, they allow individuals to make a contribution to creating something greater than themselves. For these, and many other reasons, these self-identified settlements on the electronic frontier deserve our attention.

### Online Communication and the Law

Prior to their rampage, the Columbine High School students who killed their classmates, a teacher, and themselves had posted a Web site expressing their anger with the community in which they lived, but did not feel a part. Although the media and pundits were quick to question why no one noticed the hateful proclamations uttered on the site before the tragedy struck, in the time since the event, school administrators have turned a watchful eye to the online activities of their students.

That helps explain why when Nick Emmett posted his "Unofficial Kentlake High School Home Page" in February 2000, he ended up suspended from school for 5 days (Kaplan, 2000). Emmett had included mock obituaries for a number of his friends on the page, one even having met his alleged demise from a sexually transmitted disease. After sharing the site's URL with several of his classmates, word of his dark humor quickly spread around the school. Eventually, the local television station picked up on the buzz and labeled the site a "hit list," prompting Emmett to shut down the site. However, the principal still suspended Emmett for 5 days for causing a disruption in the school.

Lawyers for the American Civil Liberties Union (ACLU) ultimately convinced a judge that in punishing him for the Web site's contents, the school had violated Emmett's First Amendment right to free speech. The ACLU successfully argued that although Emmett's site might have been in poor taste, it was not threatening any one with acts of violence. Clearly, cases such as this demonstrate just how thin the line between the virtual and the real can be. The real-life community in this case, represented by the media and the school administration, took Emmett's virtual communication as an indication of a potential problem. Censuring this behavior, even after he voluntarily acknowledged the problem, indicates just how strongly a community can react to the objectionable messages of any one of its members.

## Glossary

**Apa**: Amateur press association, an imagined community sustained by members who distribute self-published periodicals to one another.
***Gemeinschaft:*** A sense of community based on identification with the group.
***Gesellschaft:*** A community based on proximity and circumstance.
**Imagined communities**: Aggregates of people who, thanks to forms of mediated communication, perceive themselves as part of a common social unit despite the geographic distances among them.
**Lurkers**: People who observe but make no contribution to a virtual community.
**Newbie**: A newcomer.
**Netiquette**: Internet etiquette, a code of accepted behavior for virtual communities.
**Netizen**: An active participant who contributes to the growth or maintenance of a virtual community.
**Privateer**: A person who uses the Internet for profit.
**Spamming**: Cluttering a recipients in-box with irrelevant e-mail.
**Surfer**: An infrequent and detached visitor to a virtual community.
**Virtual community**: A shared understanding of inter-relatedness among participants in computer-mediated environments.
**Zines**: Fan magazines; self-published periodicals that are circulated among people sharing a common interest.

## Topics for Discussion

1. This chapter considered the past and present of virtual communities. What do you think the future holds for these organizations? Are they merely fads or will they play a role in future socialization? Respond by making three predictions about the state of virtual communities in 10 years. If applicable, identify a virtual community from the Internet that you think will still be thriving in the future.

2. In autobiographical paragraph, recount an experience where you were a "newbie" in a community (first time attending a club meeting, moving to a new town, or joining a team). When did you feel like you were a part of the community? It might be helpful to think of when you first made a contribution to the others involved or felt (or spoke of) a sense of "we-ness."

3. Participate in a chat room or review the contents of an electronic bulletin board for the next several days. Make a list of what rules of netiquette you observe governing interactions among the participants in one of these forums. Write an ethnographic essay explaining what rules you observed, and more importantly, how they might have been enforced if someone broke them.

4. Elmer (1999) suggested that Web rings could serve as a "grass-roots" approach to building connections online. Visit www.webring.org and explore one of the many Web rings presented there. As you visit various sites associated with the ring, can you find evidence that the people perceive themselves as a community or are they merely associates? Write a review of your chosen Web ring by noting what qualities the sites therein exhibited or lacked that would support a perspective of these connections as community.
5. How would you address the objections to the metaphor of the virtual community above? Take each of the arguments against the virtual community and offer support or counterpoints to them. Consider using a virtual community that you have found on the Internet in order to support your claims. Can you suggest an alternative metaphor to describe these ongoing group interactions?

## REFERENCES


Anderson, B. R. (1983). *Imagined communities: Reflections on the origin and spread of nationalism.* London: Verso Editions.

Borenstein, D. (2000). *Quoteland.com.* <http://www.quoteland.com>.

Bosky, B. (1994). Amateur press associations: Intellectual society and social intellectualism. In J. Sanders (Ed.), *Science fiction fandom* (pp. 181–195). Westort, CT: Greenwood Press.

Dibbell, J. (1993, December 21). A rape in cyberspace: Or, how an evil clown, a Haitian trickster spirit, two wizards, and a cast of dozens turned a database into a society. *Village Voice,* pp. 36–42.

Elmer, G. (1999). Web rings as computer-mediated communication. *CMC Magazine* <http://www.december.com/cmc/mag/1999/jan/elmer.html>.

Fernback, J. (1999). There is a there there: Notes toward a definition of cybercommunity. In S. Jones (Ed.), *Doing Internet research: Critical issues and methods for examining the net* (pp. 203–220). Thousand Oaks, CA: Sage.

Graham, J. (1997, April 7). Dents in the Man of Steel's ratings. *USA Today,* p. 3D.

Hamilton, K., & Gordon, D. (1999, February 1). Waiting for Star Wars. *Newsweek,* pp. 60–64.

Hauben, M. F. (1997, February). The netizens and community networks. *CMC Magazine* <http://www.december.com/cmc/mag/1997/feb/hauben.html>.

Jones, Q. (1997, December). Virtual-communities, virtual settlements & cyber-archaeology: A theoretical outline. *Journal of Computer-Mediated Communication, 3* (3) <http://www.ascusc.org/jcmc/vol3/issue3/jones.html>.

Kaplan, C. S. (2000, March 3). Judge says school may have overreacted to student's site. *Cybertimes Law Journal* <http://www.nytimes.com/ library/tech/00/03 /cyber/cyberlaw/03law.html>.

Maltz, T. (1996). Customary law & power in Internet communities. *Journal of Computer-Mediated Communication, 2*(1) <http://www.ascusc.org/jcmc/vol2/issue1/>.

Moskowitz, S. (1994). The origin of science fiction fandom: A reconstruction. In J. Sanders (Ed.), *Science fiction fandom* (pp. 17–36). Westport, CT: Greenwood Press.

Poole, M. S. (1995). Decision development in computer-assisted group decision making. *Human Communication Research, 22,* 90–128.

Post, E. (1955). *Etiquette.* New York: Funk and Wagnalls. (Original work published 1922)

Rheingold, H. (1993). *The virtual community: Homesteading on the electronic frontier.* Reading, MA: Addison-Wesley.

Riley, P., Keough, C. M., Meilich, O., & Pierson, J. (1998). Community of colony: The case of online newspapers and the web. *Journal of Computer-Mediated Communication* 4(1). <http://www.ascusc.org/jcmc/vol14/issue1/keough.html>.

Schoen, L. M., & Shoulson, M. E. (1999). *The Klingon Language Institute* <http:// www.kli.org>.

Schutz, W. (1966). *The interpersonal underworld.* Palo Alto, CA: Science & Behavior Books.

Scott, C. R., & Easton, A. C. (1996). Examing equality of influence in group decision support system interaction. *Small Group Research, 27,* 360–382.

Shea, V. (1994). *Netiquette.* San Francisco: Albion Books.

Sutton, L. A. (1996). Cocktails and thumbtacks in the old west: What would Emily Post say? In L. Cherny & E. R. Weise (Eds.), *Wired women: Gender and new realities in cyberspace* (pp. 169–187). Seattle, WA: Seal Press.

Tönnies, F. (1957). *Community and society* (C. P. Loomis, Trans.). East Lansing, MI: Michigan State University Press. (Original work published 1887)

Weinreich, F. (1997, February). Establishing a point of view toward virtual communities. *CMC Magazine* <http://www.december.com/cmc/mag/1997/feb /weinstat.html>.

# PART III

# INTERNET CULTURE AND CRITIQUE

The effects of the Internet might be easier to ignore if they only affected the worlds that exist online. However, that is not the case. Take, for example, what happened to Halfway, a town of 360 residents in Oregon's northeast corner, near the border with Idaho. In January 2000, the city council agreed to change the city's name (at least on some promotional materials) to half.com and become "America's first dot-com city" as part of a marketing deal with the Pennsylvania-based firm, www.half.com. This strange union of economics, politics, and identity has raised a few outsiders' eyebrows, but it also raised the ire of some long-time residents. One in particular criticized the decision, noting, "Not everybody's happy about this" (Young, 2000, p. H12).

The renaming of Halfway, Oregon, is but one manifestation of the effects the internet is having on cultures around the world. The introduction of this technology has meant that we have had to adapt to new economic, political, and cultural challenges. In many instances, these challenges have also presented opportunities to question traditional assumptions about the way we as a society conduct ourselves. This third and final part of the book examines how we have adapted to the presence of the Internet as a factor in our lives and further suggests how people have critiqued those adaptations. Some of the issues raised herein are at the very core of what it means to function as interdependent people, especially now that our interdependence has expanded to a global scale. Yet as the next four chapters demonstrate, in our quest to cope with our complex new communication technologies, we, too, may only have reached halfway.

## REFERENCE


Young, A. (2000, May 29). Halfway's not wholly satisfied as dot-com city. *Columbus Dispatch*, p. H12.

# CHAPTER 7

# REBUILDING CORPORATIONS ONLINE

*When Big Brother arrives, don't be surprised if he looks like a grocery clerk, because privacy has been turning into a commodity, courtesy of better and better information networks.*

—*Howard Rheingold (Borenstein, 2000)*

Charlie Chaplin hardly seems like a credible expert on the impact of computer technology on the workplace. For most folks, the most enduring memory of the "little tramp" is a bumbling, although well-meaning, goof. In fact, Chaplin was an astute social observer who used humor to make serious points about U.S. culture. In one of his most memorable movies, *Modern Times* (Chaplin, 1936) offers a vivid depiction of the social impact of mechanization on workers.

At one point in the film, representatives of an automatic feeding machine visit the boss of a plant whose employees make some sort of widget. Why waste hours of productivity as workers idle their time eating their lunches when the feeding machine can serve a hot bowl of soup right on the assembly line? Previously isolated activities like eating and working merge in Chaplin's vision of the modern factory. Even private activities in the restroom are subject to the all-seeing gaze of the boss who can view his workers through a wall-sized tele-screen. At one point, Chaplin's overworked, overstressed character gets sucked into the gears and cogs of the machine—blurring, ultimately, the distinction between people and their tools.

Is contemporary corporate life so far removed from Chaplin's nightmarish comedy? You might think so. Increasingly, scholars of the "information economy" report that knowledge work is replacing industrial work. The assembly line of old cannot churn out original ideas as quickly as it can turn out durable goods. However, in our increasingly computer-mediated society, corporate technology serves many of the functions described in *Modern Times*.

Think about how the machinery of today's workplace alters your habits and expectations. Formerly sharp divisions between home and office—illustrated by the vast differences built between suburban "bedroom communities" and urban corporate centers—are hard to differentiate as millions of Americans learn the art of telecommuting. Dining rooms and bedrooms make way for home offices filled with computers, scanners, and fax machines.

One way to understand this significant shift in how we live and work can be attributed to the emergence of the **information economy**. There was a time when the economic power of the United States was measured by its ability to build automobiles and sell washing machines. This was the age of the industrial economy, after Americans moved away from farms and filled the cities and factories in the 19th century. However, after World War II and the zenith of America's industrial might, the increasingly global economy made it difficult for the United States to compete in every field for industrial supremacy. At the same time, computer technology made it possible to envision an economy where knowledge, not durable goods, would constitute the nation's most important product.

In his germinal text, *The Control Revolution*, Beniger (1986) traces the emergence of the information economy and the more general **information society** to the 19th century and the growth of the railroads. The complexity of this undertaking—moving goods, services, and people across a continent—demanded a high degree of standardization, bureaucracy and national scale advertising. Modernization required more sophisticated mechanisms of control and feedback than had been acceptable to U.S. society before. As information became more broadly valued, it became more deeply embedded with the cohesion of national culture.

Although dating the emergence of the information economy and its corollary, the information society, is subject to historical interpretation, most economists have begun to argue that, at least since the 1960s, the United States has shifted its emphasis from the industrial to the information economy. Companies have begun to discover that information really is power. The U.S. Commerce Department seems to agree. In 1999, the department replaced a 60-year-old system designed to measure the strength of the U.S. economy that couldn't tell the difference between a computer and an adding machine. Only recently have important indicators such as the Gross Domestic Product begun to fully account for the impact of information technology on the strength of our economy. According to Robert Shapiro, former undersecretary for economic affairs at the Commerce Department: "In an information-based economy, the quality of information determines the quality of policy" (cited in Belton, 1999, B1). From a more general standpoint, we suggest that for an astute understanding of the contemporary economy and corporate world, you must understand computer technology.

In this chapter, we explore the impact of Internet communication on the work world as corporations employ computer technology to improve the quality of information in their offices and throughout their industries. At the same time, we consider the corresponding implications of corporate influence on the Internet. Our approach calls for discussion of three approaches used to study these interlocking phenomena: *discipline*, *diffusion*, and *convergence*.

## HYPERLINK: CHANGING CORPORATE CULTURES—TELEPHONY AND THE INTERNET

Throughout this book, we explore the relationship of technology, identity, and culture. Studying the emergence of the Internet as a social and cultural force is made easier when you consider the similarities between this medium and the growth of the telephone in early 20th-century America. Fischer (1991) argued that early telephone advertisements tended to stress corporate and professional uses of the electronic communications device, downplaying communal uses. Among the potential reasons for this orientation, Fischer argued, were economic and technical causes.

In terms of *cost*, phone companies were loath to allow what they perceived to be frivolous "chatting" on a device that was frequently rented on a flat-fee system. To understand this concern, place yourself in the position of a restaurant manager offering an all-you-can-eat special to someone who never leaves the premises. A second *technical* concern emerges when you recall that many phone systems depended on party lines—telephone connections shared by two or more families. The phone company manager would hardly want one person to monopolize a line shared by many. Yet, Fischer argued the primary reason for initial resistance to sociability was *corporate culture*.

The generation of phone company pioneers had come from the telegraph industry. According to Fischer, this group was accustomed to understanding the medium primarily from the perspective of short messages serving a specific purpose: "In this context, industry men reasonably considered telephone 'visiting' to be an abuse or trivialization of the service" (p. 112). By the late 1920s and early 1930s, however, corporate advertising caught up with social uses of the telephone. Rather than merely selling the phone as a tool for business, advertisements extolled the product as a way to enjoy "voice visits with friends" (p. 99).

As you might imagine, the prescribed gender of telephone usage began to change as well. Women and men were encouraged to reach out and touch someone. Can you isolate parallels between the corporate conceptualization of early telephony and that of current Internet technology?

# Telephone Tales

**BY LONG DISTANCE**

Says Bob Maguire
A noted buyer:

"I never worry, I never wait,
I never have to procrastinate.
I cover a multitude of firms
For quality, price and delivery terms.
I close the deal when I find the best
And I get the jump on all the rest.
This puts me in preferred position
Over slower competition.
How do I do it?" He cries emphatically,
"I use Long Distance systematically."

"And the other key men in our institution
Acclaim the telephone's contribution.
In sales and credit and traffic affairs,
It saves us all a lot of gray hairs."

*The Saturday Evening Post* (April 15, 1939, p. 40)

## CMC AS CORPORATE DISCIPLINE

You might remember a film called *Enemy of the State* (Bruckheimer, 1998) starring Gene Hackman and Will Smith. In the film, Smith plays a lawyer who discovers a government conspiracy and flees for his life. Throughout the film, it seems that Smith's every move is monitored by listening devices, video cameras, and computer networks. In many corporations, employees can be forgiven for feeling that they too are under close surveillance. On the same token, many corporations might be forgiven for placing less trust in their employees, especially because job turnover at the turn of the century was at an historical peak.

Many theorists striving to understand this dynamic base their studies on the concept of **discipline**. In this chapter, we approach discipline as a network of strategies employed by a person or group to maintain a specific set of power relationships. In many ways, discipline is the mechanism of control. However, as is seen here, corporate use of the Internet as a disciplinary tool can serve conflicting goals. Indeed, discipline and resistance often appear to form two sides of the same coin. It can liberate employees to pursue innovative solutions to complicated problems. However, the same technology can serve to limit their choices, particularly in how they relate to their company. The irony here is that technology is not a tool imposed on us, but one we willingly accept and use. Barker and Cheney (1994) explain that this tool (say, in the form of an e-mail network that helps us interact with one another at work) maintains inequitable and/or inhumane power relationships in a very subtle way. The subtlety of this power is its frequently hidden and ephemeral nature.

Let us consider an example in the form of online monitoring. Writing about network monitoring software that simultaneously blocks outside intrusion to the corporate network while it monitors employee actions, Blackburn (1999) provides a somewhat chilling example of how this power relationship might look:

> The software can scan every word employees write, every e-mail they send, and every Web site they visit. If the system detects an abnormality, it can instantly block the action. . . . The software also allows management to catalog employee misdemeanors for court and, if the need arises, to create a personal profile of each employee. (p. E13)

To understand this process, let's take a look at a disciplinary concept that communication researchers apply to contemporary corporations, the **panopticon**. The panopticon ("all-seeing place") was introduced in 1791 by English philosopher **Jeremy Bentham**. The first physical panopticon was designed to be an effective and humane penitentiary. In a series of letters, Bentham proposed that the building would be circular with cells lining the perimeter. Each cell would be separated by walls on either side. A window on the wall facing the building's exterior and an iron grating facing the building's interior would allow light to pass through the cell. This light would ensure constant surveillance over the activities of each individual by an inspector who was located in a tower at the center of the panopticon.

This surveillance was unidirectional, however. Bentham proposed that a set of blinders covering the windows in the inspector's tower would prevent prisoners from watching their captors. As Foucault (1979) writes in *Discipline and Punish*, "[The prisoner] is seen, but he does not see; he is the object of information, never a subject in communication" (pp. 202–203).

So, what does a panopticon have to do with Internet communication in corporate settings? A lot when you consider research from the American Management

Association (2000) stating that 73.5% of companies practice some form of electronic surveillance, which includes all forms of watching and listening—ranging from e-mail monitoring to more generic watching and listening such as the use of video cameras. When we focus on computer surveillance, the numbers reveal business practices that may surprise you:

- Monitoring Internet connections: 54.1% (first time surveyed)
- Storage and review of computer files: 30.8% (compared to 21.4% in 1999)
- Storage and review of e-mail messages: 38.1% (compared to 27% in 1999)

This process of surveillance might be defined as a panopticon of sorts, one that inspires employees to discipline their actions for fear of being observed through the computer network. Remember, the panopticon, more specifically the **electronic panopticon**, does not just impact that percentage of employees. It impacts all employees who imagine that they too are connected to a chain of electronic messages that can be deleted but never fully erased from company computers (to learn more, see Provenzo, 1992).

Botan (1996) conducted research on the impacts of electronic surveillance in the workforce. When surveying members of the International Brotherhood of Electrical Workers, he found that when workers perceive themselves to be under observation by their bosses, they feel less privacy, uncertainty about their role in the workplace, lower self-esteem, and a reduction in workplace communication. On this last finding, Botan notes: "This result is consistent with employees' being isolated within the virtual cells of an electronic panopticon and suggests that electronic surveillance may very well [reduce] workplace communication" (p. 309).

### Hyperlink: Microserfs

You might find a parallel between this form of surveillance and that described by Douglas Coupland and his description of life at Microsoft. In *Microserfs*, Coupland (1994) portrayed Bill Gates as a formless, faceless presence—unseen by most Microsoft employees. According to at least one character in the book, Bill used his powers to see but not be seen to both inspire and discipline his employees:

> Bug believes that Bill sits at his window in the Admin Building and watches how staffers walk through the Campus. Bug believes that Bill keeps note of who avoids the paths and uses the fastest routes to get from A to B, and that Bill rewards devil-may-care trailblazers with promotions and stock, in the belief that their code will be just as innovative and dashing.

The position of Bill's office as a site of surveillance is reminiscent of a panopticon. Through architectural technology, Bill's mechanism of control is mediated by corporate culture—the myths and legends about a man who is rarely seen by his employees.

## Electronic Surveillance and Anticipatory Conformity

An important implication of electronic surveillance in the workplace is defined by Lyon (1994) as **anticipatory conformity**—a practice in which an employee might adopt a docile and disciplined relationship to authority because of the potential rather than the practice of domination:

> Operators within the ubiquitous digital 'gaze' of such computer systems and without the more familiar face-to-face relationships with superiors, may seek modes of resistance, but compliance appears more common. . . . In workplaces where workers as well as management have access to the personal data collected on the systems, workers exhibit "anticipatory conformity," showing that the standards of management are internalized by workers. (p. 70)

Thus far, we have examined discipline as a network of strategies employed by a person or group to maintain a specific set of power relationships. To understand the role of computer technology in the disciplinary process, we examined some tools of the electronic panopticon. We also explored a result of this disciplinary technology: anticipatory conformity. But the question may still remain: Why would companies engage in use of the electronic surveillance to monitor the habits of their employees? Among the reasons is a trend defined by Naughton (1999) as **cyberslacking**—using corporate information technology for personal ends: "With the Internet morphing into the virtual Mall of America, day trading, Quake playing, vacation planning and hard-core porn (not to mention gateways to exciting new career opportunities) are all just a click away" (p. 62).

## Corporations and Consumers Online

To this point, we have focused on the corporate use of computer technology to observe the behaviors of employees. However, many corporations also use sophisticated computer technology to keep tabs on the habits and practices of consumers (Gandy, 1989). Their techniques range from innocent sounding devices called **cookies**, to voluntary sharing of personal information, to the somewhat more troubling practice of data mining.

**Cookies.** Every time you visit a Web site, you are not just viewing the contents of a document, you are retrieving that document from a server and displaying it on your own computer. This is a transactional process. In other words, your computer and the distant server must share information with each other to establish and maintain communication with one another. Fairly sophisticated Web sites use this connection to transmit more than the text, images, and other files you request; they also send **cookies**—files that place themselves on your hard drive. Cookies are not as nefarious as they might sound. They are most commonly used to identify you and store your Web preferences. A recent concern that has emerged with the use of cookie technology is the potential for companies to identify particular users who visit specific Web sites. Imagine, for instance, if you anonymously explored a site dedicated to mental health. While the site maintainer might simply employ cookies to customize the page to meet your preference, she or he could also use the cookie to identify your computer (and potentially yourself) to prospective companies, insurers, employers, or other entities. For this reason, the use of cookies raises substantial privacy concerns.

**VOLUNTARY DATA SUBMISSION.** Think about every free service you might enjoy on the Web. Free e-mail, calendars, database management tools, and news clipping services. Certainly, you put up with banner advertisements when you access these sites. But you pay another price as well. Almost every one of these services requests personal information from you. Typing in your name and selecting a password is hardly the limit of these requests, as you surely know. Frequently, you are invited to note your age, employment, hobbies, and even income. This data, in the context of a specific Web site, might be necessary and appropriate. The question of privacy emerges once more, however, when that data is collected and sold to a third-party who might employ it in ways you never intended. Both cookies and voluntary data submission play a role in the third practice: data mining.

**DATA MINING.** Like most technologies, data mining is not so radically new, when you think about it. What's unique about the contemporary practice, however, is how companies use computer software to develop patterns out of apparently random facts. Imagine that you are standing at the check-out line, holding a pair of jeans, a plastic container of hair color, and a DVD player. Individually, none of these purchases would necessarily provide useful insight into your personality. Even when collected, these purchases do not ensure that someone could construct a psychographic profile of you. However, some companies have developed powerful software networks that comb through multiple purchases, data entries, Web site visits, and other online choices you have made to guess your next purchase and even tell if you can afford the one you are making. Kleske (1999) provides one example:

> HNC Software in San Diego has created ProfitMax, a transaction-based monitoring system for managing the profitability of credit-card portfolios, and ProfitMax Bankruptcy, which can predict the likelihood that a cardholder might file for bankruptcy protection.
>
> The company's Falcon and Eagle systems examine transactions, cardholder and merchant data to detect credit card fraud and predict typical card use.
>
> HNC has focused on neural-network research born of its defense industry background to create software that can "learn" by indexing historical records in the databases of its customer companies and comparing broad categories of seemingly unrelated data to identify patterns.
>
> Unlike other software, though, HNC's products capitalize on real-time analysis by using 100 or more parameters to determine the validity of the transaction, says Robert North, the company's president and CEO.
>
> "We analyze these individual transactions that you make while you're still standing at the register," North says.
>
> The software then scores the transactions against past use and predictive patterns to determine if a red flag should be raised. (p. I 10)

## Are Practices of Surveillance and Data Collection Unethical?

Corporate use of cookies, voluntarily shared information, and data mining raise a host of ethical issues. Marx (1998) poses seven specific risks faced by individuals whose data is collected by corporations:

1. Unfair advantage: Companies may take advantage of information they have received about a consumer's desires or concerns. This would have added significance where information is key to bargaining (e.g., buying a car).

2. Restricted social participation: Companies or other organizations may employ information to discriminate against an individual seeking medical coverage, employment, or housing.
3. Unwarranted public embarrassment: Companies may publish or communicate information that could defame or humiliate a person.
4. Betrayal of confidence: Companies or employees may fail to maintain promised protections of privacy, illustrated by a phone companies revealing an unlisted number through Caller ID.
5. Intrusions into solitude: Companies may publish or communicate information that would result in an individual becoming the recipient of unwanted telephone calls, e-mail, or other solicitations.
6. Individualized propagandistic appeals: Companies may tailor persuasive messages to individuals. Although not illegal in itself, a risk emerges from the possibility of manipulation.
7. Waste of communication resources: Companies may use personal data to send messages via fax, e-mail, and other media that incur costs and service disruption.

Marx raised important ethical questions. Yet, he admitted that he cannot impose an ethical "Rosetta Stone of clear and consistent . . . categorical imperatives" on any of these practices (p. 182). He argued, instead, that one must consider a host of contextual issues that range from whether a particular practice may cause physical harm to whether those participating in data collection would wish for the same practices to apply to them.

Having explored corporate use of disciplinary technology, you might wonder how this approach helps you analyze corporate use of Internet communication. We propose that a disciplinary framework encourages people to study more than the functional practices of CMC. This framework insists on a critical reading of the interlocking networks of power shaped and maintained by computer networks. As a critic, you might employ this approach to reveal this subtle relationship of computers and corporate power in several ways. You can study the interplay of technology and narrative to observe how the narratives we tell to confirm or contest allegiance to a particular firm are mediated through computer networks. You might instead choose to study the impact of data collection on the marketplace of goods, services, and ideas—considering whether information has fundamentally shifted power away from persons and toward corporations. Whatever approach you take, the study of disciplinary networks in corporate settings is less a method than a framework for a critical revelation of practices that we might otherwise take for granted.

## CMC AND THE DIFFUSION OF INNOVATION

Organizational communication scholars who study the integration of computer technology and our workplace often focus on the diffusion of innovations through social systems. In this approach, the theoretical emphasis is less on the maintenance of power and more on the ways in which companies confront and seek to manage change. In his landmark book on the topic, Rogers (1995) defines the **dif-**

**fusion of innovations** as communication about new ideas through certain channels over time among members of a social system. The following examines this definition more carefully.

## Communicating New Ideas

At its heart, the diffusion of innovations is a process of communication. Rules, standards, technologies, and other factors exist and are understood within the common frame of reference generated by human sense making. This idea may seem strange at first. After all, it appears that tools are tools because of the functions they possess. However, the connotative meaning we attach to our tools—how we *feel* about them—cannot truly be separated from their denotative functions—what they *do*.

Consider the American car and its necessary counterpoint, the highway. You might remember when the Internet was called the "Information Superhighway." Long before the popularity of this cliché, however, the real highway and its vehicles illustrated best the means through which innovations become diffused throughout a community.

The automobile—an object designed to move persons great distances at high speed—emerged as a potent social force because of the narratives that surrounded it. Even though the American "frontier" had been officially closed in the 1893 Columbian Exposition, travelers still faced rugged territory beyond the towns and cities of the turn-of-the-century United States. Most Americans never ventured further than 40 miles away from their homes. The automobile served as a vehicle of innovation as it communicated an ideology—a prescription for how people should live—of limitless horizons and tamed frontiers.

## Communicating Through Channels

The channels of this innovation were not simply the roads, bridges, and highways of America's physical infrastructure. They were also the travelogues, fold-out maps, radio plays, postcards, and other means through which motorists and corporate boosters shared their enthusiasm for this radical change of how people could travel the country. Many women, for example, discovered that they could use the technology of automobiles and highways to flee 19th-century expectations for how they should live their lives. Accounts of women motorists such as Effie Price Gladding taking to the unknown outdoors inspired countless readers to try this risky innovation themselves. The channels of discourse through which stories about the automobile were told and retold provide necessary context to any analysis of the ideology of the American roadside.

## Communicating Over Time

It may seem obvious, but one must remember that the emergence of the automobile did not occur all at once. It took decades for car companies to decide whether to choose between electricity or gasoline as the fuel for their creations. During those decades, city and state officials wrestled with the government over who should pay for the roads, bridges, and other infrastructural improvements necessary for mass scale driving. Time provides a dimension to study the unfolding of events in various contexts. Yet it cannot be defined monolithically; in other words, this dimension is not experienced the same way or punctuated at the same moments for all participants. Studying the diffusion of innovation is a practice in which one must correlate multiple, overlapping, and even contradictory perceptions of time.

## Communicating in a Social System

One cannot separate the contexts of community and culture from the study of diffusion. To be sure, not every American could afford or operate an automobile in the early part of the century. The previous example of Effie Price Gladding is an exception that proves the rule of those days: Driving was primarily an activity for men. Women motorists were perceived by most auto enthusiasts and "good roads" boosters as a contradiction of terms. Moreover, the cost of purchasing and maintaining the cranky automobiles of the day all but ensured that the social system through which this innovation diffused would be shared by rigid distinctions and expectations of class.

From this perspective, the automobile illustrates the diffusion of innovations. Studying its technology demands careful attention to its unique idea, the channels through which that idea is communicated, the multiple histories in which that communication takes place, and the social systems that shape that discourse. As a theory, diffusion of innovations provides a set of questions and a necessary context to understand the management and implications of change.

The computer—the vehicle of the Information Superhighway—has also served as a conduit of diffusion. But there is no assurance that computers ensure that a company can successfully adapt to change. To illustrate this point, Rogers describes the challenges faced by researchers at the Xerox Palo Alto Research Center (PARC). Working among some of the brightest minds in the computer industry, PARC researchers were free to envision solutions to problems that did not yet exist. During the late 1960s and early 1970s, few people imagined that the average person would need personal access to a computer; fewer still thought that "head-in-the-cloud" researchers hired by a company that made copy machines could offer society anything much of substance. But PARC revolutionized computing by developing the laser printer, the mouse, and the Graphical User Interface.

Why isn't Xerox a key player in the computing industry today? Among the answers to this question, Rogers noted the **physical distance** between decision makers in the Xerox corporate headquarters, the excessive **rapidity** of change overtaking the industry as innovation outpaced most managers' wildest expectations, the **opposing internal cultures** of Xerox employees living and working on opposite coasts, and the **inflexible corporate identity** of Xerox—a copy machine company, not a computer company.

Think about factors that have slowed the diffusion of innovation in any industry: solar power in the automobile industry, standardization in the hotel industry, online stock management in the financial industry. You'll probably find a combination of two or more of these factors responsible for the paralysis that affects managers and other "experts" as old ideas give way to new ones.

Drawing from Rogers' work, Papa (1990) conducted research in two insurance companies that introduced new computer systems to their employees. He found that about one third of computer systems introduced to corporate settings fail to improve efficiency. So what are the factors necessary for computer-mediated diffusion of innovations? According to Papa, **interaction** and **diversity**. These two factors are more important than employees' previous experience with technology: "Put more simply, the more diverse an employee's network was, the more coworkers he or she talked to about the new technology, and the more frequently he or she talked about the new computer, the more productive that employee was likely to be using the new system" (p. 361). This should remind you of Jones' four qualities of virtual communities, described in chapter 6.

Here a question emerges, is it possible for a diverse and active network of employees to maintain the corporate status quo? The role of diversity becomes central to this issue. Papa found that employees who interact across traditional functional lines of division—chatting in the hallway among members of different corporate departments, for example—are more successful in finding new and improved ways to utilize the technology than they would in networks of close colleagues. Might not these networks provide the means for isolated individuals and groups to find common interests in their relationship with the company? On the other hand, does technology as a motivator of human interaction serve merely to allow a more efficient transmission and maintenance of corporate discipline?

When studying the diffusion of innovations from the perspective of corporate Internet communication, you are challenged to reveal the functional relationships between persons and groups in a corporate setting and to analyze the restrictions and flow of human communication as mediated by computer technology. This approach might best be served when you assume the position of an auditor rather than a critic. Your primary goal is to observe practices at the level of lived and functional experience and to analyze how persons make sense of the machines in their midst. There is room for your individual response to the ideological implications of a corporate environment, but the ultimate goal of the diffusion perspective is to bring to sharp relief the ways in which discourse and change are channeled or blocked in a social setting.

## CMC AND CORPORATE CONVERGENCE

A third perspective concentrates on *corporate convergence*. Here, one studies the ways in which computer technology in general (and Internet communication, specifically) blur existing relationships and create new ones. From the perspective of the corporate "bottom line," convergence appears to be the watchword in Internet communication. In this case, **convergence** refers to a process in which industries, formerly considered to offer distinct services, merge their products and distribution networks.

An example might be if your local cable company coordinated with your long distance phone company. The cable company could carry telephone communication through their wires; the phone company could use those wires to bypass the near-monopoly enjoyed by local telephone companies. As you can guess, this very scenario is being explored by many companies—a recent example being long distance telephone carrier American Telephone and Telegraph's (AT&T) purchase of cable giant Tele-Communications Inc. (TCI). New media giant America Online's purchase of old media stalwart TimeWarner offers an even more recent example. Schiller (1999) explains how Internet convergence mirrors a larger economic trend that began in the 1980s:

> In a cascade of huge mergers and acquisitions, multibillion dollar media properties—film studios, broadcast networks, program packagers, cable systems, satellite channels—changed hands like marbles. Such vertically integrated megamedia as TimeWarner, Disney, and News Corporation were created to fulfill the strategic goal of cross-promotion and cross-media program development. In their search for profit maximization, these powerhouse firms typically try to design and move program products across individual media boundaries. (p. 99)

In Fall 2000, AT&T illustrated the difficulty of convergence by announcing plans to split into several companies. At the same time, however, AOL reaffirmed its plans to continue its acquisition of TimeWarner.

This trend toward media convergence spells out important changes in how you'll be entertained, informed, and connected. Today's major media corporations are jockeying for position to build the much-vaunted Information Superhighway. We are not referring merely to the Internet, but to a convergence of all kinds of data: local phone calls, cable television shows, dial-on-demand movies, web documents, and other forms of mediated communication.

The emergence of portals illustrates the broader scope of this phenomenon. As you read this, major companies in all aspects of the **infotainment** industry (the blurring of information and entertainment) are gobbling up Internet portals to services like search engines, free e-mail, and the like. Internet portals reflect the same kind of convergence as the AT&T–TCI deal; each promises a bundle of services to lure you to their network of money-making opportunities. Portal managers want their pages to be your doorways to the World Wide Web—and a world of advertising.

## Convergence and Clusters of High-Tech Jobs

Another kind of convergence is taking place as specific geographic locations vie for dominance in construction of computers, the development of software, and the envisioning of new Internet applications. In late 1999, the New York Stock Exchange ran a commercial in which a precocious pre-teen went searching for the center of the high-tech world. After visiting stuffy economics lecture halls, watching NASA shuttle launches, and experiencing interactive video games, the kid remains unsatisfied. Surely there must be one place where the digital age resides. In the spot, he discovers Wall Street where the major tech companies sell stock to investors racing to take advantage of the Internet stock boom of the late 1990s. Maybe he's right. But even in an age when currency seems to respect no boundaries, most analysts of the Internet Age are still drawn to geographies of human capital.

Perhaps the place to start is Silicon Valley. Like most nicknames, **Silicon Valley** is based on an historical reference more than a contemporary reality. Although you won't find Silicon Valley on most maps, most people agree that it is composed of a cluster of cities stretching south from the San Francisco bay that include Menlo Park, Palo Alto, Cupertino, San Jose, and Campbell, California. Of course, as Winner (1999) wrote: Silicon Valley is "less a specific geographical location than a state of mind" (p. 36). Certainly, semiconductors and hardware are still manufactured in the Valley thanks to companies like Hewlett-Packard, Sun Microsystems, and Cisco Systems. However, some of the fastest growing companies like eBay, the online auction firm, and Yahoo!, the popular search engine company, illustrate how the Valley has begun to face a global economy that follows cheaper wages than can be paid in the United States. During the first half of 1999, the region received almost 40% of all high-tech venture capital funds distributed in the United States (Jaffe, 1999).

A.T. Kearney (1999), a management consulting firm, surveyed more than 100 executives for Internet-based firms searching for **high-tech clusters**—sites that draw highly educated workers, inspire technological innovation, and concentrate venture capital—seed money to grow businesses—in the United States. The results of this research produced seven centers of the Internet industry that compete with Silicon Valley as high-tech clusters: Seattle's Silicon Forest, San Francisco's Multimedia Gulch, Los Angeles' Digital Coast, Austin's Silicon Hills, Boston's Route 128, New York City's Silicon Alley, and Washington, DC's Silicon Dominion (see Fig. 7.1). These sites represent a particular kind of convergence—of location, culture, talent, and luck.

Although we discuss each cluster, it is important to remember the risk that follows any examination of high-tech business: constant change. Consider **Moore's Law**, which states that every 18 months, the number of transistors that will fit on a silicon chip doubles (Markoff, 1999). Some scientists report that Moore's Law cannot break the laws of physics; the challenges of molecular and atomic level computing will slow the pace of innovation in the near future. However, the growth of high technology on the macroscopic level is unlikely to slow down any-

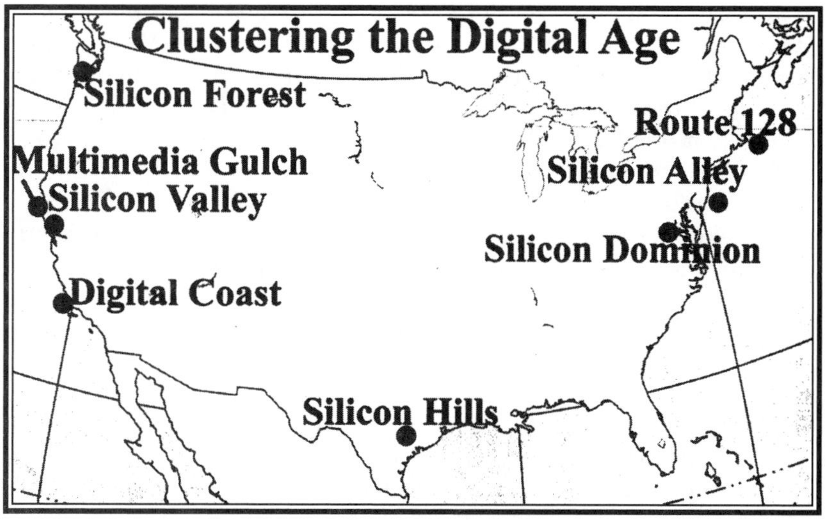


FIG. 7.1. Clustering the digital age.

time soon. Like mushrooms after a spring rain, high-tech clusters seem to grow faster than they can be counted. Thus, extrapolating from Moore's Law, one must take this list of high-tech centers as merely a snapshot of the digital economy at the turn of the century.

**Silicon Forest.** The center of Microsoft's business empire, Seattle–Redmond is also the headquarters of Amazon.com, the online bookseller, and Vulcan Ventures Real-Networks, the music software company. But Microsoft is the gravitational center of this region. Its Windows software is run on about 90% of the computers on the planet. Over the past several years, the Justice Department has sought to punish Microsoft and its co-founder, Bill Gates, for alleged monopolistic practices. Some analysts have even envisioned Microsoft being broken into smaller companies—Baby Bills—just like AT&T in the 1980s was forced to wean regional "Baby Bells" from Ma Bell. However, even in an increasingly competitive and litigious environment, Seattle–Redmond is unlikely to lose its tech influence anytime soon.

**Multimedia Gulch.** The region south of San Francisco's Market Street (SoMA) has been called **Multimedia Gulch**. Cresting and surfing the undulating streets of the city, you'll find, *Wired Magazine,* Macromedia, the maker of Flash and ShockWave software, and even the understated Dolby Laboratories—a firm whose sound system technology contributes to a $100 million-a-year success story (Greenberg, 1999). The Gulch's 120,000 square-foot New Media Campus features innovations like the Women's Technology Center, a business incubator (a site where new businesses are grown) for female entrepreneurs: "Like other business incubators, the cluster will provide practical low-cost assistance—such as office space and services, and mentoring and peer support—to help new businesses through initial growing pains" (Evangelista, 1998, p. B1).

**The Digital Coast.** Los Angeles and Orange County claimed $640 million in venture capital during the first half of 1999 as entrepreneurs and business incubators have taken root in the **Digital Coast**, the region between Ventura County and Orange County, California (Jaffe, 1999). The nickname was coined by Los Angeles Mayor Richard Riordan in an effort to convince financiers to visualize Southern California for more than its movie studios. So far, Riordan appears to have been successful. Major firms in the region include Paramount Digital Entertainment, DreamWorks Interactive, and GeoCities, the personal homepage company now owned by Yahoo. Of course, the same gravity that has attracted so much attention to the Digital Coast has also attracted stratospheric housing costs.

**Silicon Hills.** Austin, Texas is an anchor for firms such as Dell Computer, Motorola, and Advanced Micro Devices. The rapidity of change that has overtaken this high-tech center is astonishing. In 1986, the town boasted 100 software companies. At the end of 1999, Austin could boast more than 900 (Reuteman, 1999). Mayor Kirk Watson explains that the key to Austin's growth—along with venture capital firms and incubators found in other high-tech towns—is epitomized by Dell Computer. Hungry to attract the firm, Austin turned a two-lane country road into a major highway so that Dell could build world-class headquarters: "Now you can't swing a dead cat around here without hitting a Dell employee. Those 'Dellionaires' walk around with a smirk on their face like an armadillo that learned how to kill cars" (p. G2).

**Route 128.** Named after the corridor that cleaves through the southwest quarter of the Boston metropolitan region, Route 128 is known for marquee firms like Digital Equipment, Wang Laboratories, and Data General. However, as those firms faced shifting fortunes toward the end of the decade, Boston's new fame became the amount of money poured into the region. In 1999, Route 128 ranked just beyond Silicon Valley in high-tech venture capital (Judge, 1999). One reason for the amount of money that flows into Route 128 is its proximity to MIT—a similar advantage enjoyed by Silicon Valley, which is the home of Stanford University.

**Silicon Alley.** In Manhattan, Internet companies like iVillage, an online community for women, and CDNow, an online music vendor, struggle with long hours, sky-scraping real estate costs, and explosive growth. An editor of an online magazine commented on the almost surreal turn of events: "Just a few years ago, we were dance or literature majors, actors with day jobs. Now we live in a strange world where it seems as if every 10th person has won the lottery" (Harmon, 1999, p. A1). A major draw noted by Silicon Alley boosters is the close proximity of regional engineering schools and Wall Street financing operations. The convergence of academics and corporations is well illustrated by this cluster.

**Silicon Dominion.** Perhaps the most improbable cluster of high-tech innovation is in Washington DC—known more for bureaucratic wrangling and the social and economic problems that have beset the district over the past three decades than overnight start-up firms. However, the region between northern Virginia and Washington DC (sometimes described as Silicon Swamp) hosts industry giants such as America Online, MCI WorldCom, UUNet, and Network Solutions. As one economist notes: "Networking in Washington used to mean cocktails in Georgetown. It now means building the Internet infrastructure for the next century" (Yang, 1999, p. 168).

## What Are the Factors Necessary to the Development of High-Tech Cluster?

Here, the notion of convergence takes a predictive tone. As a researcher in this framework, you are encouraged to define parameters that shape and constrain the emergence of new clusters and analyze the passing of existing ones. In the section that follows, we present management consulting firm A.T. Kearney's (1999) four components that must converge for a high-tech cluster to be successful: access to talent, proximity to other industries/support services, access to capital, and high quality of life.

**Access to Talent.** Three quarters of surveyed executives state that well-educated, motivated employees are essential for a high-tech cluster to thrive. This explains why so many clusters form in the intersection of several top-notch universities. Access to talent is particularly critical in an age of increased demand and decreasing supply of labor. In Silicon Valley, for example, too many jobs chase too few viable workers in most fields, resulting in escalating salaries and perks—and declining loyalty to the boss.

**Proximity to Other Industries and Support Services.** High-tech clusters cannot survive on brainpower alone. They need access to good airports, media firms, advertising agencies, warehouses (data and physical), and other business-essential sites. Beyond the obvious support system necessary for a cluster to thrive, high-tech industry cannot endure without a secondary network of teachers, police officers, fire fighters, mechanics, and the other people who keep a community going. Turning once more to our Silicon Valley case study, rising salaries and limited housing have contributed to a struggle to keep secondary support services. For many folks who aren't awash in Internet-related earnings, it's just too expensive to live where they work. The result is a threat to this cluster's ability to endure.

**Access to Capital.** Entrepreneurs with big plans and workers willing to turn the visions into reality may be the heart of a high-tech cluster, but funding is the circulatory system. This is particularly true when Internet businesses incur huge costs in rent, equipment, and (of course) talent but do not plan to make money for several years. Thus, clusters thrive near investment centers and investors who don't fear risking millions on a new idea. Returning to Silicon Valley, we see a partial explanation for success given that an estimated one fourth of venture capital invested in the United States comes to the land of Apple Computer, Cisco, and Yahoo!.

**Quality-of-Life Issues.** A high-tech cluster cannot endure on work, support, and money alone. Other somewhat more intangible factors play into their success. Flush with cash, many Internet-age workers seek a combination of outdoor activities, cultural opportunities, and luxury items. On the same token, a cluster will suffocate in traffic, escalating housing costs, and stress. For this reason, many Internet business watchers cast a wary eye on the potential for Silicon Valley to dominate the computer and software industries for another 20 years.

The study of corporate convergence is the analysis of how disparate forces and personalities form networks. The method of your study stems less from ideology or auditing than your ability to analyze systems whose members do not necessarily plan their interactions. Certainly, some forms of convergence are organized in the forms of mergers and portals. However, convergence is frequently the study of serendipity and unplanned synchronicity as commercial, educational, and political entities align themselves. We highlight this approach here because of the increasing role of Internet communication in the emergence of these corporate networks that blur apparently insurmountable obstacles. As a student of Internet-inspired convergence, your primary goal is to invoke constellations where other people see random stars.

## CHAPTER SUMMARY

This chapter examined the impact of Internet communication on the corporate world as the United States shifts from an industrial economy to an information economy. We examined the roles of control and feedback mechanisms that precipitated this change and contextualized this revolution in light of changes that occurred after the World War II. To examine the cultural implications of this new economy, we proposed three theoretical approaches: discipline, diffusion, and convergence.

An emphasis on discipline mandates a critical approach that asks how computer technology serves to render docile the bodies and habits of employees and consumers in response to powerful corporations. Studying the use of hardware and software to monitor the activities of employees and consumers, we proposed the electronic panopticon as a metaphor to illustrate the process through which people are disciplined through individuation and disembodied influence resulting, ultimately, in anticipatory conformity. The techniques we examined through which consumers are monitored are the use of cookies, voluntary data submission, and data mining. We concluded this section with a review of ethical issues that arise from the use of disciplinary technology.

We explored diffusion of innovation theory as a means to study the ways in which new technology reflects and inspires social and cultural change within corporations and other cultures. After defining diffusion as communication about new ideas through certain channels over time among members of a social system, we examined factors that can hinder this process such as physical distance, excessive rapidity of change, opposing internal cultures, and inflexible corporate identity. Then we described two factors linked to the effective diffusion of innovation: interaction and diversity.

The third section of this chapter identified corporate convergence as a standpoint for the study of Internet communication. In terms of method, corporate convergence calls on researchers to interpret historical and economic forces with an eye on the social impacts of these new megafirms. As a brief illustration, we noted the growth of Internet portals as tools of cross-promotion and cross-media program development. We also discussed the growth of high-tech clusters, profiling Silicon Valley and outlining seven other regions of Internet innovation at the turn of the century: Seattle's Silicon Forest, San Francisco's Multimedia Gulch, Los Angeles' Digital Coast, Austin's Silicon Hills, Boston's Route 128, New York City's Silicon Alley, and Washington, DC's Silicon Dominion. We cited research that found four major factors contributing to the growth of these clusters: access to talent, proximity to other industries/support services, access to capital, and high quality of life.

In this chapter, we identified three frameworks for the study of how power is concentrated, diffused, and networked. What has been lacking is a careful analysis of how Internet communication might reflect and amplify social distinctions and inequities throughout U.S. culture. In the next chapter, we take on this issue directly.

## Online Communication and the Law

Does a company have the right to fire you for using the office Internet account for personal business? Currently, many firms require employees to sign agreements that specify which uses of Internet access are appropriate and which ones violate corporate policy. Thus far, the courts have sided with companies, agreeing with corporate claims that computer networks owned by businesses do not constitute public space or demand personal freedom of expression.

As a result, several companies have successfully fired employees for improperly using their networks. In 1999, the investment firm of Edward Jones fired 18 employees and warned 41 others after an investigation in which a worker claimed to have received an inappropriate message through the company network.

Writing in *The New York Times*, Mendels (1999) notes that the American Civil Liberties Union receives six to seven employee complaints of workplace surveillance a week: "Among those complaints was one from a woman who found that intimate messages she had sent to her boyfriend through the company e-mail system had been printed out and posted on a bulletin board by her boss, who had monitored the messages" (n.p.). Despite these risks, the courts generally uphold corporate concerns that Internet networks might be used by some employees to waste time, reveal company secrets, or harass colleagues.

You should remember that any messages you send from your corporate network are likely to be saved on a server, even if you delete the message from your own computer. Indeed, many firms have used data-retrieval software to reconstruct "deleted" messages for use in lawsuits against employees or other companies.

## Glossary

**Anticipatory conformity**: Adopting a docile and disciplined relationship to authority because of the potential rather than the practice of domination.

**Corporate convergence**: The blurring of previously disparate industries. Convergence commonly occurs within and between communications, information, and computer industries. A recent example of corporate convergence is the creation of MSNBC—a blurring of information technology and a news and entertainment company. Goals of corporate convergence include cross-promotion and cross-media program development.

**Cookies**: Pieces of software downloaded from a computer network or Web site used to track your individual computing habits. Cookies are frequently used to generate customized browsing experiences on the World Wide Web.
**Cyberslacking**: Using corporate information technology for personal ends.
**Diffusion of innovations**: Communication about new ideas through certain channels over time among members of a social system.
**Digital Coast**: Technology cluster between Ventura and Orange Counties; headquarters of Param Diount Digital Entertainment, DreamWorks Interactive, and GeoCities
**Data mining**: Process through which disparate pieces of information from multiple sources are gathered, stored, and sold to develop an evolving construct of a person's habits and personality.
**Disciplinary technology**: A critical perspective on CMC that studies the ways in which machines serve to reflect and reinforce power relationships between individuals and groups.
**Electronic communications monitoring**: Storage and review of e-mail, recording and review of telephone conversations, storage and review of voice mail messages, storage and review of computer files, and video recording of employee job performance (definition adopted from American Management Association).
**Electronic panopticon**: An extension on the panopticon concept (see definition of panopticon) through which computer technology serves to deindividuate, isolate, and monitor the behaviors of persons, generally in a corporate context.
**High tech clusters**: Concentrations of technological innovations such as Silicon Valley and Multimedia Gulch that generally depend on by four factors to thrive: access to talent, proximity to other industries/support services, access to capital, and high quality of life.
**Information economy**: Economy marked by emphasis on knowledge and symbol manipulation in contrast to an economy whose success is measured by the production of physical goods.
**Information society**: Broader term for society whose cohesion may be traced to a dependence on standardization, bureaucracy, and national scale advertising rather than oral traditions and regional ties.
**Infotainment**: An example of convergence: The blurring of information and entertainment.
**Moore's Law**: Claim first made in 1965 by Intel co-founder Gordon Moore that every 18 months, the number of transistors that will fit on a silicon chip doubles.
**Multimedia Gulch**: Technology cluster in San Francisco's SoMA district; headquarters of *Wired Magazine* and Macromedia.
**Panopticon**: Architectural notion of a humane penitentiary that disciplines prisoners through the constant sense of surveillance and isolation rather than physical punishment.
**Portals**: Web sites where a consumer can access multiple services such as e-mail, online calendars, and instant messaging that previously had been available separately.
**Route 128**: Technology cluster near Boston; headquarters of Digital Equipment, Wang Laboratories, and Data General; near MIT.

**Silicon Alley**: Technology cluster in Manhattan; headquarters of iVillage and CDNow.

**Silicon Dominion**: Technology cluster in Washington DC; headquarters of America Online, MCI WorldCom, UUNet, and Network Solutions.

**Silicon Forest**: Technology cluster in Seattle–Redmond; headquarters of Microsoft and Amazon.com.

**Silicon Hills**: Technology cluster in Austin, Texas; headquarters of Dell Computer, Motorola, and Advanced Micro Devices.

**Silicon Valley**: Technology cluster in Palo Alto, Cupertino, and San Jose; headquarters of Apple Computer, Yahoo!, and eBay and location of Stanford University.

## Topics for Discussion

1. Does the emergence of the information economy mandate a different kind of educational system than that which dominated during your parents' youth? Generate a list of the top five competencies required in today's workplace and propose ways in which modern schooling might better meet those needs.

2. In our discussion of the panopticon, we explored the roles of individuation and surveillance as tools to discipline the bodies of prisoners. Rank-order five examples of communication technology (e.g., voice mail, instant messaging) to determine which corporate tools contribute most to the construction of an electronic panopticon.

3. Data mining is a rapidly growing tool to determine a consumer's interests and habits. During a 24-hour period, keep a notepad with you and make a notation of every instance you feel that your personal information is being collected by someone else. Which occasions of data mining appear to be appropriate? When is data mining inappropriate?

4. In this chapter, we discussed the role of interaction and diversity in the diffusion of innovations. How might you employ communications technology such as the World Wide Web or instant messaging to increase one of these components of your workplace? In a paragraph, outline the specific approach you might take and anticipate problems you might face.

5. A common theme in this chapter's discussion of high-tech clusters of innovation is computer technology. Compare the geography of these clusters (you might wish to review the map in Fig. 7.1) to the geography of the industrial age when steel and automobiles were ever more major components of the U.S. economy than they are now. How have these economic geographies shifted? Why have they shifted?

## REFERENCES


American Management Association (1999, April 14). *More U.S. firms checking e-mail, computer files, and phone calls, says American Management Association survey.* <http://www.amanet.org/research/specials/monit .htm>.

A. T. Kearney. (1999, June 21). *New study analyzes challenges to Silicon Valley's Internet industry leadership.* <http://www.atkearney.com/about /press/072199 .html>.

Barker, J. R., & Cheney, G. (1994). The concept and the practices of discipline in contemporary organizational life. *Communication Monographs, 61,* 19–43.

Belton, B. (1999). U.S. brings economy into information age. *USA Today,* p. B1.

Beniger, J. R. (1986). *The control revolution: Technological and economic origins of the information society.* Cambridge, MA: Harvard University Press.

Blackburn, N. (1999, January 19). Beware, your employer may be watching you. *Jerusalem Post,* p. E13.

Borenstein, D. (2000). *Quoteland.com.* <http://www.quoteland.com.>.

Botan, C. (1996). Communication work and electronic surveillance: A model for predicting panoptic effects. *Communication Monographs, 63,* 293–313.

Bruckheimer, J. (Producer), Scott, T. (Director). (1998). *Enemy of the State* [film]. Jerry Bruckheimer Films.

Chaplin, C. (Producer), Chaplin, C. (Director). (1936). *Modern Times* [film]. United Artists.

Coupland, D. (1994). *Microserfs.* New York: ReganBooks.

Evangelista, B. (1998, December 11). Multimedia Gulch to get area focal point. *The San Francisco Chronicle,* p. B1.

Fischer, C. S. (1991). "Touch someone": The telephone industry discovers sociability. In M. C. LaFollette & J. K. Stein's (Eds.), *Technology and choice* (pp. 87–116). Chicago: University of Chicago Press.

Foucault, M. (1979). *Discipline and punish: The birth of the prison.* New York: Vintage Books.

Gandy, O. H. (1989). The surveillance society: Information technology and bureaucratic social control. *Journal of Communication, 39*(3), 61–76.

Greenberg, I. (1999, March 22). Crank up the volume. *U.S. News and World Report,* p. 52.

Harmon, A. (1999, May 31). Stocks drive a rush to riches in Manhattan's Silicon Alley. *The New York Times,* p. A1.

Jaffe, G. (1999). The new map of high tech: From Billville to Silicon Alley, the 13 hottest regions in America. *The Wall Street Journal,* pp. B1, B12.

Judge, P. (1999, October 18). Boston's Route 128 is humming again. *Business Week,* p. 190.

Kleske, A. (1999, August 22). The data miners; Software advances are making recovery of your most intimate and minute buying decisions readily available to corporate America. *The San Diego Union-Tribune,* p. I10.

Lyon, D. (1994). *The electronic eye: The rise of surveillance society.* Minneapolis: University of Minnesota Press.

Markoff, J. (1999, October 9). Chip progress forecast to hit a big barrier. *The New York Times*, p. C2.

Marx, G. T. (1998). Ethics for the new surveillance. *The Information Society*, 14, 171–185.

Mendels, P. (1999, May 14). *E-mail abuse leads to firings at investment firm*. <http://www.nytimes.com/library/tech/99/05/cyber/cyberlaw/14law.html>.

Naughton, K. (1999, November 29). Cyberslacking. *Newsweek*, pp. 62–65.

Papa, M. J. (1990). Communication network patterns and employee performance with new technology. *Communication Research*, 17, 344–368.

Provenzo, E. F. (1992). The electronic Panopticon: Censorship, control, and indoctrination in post-typographic culture. In M. C. Tuman (Ed.), *Literacy online: The promise (and peril) of reading and writing with computers* (pp. 167–188). Pittsburgh: University of Pittsburgh Press.

Rogers, E. (1995). *Diffusion of innovations*. New York: The Free Press.

Reuteman, R. (1999, November 14). Austin upgrades to high-tech capital. *Denver Rocky Mountain News*, p. G2.

Schiller, D. (1999). *Digital capitalism: Networking the global market system*. Cambridge: MIT Press.

Yang, C. (1999, August 30). Between Silicon Valley and Silicon Alley. *Business Week*, p. 168.

Winner, L. (1999). Silicon Valley mystery house. In M. Sorkin (Ed.), *Variations on a theme park* (pp. 31–60). New York: Hill & Wang.

# CHAPTER 8

# ACCESSING THE MACHINE

*The World Wide Web has turned out to be nowhere near as diverse as the number 7 train I ride home every night.*

—*Max Padilla (Borenstein, 2000)*

The Manassas Mall in northern Virginia offers a typical range of storefronts, a Montgomery Ward, a Radio Shack and more than 100 specialty stores. But the mall also provides local residents something unique, a 2,500 square-foot high tech computer center with Internet access and computer training. The center features more than two dozen computers, along with scanners and printers. The services, except for a nominal fee to print documents, are free. On some evenings, representatives of the Department of Social Services meet with folks looking for work, offering resume advice and computer skills training. Library Director Richard Murphy explains: "There are a lot of people who don't have access to computers. . . . We're responding to a need we saw in the community" (Stockwell, 1999, p. V03).

In Milwaukee, the Boys and Girls Clubs have begun developing ties to regional corporations to provide computer access to local children. At one location, the clubs have teamed up with Ameritech to create a "Cyberplace" in the middle of a housing development for lower income families. There, students experiment with digital cameras, learn about computer hardware, develop multimedia presentations, and master Web site design. One of the programs at the Milwaukee Cyberplace is called "Girls Only." It is designed to meet the needs of young women who might not pursue jobs in science and engineering. Kim Callhan, director of another Milwaukee Cyberplace explains: "It's such a digital divide between the haves and have nots. The world is technical, and if you don't have any experience base with that, you'll have a lot of problems finding jobs" (Parchia, 1999, p. MJSTECH1).

In suburban malls and downtown agencies, **community access centers** (CACs) are striving to bring Internet access to individuals and groups who have missed out on the Internet revolution. According to the Commerce Department's National Telecommunications and Information Administration (2000), more than half of Americans at the end of the 1990s remained offline, leaving about 44% who reported access to the Internet from their homes, workplaces, or other public settings.

At the turn of the century, it is clear to many observers of Internet communication and commerce that this medium will have the same impact on national and global economy as the introduction of locomotives to the 19th century world. Black (1999) quotes Microsoft Chief Technology Officer Nathan Myhrvold: "E-commerce is an enormous equalizer . . . It does not matter if you are in Dakar or Bombay. The Internet will be as important for the next 100 years as the railroad was for the last 100 years" (p. C2).

In this chapter, we explore efforts by organizations and governments to increase access to Internet communication for disadvantaged and under represented groups—in short, we explore attempts to close the digital divide. The **digital divide** refers to a statistical difference in access to computer technology between various demographic groups. Initially, we analyze differing historical experiences of women and men on the Internet. We then explore the racial and economic dimensions of the digital divide. Afterward, we examine efforts to close the divide through public–private efforts in U.S. schools. Following this discussion, we analyze critiques of the digital divide thesis, focusing on claims that advocates for federal involvement in the wiring of schools and communities overstate concerns about racial divisions online while ignoring regional divisions in high speed Internet access. We conclude this chapter with comments about the global divide between information "haves" and "have nots." Our purpose here is to continue a theme expressed throughout this text—to study the intersection of technology, identity, and culture within Internet communication. Even as the number of Internet users grows year by year, are some individuals and communities more likely than other to have access to online communication?

## A CHICKEN IN EVERY POT AND AN INTERNET-CAPABLE COMPUTER IN EVERY HOME?

That certainly seems to be a goal of those who claim that access to computers and information networks has become a human rights issue for the new century. During the 1980s and early 1990s, many communication scholars concentrated on the differing levels of access to technology experienced by women and men (Baran, 1985; Jansen, 1989; Rakow, 1988; Rakow & Navarro, 1993). A common thesis to many of these works states that technology, although not necessarily the domain of man in an essentialist sense, has nonetheless been used to observe, limit, and control the movements of women in and out of the public sphere. Marvin (1988) provides an historical object lesson for this kind of study, describing the Electric Girl Lighting Company that in 1884 supplied "illuminated girls" for indoor occasions: "women's bodies were . . . decorated with electric light, logically extending their conventional adornment and not less frequently their cultural objectification" (p. 137). Here, one imagines that women in the Victorian period could adorn themselves with electricity, but none could control the power.

As the United States industrialized in earnest during and after World War II, many technologies of work maintained their gendered natures—their appropriate uses defined by patriarchal assumptions. Toffler (1990) defines the industrial ideology that reinforced this state of affairs as "material-ismo" in which "the manufacture of goods—autos, radios, tractors, TV sets— was seen as 'male' or macho, and words like practical, realistic, or hardheaded were associated with it" (p. 79). Communication scholars would expand from Toffler's analysis to explore the metaphors and practices that serve to perpetuate this gendered notion of technology.

In the first years of popular Internet use, many women found that the same gender divide crippled their chances to enjoy equal access to the online medium. Kramarae (1998) noted:

> Looking at the programs and the discussions of computer technology, we see that women are in this cyberspace but in the same basic ways they have been in the rest of men's technology creations, not as primary decision makers but primarily as tools or concepts to be used in the creations of men. (p. 107)

Although it is difficult to fully account for the qualitative experiences of women online, it is possible to state that the numerical gender gap of Internet users has disappeared in general terms. A 1995 survey of Internet usage reported that the ratio of women and men Internet users as 30:70. By 2000, the ratio had evened at 50:50. It is important to remember that these numbers reflect U.S. Internet users. International numbers still diverge significantly (NUA, 1999). One should also remember that access to the Web does not mean the same thing to women and men. Intriguing research agendas await scholars who wish to pursue how subtle markers of gender continue to become inscribed in Internet communication. Moreover, it is important to realize that even as the digital divide has largely disappeared from a gendered perspective, it remains in other contexts.

## Race, Class, and Internet Usage

In Fall 2000, the National Telecommunications and Information Administration (NTIA) released a report entitled, *Falling Through the Net: Toward Digital Inclusion*. The annual report analyzed Census Bureau surveys of 50,000 households with questions that included the amount and usage of telephones and computers in respondents' households, locations where family members might access the Internet, and reasons for Internet use.

The report was released in an environment of increasing federal involvement in the wiring of Internet connections to homes, schools, and public locations. Previous studies indicated a large and growing divide among Internet access, particularly when race and income were considered. Speaking before a group of communications industry executives in December 1999, former President Bill Clinton remarked:

> Together we have the power to determine exactly what we want the internet to become, and what we want it to do is to be an instrument of empowerment, education, enlightenment, and economic advance and community building all across America, regardless of the race, the income, the geography of our citizens. (Clinton, 1999, n.p.)

The numbers in the NTIA report were positive but, as the new century began, government and industry leaders continued to intensify their efforts to close the digital divide.

The NTIA found that computer usage and Internet access for all U.S. residents grew significantly from 1998 to August 2000. The overall percentage of Internet access alone grew 58% over a 2-year period. In 1998, 26.2% of U.S. households had Internet access. In 2000, that number climbed to 41.5%. The rate of growth is particularly significant among individuals who are 50 or older.

## Table 8.1

**2000 Percent of U.S. Households With Internet Access**

| | August 2000 | December 1998 |
|---|---|---|
| All | 41.5% | 26.2% |
| White non-Hispanic | 46.1% | 29.8% |
| Black non-Hispanic | 23.5% | 11.2% |
| Asian American and Pacific Islander | 56.8% | 36.0% |
| Hispanic | 23.6% | 12.6% |

*Note.* Adapted from National Telecommunications and Information Administration report, *Falling Through the Net: Toward Digital Inclusion*, p. 31. Available online: http://search.ntia.doc.gov/pdf/fttn00.pdf

Despite these positive numbers, the report found that the gap between some "information-rich" and "information-poor" groups remains. Among its most important findings, the NTIA reports that Whites and Asian/Pacific Islanders are more likely than Blacks or Hispanics to have Internet access from home (see Table 8.1). Moreover, the gap between Blacks and the national average grew about 3%, whereas the gap between Hispanics and the national average grew about 4%. Most intriguingly, this gap between Internet access for both Black and Hispanic households and their White counterparts increased according to income, only dropping in the $75,000+ income bracket (see Table 8.2).

Even with the explosion of computer ownership and Internet usage across demographic groups, why does there appear to be a racial divide among Internet users? There are no definitive answers to this question. But, socioeconomic factors such as the presence of a computer at home—and the ability to afford access to an ISP—seem to be more significant indicators of the digital divide than culture of communication styles. Indeed, the NTIA stated that in the year 2000, more than half of Whites had access to computers in the home, compared to one third of Blacks and one third of Hispanics.

## Table 8.2

**2000 Percent of U.S. Households With Internet Access By Income, By Race/Hispanic Origin**

| | Income Under $15,000 | Income $15,000–$34,999 | Income $35,000–$74,999 | Income $75,000+ |
|---|---|---|---|---|
| White non-Hispanic | 16.0% | 31.0% | 56.7% | 78.6% |
| Black non-Hispanic | 6.4% | 17.9% | 38.7% | 70.9% |
| Hispanic | 5.2% | 17.7% | 41.5% | 63.7% |

*Note:* Adapted from National Telecommunications and Information Administration report, *Falling Through the Net: Toward Digital Inclusion*, p. 99. Available online: http://search.ntia.doc.gov/pdf/fttn00.pdf

The NTIA concluded that despite the apparent growth in telephone usage, computer access, and Internet availability, the racial and economic divides between various demographic communities represent a significant concern in our increasingly computer-mediated society. The study offers a compelling argument that expanding public–private CACs is a necessary first step to closing the gap.

### HYPERLINK: THE PEN AND ELECTRONIC DEMOCRACY

In 1989, the city of Santa Monica introduced a municipal computer network called **Public Electronic Network** (PEN) and almost immediately its online participants used the forum to comment on economic problems facing the city. Rheingold (1994) recalled that a PEN action group turned its attention to the city's homeless—several of whom participated in the dialogue—and the physical divides that kept them from becoming full-fledged members of the Santa Monica community.

As PEN participants discussed the issue, it became apparent that homeless members of the Santa Monica community had little chance of finding work because they had no place to prepare for interview, clean their clothes, or store their belongings. Group members decided to advocate the formation of SHWASHLOCK, an acronym for SHowers, WASHing machines, LOCKers. Using PEN to hone their arguments, SHWASHLOCK advocates went to city hall and got funding for their project.

PEN provides a powerful example of how crossing the digital divide—by making computer access free and publicly available—can help reduce economic inequities. However, as Varley (1998) noted, the online community dealt with plenty of problems including hard core participants to dominate the conference proceedings and online sexism. Even so, 10 years later, the city of Santa Monica celebrated its enduring experiment in electronic democracy.

In this section, we examined research that suggests a persisting digital divide among racial and income groups has eclipsed the gender gap. For many advocates and researchers, the issue is more important than statistics or demographics. Reporting on their research on the introduction of Internet technology to disadvantaged people, Bier, Gallo, Nucklos, Sherblom, and Pennick (1997) report that closing the digital divide can empower individuals by providing them tools to manage and transform their lives. What remain to be studied are strategies undertaken to bridge the digital divide. For many people concerned with this issue, the solution begins in school.

## WIRING THE SCHOOLS OF THE 21ST CENTURY

In 1996, former President Clinton called for every school to be connected to each other and to the Internet by the year 2000—a goal yet to be fully realized even now. During the same year, the United States Congress passed the **Telecommunications Act of 1996**. The act was designed to increase competition among telecommunications companies through deregulation. An amendment to the act mandated that "consumers in all the regions of the Nation, including low-income consumers and those in rural, insular, and high cost areas, should have access to telecommunications and information services . . . that are reasonably comparable to those services provided in urban areas" (U.S. Congress, 1996).

Clinton's goal of wiring every school flowed in part from language in the 1996 act that authorized the use of public funds to increase telecommunications access to schools and libraries. It was an ambitious goal, especially because the cost of installing the wires in California alone was conservatively estimated to be about $1 billion (out of a $16 billion operating budget). In 1994, 35% of all public schools reported access to the Internet, although only 3% of all classrooms had Internet access. In 1998, after the success of public–private efforts like **NetDay** (see the following Hyperlink), the number of schools with Internet access jumped to 89%, whereas the number of individual classrooms with Internet access increased to 51% (National Center for Education Statistics, 1999).

A question that remains concerns teaching. Specifically, now that so many schools have rooms full of computers and are wired to the Internet, should teaching styles and strategies change? Predictably, educational scholars have proposed plenty of options (Laurillard, 1987; McComb, 1994; Shedletsky, 1993).

Recently, and with some controversy, teachers have called for lessons in **information literacy** (sometimes called "information competence" or "information awareness"). Information literacy calls for students to learn skills necessary to access, gather, analyze, synthesize, evaluate, and present information from a variety of oral, text, and electronic resources. Schools and universities across the nation are struggling with the question of whether information literacy calls for new kinds of student learning skills. Should they be trained to *think* differently in an increasingly online environment?

A common response appears to be that students should practice the art of evaluation as they integrate online information in their scholarly efforts. This sentiment represents a shift in the dominant theme of information literacy conversations—away from questions of access and toward concerns about critical decision making. Still, as we explore more fully later in this chapter, there are still many schools around the nation that lack even adequate access to the Internet.

### HYPERLINK: NETDAY 96

Wearing a sweatshirt that read "Nothin' But Net," Henry Meyer, an employee of Rockwell International joined more than 20,000 volunteers to help wire 2,500 California schools on the first NetDay in March 9, 1996 (Colvin, 1996).

The massive effort that inspired public–private projects throughout the nation began when Michael Kaufman (formerly the director of information services at the San Francisco public broadcasting station) and John Gage (director of the science office at Sun Microsystems), discussed the irony that California, with its world-renowned high-tech industry, seemed unable to connect its students to the Internet. They lamented the growing gap between industry and education that resulted in fewer and fewer students demonstrating a readiness to enter the contemporary workplace. Both Kaufman and Gage had been activists in the 1960s and knew firsthand the power of public demonstrations. What if thousands of students, parents, administrators, and engineers received free or bulk-price materials and spent a day wiring their own schools?

Using Internet web pages and corporate sponsorship, Kaufman and Gage spread the word until volunteers pledged to wire 5,000 schools in California in one day. Speaking before volunteers at Ygnacio Valley High School, President Clinton said: "In a way, NetDay is a modern version of an old-fashioned barn-raising" (Mathis, 1996, p. A27).

## CRITIQUING THE DIGITAL DIVIDE

Claims of a growing divide between information "haves" and "have nots" understandably raise great concerns about inequalities hidden by the popular embrace of Internet communication. However, some critics have been effective in calling into question the existence and focus of digital divide concerns. We address two of these responses: the **snapshot critique** and the **place, not race critique**.

### Snapshot Critique: Have Nows and Have Laters

There are plenty of critics of the digital divide thesis. Some argue that it overstates the "racial ravine"; others claims that it misses the real gap. Boaz (1999), executive vice president of the libertarian Cato Institute, argues that the distinction between groups' access to the Internet should be defined less as "haves" and "have nots," but rather "haves" and "have laters." He argues that the NTIA study should be viewed as a snapshot of a rapidly changing environment.

To be sure, the time necessary for technological innovations to reach a critical mass of Americans has become small and smaller. Indeed, it took 4 years for the

Internet to reach 50 million users, almost 10 times faster than it took radio to reach the same number of people (Tonti, 1999; see Fig. 8.1).

Boaz (1999) argues that statistics indicating a growing divide between Whites, Blacks, and Hispanics (except among the wealthy) obscure the overall growth in Internet access among all groups: "What is really happening is that computer ownership and Internet access are spreading rapidly through society, with richer households getting there first" (n.p.). Perhaps the divergence between Blacks, Hispanics, and Whites in Internet usage will become smaller, following the trend in other media.

## Place, Not Race Critique

There is another response to the digital divide thesis that suggests that the real problem is less a question of race or even income and more a matter of geography. The Center for the New West, a think tank devoted to regional issues, reports that downtown centers and edge cities with their high density business parks enjoy much faster Internet connections than do small towns, rural areas, reservations, and inner-city neighborhoods: "The 'other' digital divide refers to the gap between large business enterprises, which are largely connected by high-speed on-ramps to the information superhighway versus small and mid-sized enterprises . . . that still use electronic dirt roads" (Center, 1999). A recent *USA Today* study appears to support this claim, noting that approximately 86% of U.S. Internet delivery capacity is concentrated in the 20 largest cities. Lieberman (1999) quoted Mitchell Moss of New York University's Taub Urban Research Center: "The entire Midwest is simply not part of the information highway. . . . It's the whole Great Plains, all the places that voted for Bob Dole" (p. B1).

Chances are, however, that you do not have to go far to cross a subtle but significant geography of the digital divide. Surrounding some of the most affluent

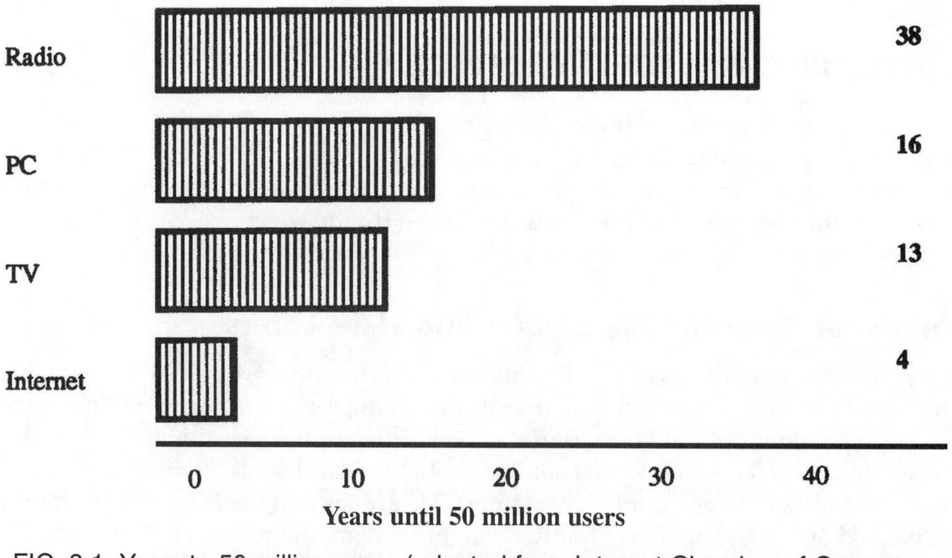


FIG. 8.1 Years to 50 million users (adapted from Internet Chamber of Commerce. Available online: http://www.icc.org/meetings/notes/062999/sld033.htm).

communities, you may find rings of people who have yet to be wired to high speed, high-bandwidth Internet connections. Writing in *Business Week*, Stepanek (1999) provides the following case study:

> Blacksburg [Virginia] is the most wired town in the nation. Over the span of only five years, more than 85% of its 36,000 residents, including 24,000 students at Virginia Tech, have gone online—far above the [national average]. By contrast, in the region surrounding Blacksburg, only some 14% are connected to the Net. In fact, only an estimated 20% even have access to a computer, mostly through schools just starting to install them. The African American residents of low-income Christiansburg, on the other side of Montgomery County, lag even further behind. (p. 188)

It appears that phone and cable companies—not the federal government—sit on the frontlines of the decision-making process to extend high-speed Internet access beyond the corporate corridors and university communities.

## HYPERLINK: MAPPING THE NEW ECONOMY

In chapter 7, we examined emerging high-tech clusters like northern California's Silicon Valley and Austin Texas's Silicon Hills. But, aside from these specific locations, are there regions in the United States that are more likely to be wired than others? The Progressive Policy Institute (1999), a Democratic Leadership Council think tank, decided to find out by creating a **New Economy Index**: a study that compares the states along five criteria:

1. The number and quality of "knowledge jobs."
2. The extent to which a state is involved in the global economy.
3. The economic dynamism of state companies—epitomized by the number of **gazelle firms**, companies who thrive on rapid change.
4. The degree to which its citizens are online.
5. The amount of innovation generated by state companies.

According to the Institute, the five states that have most embraced the new economy are Massachusetts, California, Colorado, Washington, and Connecticut. The five states most dependent on the traditional economy are Mississippi, Arkansas, West Virginia, Louisiana, and Montana. On a regional basis, the hottest spots are on the Pacific Coast and Northern Atlantic seaboard. The lowest rankings according to the New Economy Index are found in the deep south and upper midwest. Adaptation to change seems to be the essential indicator of whether a state will find itself on the right side of the digital divide: "A high rate of 'creative destruction'—the shedding of old practices while embracing the new—is the key to economic transformation in the private, public, and non-profit sectors" (Progressive Policy Institute, 1999, n.p.).

Thus far, we have analyzed educational responses to the digital divide, exploring grassroots initiatives liked NetDay and pedagogical discussions of information literacy. We too also examined two critiques of the digital divide thesis: the snapshot critique and the place, not race critique. What remains to be studied may be termed a third critique—the emphasis in U.S. press on the domestic divide. Worldwide, researchers report that a more significant divide separates international "haves" and "have nots."

## REDISCOVERING THE "WORLD" IN THE WORLD WIDE WEB

The UN *Human Development Report* (United Nations, 1999) posited three implications of an increasingly networked world: decentralization versus recentralization, fragmentation versus integration, diversity versus homogenization. The existence of a digital divide on the national level may be debatable, but it can hardly be questioned on a global scale. As we briefly highlight each of the three implications of information networking around the world, consider this question: Does Internet communication challenge or merely mirror inequitable power relationships?

### Decentralization Versus Recentralization

These terms refer to the relative control exerted by a "center" of power over those people and institutions that surround it. To illustrate this point, consider the shifts in power in U.S. society from the Washington DC beltway to states and cities—and back from those institutions to the capital—through U.S. history. This process of expansion and retraction might be defined as centralization versus recentralization. On a broader stage, consider nation states.

Nation states are a relatively recent phenomenon. As you may recall in chapter 6, they might be considered a form of imagined community, woven together through shared texts. However, the nation state is challenged by supranational organizations who use network communication (and a weak international legal structure) to cross borders and bypass local restrictions (Mathews, 1997). International financiers can strengthen or crush national and regional economies through the use of virtually instantaneous information and money transfers. The result is a simultaneous decentralization of government control and a tightening grip by newer entities.

### Fragmentation Versus Integration

Fragmentation and integration refer to the relative degree of cohesion, of closeness and familiarity, experiences by ethnic, religious, racial, and social groups. Is the United States truly one nation, or a patchwork quilt of many peoples? On the international stage, it appears that a new tribalism composed of groups and organizations who share no common geography or political structures—only a unifying set of principles, interests, or aspirations—has begun to fragment traditional social networks. Global online communities challenge or simply ignore governments and national identities by using the Internet to communicate. In doing so, they enable the integration of closely knit interest groups on a global scale.

## Diversity Versus Homogenization

These terms refer to the relative sameness of human experience shared by individuals and groups. If every member of a community watches the same television shows, reads the same newspapers, and laughs at the same jokes, it may be considered homogenous. If, however, a society has many overlapping and contradictory notions of entertainment, news, and humor, it is diverse.

Just as media companies converge their interests and ownership until a relatively small number of conglomerates produce the same bland mix of news and entertainment, individuals and groups around the world have begun to exploit the comparatively cheap communications infrastructure to craft and distribute ethnically diverse music, microlanguage news, and hyperspecific activism.

These are exciting times! Yet, the question emerges in the international setting, much as it does in the United States. Does cyberspace, that supposedly formless void of relatively cheap information, innovation, and interaction, actually follow a topology that divides "haves" and "have nots"? The UN *Human Development Report* (United Nations, 1999) warned that a global digital divide does indeed exist, stating the Internet revolution has bypassed the vast majority of people on the planet: "In mid-1998 industrial countries—home to less than 15% of people—had 88% of Internet users. North America alone—with less than 5% of all people—had more than 50% of Internet users. By contrast, South Asia is home to over 20% of all people but had less than 1% of the world's Internet users" (p. 62; see Table 8.3).

**Table 8.3**
**Global Internet Usage**

| | Population (Regional Percentage of World Population) | Internet Users (Percentage of Regional Population) |
|---|---|---|
| United States | 4.7% | 26.3% |
| OECD (excluding the U.S.)[a] | 14.1% | 6.9% |
| Latin America and Caribbean | 6.8% | 0.8% |
| South-East Asia and the Pacific | 8.6% | 0.5% |
| East Asia | 22.2% | 0.4% |
| Eastern Europe and the CIS[b] | 5.8% | 0.4% |
| Arab States | 4.5% | 0.2% |
| Sub-Saharan Africa | 9.7% | 0.1% |
| South Asia | 23.5% | 0.04% |

*Note:* Adapted from United Nations Development Program (1999) *Human development report*. Adobe Acrobat document available online: http://www.undp.org/hdro/99.htm

[a]Organization for Economic Co-operation and Development (OECD) includes Australia, Austria, Belgium, Canada, Czech Republic, Denmark, Finland, France, Germany, Greece, Hungary, Iceland, Ireland, Italy, Japan, Korea, Luxembourg, Mexico, Netherlands, New Zealand, Norway, Poland, Portugal, Spain, Sweden, Switzerland, Turkey, the United States, and the United Kingdom.

[b]CIS stands for Commonwealth of Independent States (former Soviet Union).

Consider these statements:

- "There are more telephone lines in Manhattan than in sub-Saharan Africa" (O'Connor, 1998, p. 272).
- "The U.S. has more computers than the rest of the world combined" (Chapman, 1999, p. C1).
- "Under 10 per cent of [the Internet's] content is of Asian origin, yet Asia represents almost half of the world's population" ("Wiring," 1999, p. COMP17).

Spender (1998) describes a recommendation drafted by Women, Information Technology and Scholarship arguing that access to information is a human right: "As an extension of the aim of universal literacy, universal '**informacy**' could be readily accommodated by UN policy" (p. 268). All that remains to accomplish this goal, it appears, is careful construction of policy and planning.

But we also return to notions of communication and culture. As discussed in chapter 1, so much of the discourse that surrounds the Internet concerns its apparent openness—its frontier spirit where anyone can speak their mind, plant their stake, and build their homestead. Yet, as Carstarphen and Lambiase (1998) remind us, it is impossible to ignore a topology to online communication.

Online communication is *shaped* by discourses and practices that manifest themselves in class, race, and gender: "the Internet itself is established on a hierarchy of protocols and codes, with much of its communication overseen by webmasters, dungeon masters, listowners of electronic discussions, and hackers" (p. 125). What are the impacts on a cyberspace whose topology seems so drastically slanted toward English-speaking industrial powers? We are only now discovering the answer to that question.

## CHAPTER SUMMARY

In this chapter, we examined recent research on the digital divide—focusing closely on dimensions of gender, race, and income. We concluded that, although the gender divide has largely disappeared in Internet access, work remains to be done on the digital divide when race, ethnicity, and class are considered. Turning to educational initiatives, we found that grassroots efforts such as NetDay and scholarly inquiries into information literacy reveal a necessary balance between schoolyard priorities. Wiring the schools with high-speed networks and powerful computers cannot proceed without simultaneous concern for students' astute evaluation of information technology. Finally, we explored critiques of the digital divide thesis claiming that researchers are either too concerned about race or not nearly concerned enough about geography. Adding to these critiques, we concluded with a study of the global divide in information access. An appropriate next step for chapter 9 is an analysis of ways in which individuals and groups have begun to challenge the digital divide on their own terms. You may find that some of their tactics are quite surprising.

## Online Communication and the Law

On the cutting edge of the debate over the government's role in securing access for its citizens to the digital economy is a debate concerning the 1990 **Americans with Disabilities Act** (ADA) and ISP, America Online (AOL). In 1999, the National Federation of the Blind (NFD) sued AOL on the grounds that the company does not make a reasonable effort to ensure that its online environment is accessible to visually impaired people (Kaplan, 1999).

According to the suit, AOL's software is incompatible with software used by visually impaired persons to translate text and images into synthesized speech or Braille. The broader issue raised by the suit is whether AOL's online services that include Web access, e-mail, and instant messaging constitute a public place—and is thus covered by ADA's definition of public accommodation in the same manner as a hotel, restaurant, or movie theater.

Attorneys for the NFD argue that framers of the public accommodation concept did not intend to limit its meaning to brick and mortar establishments, noting that a blind person should enjoy the same access to a business over the phone as she or he would in person. Organizations that conduct their businesses entirely by way of telecommunication media would naturally be subject to ADA requirements. Opponents respond that a positive ruling for the NFD would create chaos for ISPs and, potentially, other Web site maintainers. The fundamental question that emerges from this litigation concentrates on whether corporations have an interest, or perhaps an obligation, to help reduce the digital divide. Should ISPs be required to ensure reasonably priced Internet access to economically depressed regions? Should companies ensure that their Web sites are accessible to persons with disabilities? Should the federal government continue its activism for universal access to the Internet?

AOL provided a partial answer to those questions by promising to ensure that its newest version software would be more compatible with technology used by visually impaired Internet users. Because of this compromise, the NFD withdrew its suit. However, the Commerce Department more recently reported that Internet use is only half as common among persons with disabilities as with other people (National Telecommunications and Information Administration, 2000). So, the larger issue remains. Can the Internet become "public place" for all people, or is it destined to become fixed as a market between information haves and have nots?

## Glossary

**Americans with Disabilities Act**: 1990 law prohibits denial of access to employment, state and local services, and private goods and service, and commercial facilities because of disability.

**Community access centers**: Public sites including libraries, schools, and malls where information technology is made available to the public at little or no cost.

**Digital divide**: A statistical difference in access to computer technology between various demographic groups.

**Gazelle firm**: A fast-growing company, typically at a rate of 20% per year for 4 years.

**Information literacy**: Movement in educational circles to facilitate student abilities to access, gather, analyze, synthesize, evaluate, and present information from a variety of oral, text, and electronic resources.

**Informacy**: Extension of literacy, a universal right to information.

**NetDay**: A grassroots response to lagging Internet connectivity within U.S. schools; initiated in 1996 by Michael Kaufman and John Gage.

**New Economy Index**: Progressive Policy Institute index of states' relative transformation from traditional to contemporary growth strategies along five criteria: knowledge jobs, globalization, dynamism, online access, and innovation.

**Place, not space critique**: Critique of the digital divide thesis claiming that disparities in geographical access to high-speed Internet access are more significant a measure of the digital divide than comparative access of demographic groups.

**Public Electronic Network**: An early experiment in online democracy pioneered by the city of Santa Monica. Noteworthy for its SHASHLOCK project designed to provide homeless persons access to showers, washing machines, and storage lockers.

**Snapshot critique**: Critique of the digital divide thesis responding that statistics used to prove a growing disparity in Internet access between demographic groups do not reflect historical trends.

**Telecommunications Act of 1996**: Overhaul of the 1934 Communications Act designed to stimulate competition in the communications industry through federal deregulation.

## Topics for Discussion

1. Many individuals and groups concerned about the digital divide have called for the federal government to increase its aid to states and organizations trying to get Internet access to disadvantaged and underrepresented groups. Generate a list of reasons for and against

government activities to expand Internet access. What seems to be the trend in your responses?

2. Conduct a survey of local and private organizations that have set up CACs near your college or hometown. Generate a set of suggestions for how your class might contribute knowledge and or labor to one of these centers.
3. Read the NTIA report online (http://search.ntia.doc.gov/pdf/fttn00.pdf). Can you find a demographic category or group of persons not adequately addressed by the report findings? Be prepared to explain your answer.
4. Examine the Progressive Policy Institute New Economy Index (http://www.neweconomyindex.org/states/) and explore the position of your home state to others. What are three factors that explain your state's relative position?
5. Some international activists have begun to claim that information access is a human right on par with the right of free speech and religious expression. Do you agree that access to online information should be included as a basic human right? Develop a 3-minute presentation for an imagined audience of folks opposed to the notion that information should be freely accessible. What strategies should you use?

## REFERENCES

Baran, B. (1985). Office automation and women's work: The technological transformation of the insurance industry. In M. Castells (Ed.), *High technology, space, and society* (pp. 143–171). Beverly Hills, CA: Sage.

Bier, M., Gallo, M., Nucklos, E., Sherblom, S., & Pennick M. (1997, Winter). Personal empowerment in the study of home Internet use by low-income families. *Journal of Research on Computing in Education*, 107–132.

Black, G. (1999, November 30). Sharing a goal to close the world's digital divide. *The Seattle Times*, p. C2.

Boaz, D. (1999). A snapshot view of the world. *CATO commentary*. <http://www.cato.org/dailys/07–17–99.html>.

Borenstein, D. (2000). *Quoteland.com*. <http://www.quoteland.com>.

Carstarphen, M. G., & Lambiase, J. J. (1998). Domination and democracy in cyberspace: Reports from the majority media and ethnic/gender margins. In B. Ebo (Ed.), *Cyberghetto or cybertopia? Race, class, and gender on the Internet* (pp. 121–135). Westport, CT: Praeger.

Center for the New West. (1999, September). *The "other" digital divide*. <http://www.newwest.org/technology_society/digital_divide/digital _divide_1.html>.

Chapman, G. (1999, July 19). The cutting edge. *Los Angeles Times*, p. C1.

Clinton, B. (1999, December 9). Remarks by the president on bridging the digital divide. <http://www.whitehouse.gov/WH /New/html/19991209.html>.

Colvin, R. L. (1996, March 16). Volunteers wire 2,500 schools on netday. *Los Angeles Times*, p. A1.

Jansen, S. C. (1989). Gender and the information society: A socially structured silence. *Journal of Communication, 39*(3), 196–215.

Kaplan, J. (1999, November 12). Is cyberspace a "public accommodation"? *The New York Times*. <http://www.nytimes.com/library/tech/99/11/cyber/cyberlaw/12law.html>.

Kramarae, C. (1998). Feminist fictions of future technology. In S. Smith (Ed.), *Cybersociety 2.0: Revisiting computer-mediated communication and community* (pp. 100–128). Thousand Oaks, CA: Sage.

Laurillard, D. (1987). Computers and the emancipation of students: Giving control to the learner. *Instructional Science, 16*, 3–18.

Lieberman, D. (1999, October 11). America's digital divide. *USA Today*, B1.

Marvin, C. (1988). *When old technologies were new: Thinking about electric communication in the late nineteenth century*. New York: Oxford University Press.

Mathews, J. T. (1997). Power shift. *Foreign Affairs, 76*(1), 50–66.

McComb, M. (1994). Benefits of computer-mediated communication in college courses. *Communication Education, 43*, 159–170.

Mathis, N. (1996, March 10). Campaign 96. *The Houston Chronicle*, p. A27.

National Center for Education Statistics. (1999, February). *Internet access in public schools and classrooms: 1994–98*. Washington DC: U.S. Department of Education. <http://nces.ed.gov/pubs99/1999017.html>.

National Telecommunications and Information Administration. (2000). *Falling through the net: Toward digital inclusion*. Washington D.C.: United States Commerce Department. <http://search.ntia.doc.gov/pdf/fttn00.pdf>.

NUA. (1999). *NUA Internet surveys*. Available online: http://www.nua.ie/surveys/

O'Connor, R. J. (1998). Africa: The unwired continent. In R. Holton (Ed.), *Composing cyberspace: Identity, community, and knowledge in the electronic age* (pp. 270–274). Boston: McGraw-Hill.

Parchia, M. (1999, September 14). Digital divide: Computer clubhouse hopes to reverse trend. *Milwaukee Journal Sentinel*, MJSTECH,1.

Progressive Policy Institute. (1999). *State new economy index*. <http://www.neweconomyindex.org/states/>.

Rakow, L. F. (1988). Gendered technology, gendered practice. *Critical Studies in Mass Communication, 5*, 57–70.

Rakow, L. F., & Navarro, V. (1993). Remote mothering and the parallel shift: Women meet the cellular telephone. *Critical Studies in Mass Communication, 10*, 144–157.

Rheingold, H. (1994). *The virtual community: Homesteading on the electronic frontier*. New York: HarperPerennial.

Shedletsky, L. (1993). Minding computer-mediated communication: CMC as experimental learning. *Educational Technology, 33*(12), 5–10.

Spender, D (1998). Social policy for cyberspace. In R. Holton (Ed.), *Composing cyberspace: Identity, community, and knowledge in the electronic age* (pp. 266–269). Boston: McGraw Hill.

Stepanek, M. (1999, October 4). A small town reveals America's digital divide. *Business Week*, p. 188.

Stockwell, J. (1999, November 17). New library fits needs of digital age. *Washington Post*, p.V03.
Toffler, A. (1990). *Powershift: Knowledge, wealth, and violence at the edge of the 21st century*. New York: Bantam Books.
Tonti, G. (1999, June 29). *Gaining competitive advantage through Internet business solutions*. Presentation to the Internet Chamber of Commerce. <http://www.icc.org/meetings/notes/062999/sld003.htm>.
United Nations Development Program. (1999). *Human development report*. <http://www.undp.org/hdro/99.htm>.
U.S. Congress. (1996). *Telecommunications Act of 1996*. <http://www.fcc.gov/Reports/tcom1996.pdf>.
Varley, P. (1998). Electronic democracy: What's really happening in Santa Monica. In R. Holton (Ed.), *Composing cyberspace: Identity, community, and knowledge in the electronic age* (pp. 244–252). Boston: McGraw Hill.
Wiring a divided world. (1999, April 5). *Irish Times*, p. Comp17.

# CHAPTER 9

# CARVING ALTERNATIVE SPACES

*I do not fear computers. I fear lack of them.*

—*Isaac Asimov (Borenstein, 2000)*

In 1999, as Serbia braced itself for war with NATO allies, its leadership sought to stifle dissent within its own borders. Since 1989, Serbian radio station, B92, fought to maintain an independent voice on Serbian airwaves, even as the government grew more and more isolated and paranoid. Like any radio station, B92 sponsored concerts and played the hits. However, unlike most stations, B92 also spoke against its government and warned its increasingly fearful listeners: "Trust no one—not even us." Rallying antigovernment protestors and critiquing the policies of former Serbian President Slobodan Milosevic, the radio station stood as a lone voice of dissent among state-controlled media.

Once NATO bombs began to fall, the Serbian government moved against B92, unwilling to allow the independent station to speak against the state and its war effort. Plain-clothed police officers stormed the station's offices and replaced its management with government-approved personnel. It looked like the 10-year career of radio resistance was over for B92.

However, the radio station found new life on the Internet when an Amsterdam-based ISP offered its services. As the Serbian government restricted the communications of its dissidents, B92 aired its programs over the Internet, telling listeners about NATO bombings and Serbian responses. After the bombing campaign, the station continued to run from the 440 square-foot apartment of Sinisa Rogic who states: "Without the Internet, we would not even be in this country anymore" (Engardio, 1999, p. 144).

Around the world and across the United States, activists who might have been shut out of the public arena have found a powerful tool in the Internet (Coombs, 1998). Certainly, this network of networks can be blocked by various means. Many companies protect themselves by **firewalls**—software and hardware barriers that restrict access to and from their internal networks. Many parents, schools, libraries, and workplaces employ **filtering software** designed to restrict access to certain Web sites. Many national government's regulate their citizens' use of the Internet, fearing that their cultural and political harmony (and control) might be thwarted by foreign ideas. However, as discussed earlier, the Internet is not like any other communications medium. It is designed to regulate itself with little governance from a central location. When you think about CBS, *The New York Times*, or your favorite radio station, you can probably imagine a specific anchor person, building, or broadcasting tower. Internet communication, by contrast, pulses through many conduits. Close one, and it finds another.

In this chapter, we examine ways in which individuals and organizations have used Internet communication to carve alternative spaces for themselves in an increasingly global and centralized world. Much of this chapter focuses on the manner in which disparate groups, marginalized by small size, are forming communities of like-minded people to confront problems on the global stage (Warf & Grimes, 1997). In many ways, this chapter serves to bookend chapter 8. Chapter 8 outlined some critics' concerns that a digital divide separates information "haves" from "have-nots." Considering that so many communications networks are merging and growing, it may appear that this process is irreversible. We respond to this sense by outlining a notion of discursive resistance that emerges when individuals and groups use technology to create spaces of community and protest. Second, we analyze two specific rhetorics employed to shape these spaces: agonistic and utopian discourse. Finally, we evaluate a dangerous intersection of agonistic and utopian rhetoric online, the use of computer networks to disseminate hate speech.

## DISCURSIVE RESISTANCE: CRAFTING ALTERNATIVE SPACES WITHIN DOMINANT PLACES

**Discursive resistance** is a process through which text, oral, nonverbal communication, and other forms of meaning-making are employed to imagine alternatives to dominant power structures. This definition rests on a conception of **discourse**—communication that shapes or influences human relationships. Of course, all communication may be considered discursive to some degree; some are just more obvious than others. This form of resistance may confront and reject those structures, but it seldom attacks them directly. Ironically, current trends reveal that the Internet may be an unlikely site of discursive resistance.

For some observers, the Internet will inevitably become ubiquitous and indistinguishable from other social institutions. Rather than maintain its cultural mystique as a lawless frontier where anybody can put down a homestead, the Internet will become domesticated, controlled, and part of disciplined society. David Plotnikoff (1999) writes in the *San Jose Mercury News* that the Internet will become "an ubiquitous component of the economic and social landscape (or, to look at it another way, as economic and social affairs become part of the Net's landscape) all this technology will recede to the back of our consciousness and seem utterly unremarkable" (n.p.). If Plotnikoff is right, will there be room left in this medium for individuals and groups who resist dominant society?

To answer this question, we first outline our notion of alternative spaces online as discursive resistance against dominant culture. These forms of resistance may not enjoy wide popular support; they may not even be successful in literal terms. However, they succeed insofar as they enable some form of critique against powerful places that might otherwise obstruct or even eliminate any form of dialogue.

Hopefully, at this point, you have noticed that we use "space" and "place" somewhat specifically. These concepts are examined more carefully next.

## Places of Control: Spaces of Resistance

**Place** works to formalize, authorize, and make permenant the processes through which dominant interests maintain their influence. We approach this definition from the perspective outlined by de Certeau (1984), who studies the way in which abstract institutional power—architectural drawings, maps, census data, and the like—is rendered concrete in places. When you think of a place, think of a shopping mall whose architectural design serves a singular purpose—to consume. You can think of other uses of the mall, but the place—its laws, habits, and organization—works hard to limit your choices. Toulmin (1990) further described the power of modern places to affirm "universal, timeless concepts" (p. 75). Places justify ideology and power by attaching a sense of permanence to them. When Blair, Jeppeson, and Pucci (1991) describe the modernism as a process through which dominant powers maintain their identities by invoking comprehensiveness of purpose and intent, we imagine place as a site where that process occurs.

**Space**, in contrast, is a localized, particular, momentary response to place. Space is a set of options for the individuals and groups who struggle to find meaning and identity within (and despite) physical places. For de Certeau (1984), space is a profoundly personal and fluid experience: "the [place called 'street' is ] geometrically defined by urban planning [yet] transformed into a space by walkers" (p. 117). Within that space, ideally, the places that surround us might be transformed. Here is an example: Imagine that you live in a country where any sign of protest would be met with violent police response. If you enter the public square and hoist banners and placards, you might be harmed or killed. But what if you enter that square and merely stand your ground—making no obvious protest? That's what the Mothers of Plaza de Mayo did when they occupied public arenas in silent protest of the military and economic brutality of an Argentinean dictatorship during the 1970s. Their construction of a rhetorical space through the astute manipulation of an architectural place blurred the distinctions between public and private. Their inner pains were revealed, but not spoken. Doing so, the space of their stance in public locales made it possible for disenfranchised women to seize the public sphere, even if only for a moment (Fabj, 1993). As Lefebvre (1991) reminds us: "Space is becoming the principle stake of goal-directed actions and struggles" (p. 410). Place and space might best be related in this manner: Places constrain and affect the movements of people who construct spaces in response.

When we speak of Internet communication "carving alternative spaces," we refer to the use of computer networks to construct discursive resistance to dominant forces—to build alternative paths, hiding spaces, impromptu monuments, and unauthorized meeting places online.

We approach this notion from an historical and theoretical perspective that posits that technological innovation has long served to challenge existing social orders. This does not mean that technology is the single engine of social change, only that technology plays a critical role in shaping changes in society. Consider the introduction of the printing press to western society. Historians such as Lewis Mumford argue that moveable type is second only to the clock in its impact on our culture and worldview. With mass production of the written word, access to new ideas becomes available to all people. Control over the press, literacy, and the public forum where the written word may be displayed and archived remained a critical factor that limited the potential of this technology to significantly affect human relationships. Thus, it should come as no surprise that the Protestant Reformation began when Martin Luther posted his 95 Theses (or arguments) in the public forum of a church door.

In the last 25 years alone, the technology of communication served to challenge cultures of control. In the 1970s, taperecorders carried illegal speeches by Iranian holy men who rejected their nation's government. In the 1980s the fax machine became a critical tool of anti-Communist leaders in the former Soviet Union. In the 1990s, the Internet carried appeals by the Zapatista insurgency for global attention to their stand against the Mexican government. In each case, individuals and groups shaped discursive spaces that acted to resist dominant places in their societies.

## Hyperlink: Laptops in the Jungle

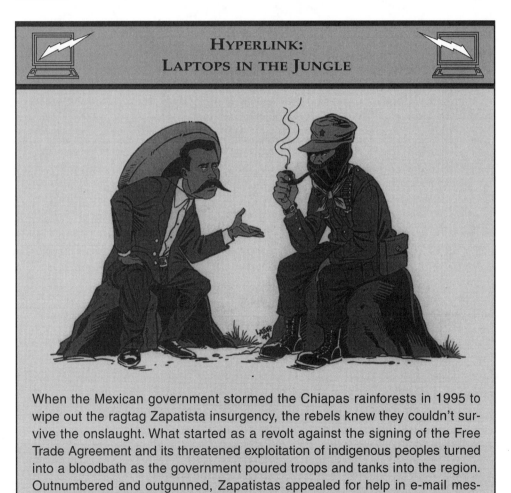

When the Mexican government stormed the Chiapas rainforests in 1995 to wipe out the ragtag Zapatista insurgency, the rebels knew they couldn't survive the onslaught. What started as a revolt against the signing of the Free Trade Agreement and its threatened exploitation of indigenous peoples turned into a bloodbath as the government poured troops and tanks into the region. Outnumbered and outgunned, Zapatistas appealed for help in e-mail messages forwarded around the world.

They accused the Mexican government of pillaging the poor state and brutalizing its people during the crackdown. Almost immediately, the government backed down and began peace talks. They had been beaten by the written word that connected guerillas to academics, journalists, and peace activists around the globe. Cleaver (1995, also see Cleaver, 1998), an economist at the University of Texas at Austin compared the Zapatista revolt online to postcolonial revolts in the second half of the 20th century:

> In cyberspace just as in the geographical frontiers of the Americas (the North American West, the South American Pampas or Rainforests) there has been a dynamic struggle between the pioneers and the profiteers. Just as mountain men, gauchos and poor farmers have sought independence through the flight to and colonization of new lands, so cyberspace pioneers have carved out new spaces and filled them with their own activity.

By 2000, you could find more than 40 Web sites dedicated to the Zapatista cause (see, e.g., http://www.ezln.org/). The Zapatista leader known as Subcommander Marcos explains how these sites can alter the balance of power between a government and its opponents. Social control can no longer be maintained by force: "What governments should really fear . . . is a communications expert" (Watson, 1995, p. 36).

How might studies of space and place sharpen your analysis of online communication? Consider cyberspace as a site where individuals and groups craft alternatives to dominant places that shape their interaction. These spaces may be individual Web sites or constellations of sites located on servers around the world. Some of these sites enable discursive resistance by advocating direct action: Some ask you to join boycotts against oil companies, purchase locally grown fruits, or support charitable causes. As discussed later, some advocate far more radical responses to perceived moral decay of a people.

However, as we also discover, not all alternative spaces work so publicly. Some sites achieve some measure of success merely by providing a location where intentional and ad-hoc communities may form. **Intentional communities** are those comprised of persons who elect to join one another for a specific cause. Typically, they are unified by some shared geography, language, or cultural practice. These sustain themselves long enough to accomplish some goal—even when the goal is continued interaction.

**Ad-hoc communities** are those groups who form spontaneously, often in response to a traumatic or threatening event. Online, these communities may be composed of strangers who may never meet face to face. Bereaved family members and friends who fashion virtual shrines after a disaster (such as the destruction of TWA Flight 800) may be defined as ad-hoc communities. In many important ways, this type of community serves as a site and means of protest. In the example of the air disaster, many bereaved individuals who lost loved ones in TWA crash found themselves doubly victimized by an airline they perceived to be too slow in releasing information and too insensitive in helping them cope with their grief. Posted Web sites that responded to this tragic turn of events and allowed strangers to form a short-lived community carved an alternative space of shared grief and anger.

Thus far, the discussion has focused on the site of Internet protest. The language of space and place provides a metaphoric means to identify how alternative and contradictory messages may possess the same discourse. As a student of communication, you might examine local examples in which individuals and groups craft an alternative space within a dominant place. What we need to examine at this point, however, is the process through which those resistant discourses are shaped. Do they seek to redeem a failed institution by confronting its limitations? Or, perhaps, do they concentrate their appeal to the evocation of an ideal social order that can be realized online, if not in the real world? Here we turn to agonistic and utopian rhetorics. But, remember, redemption and idealism do not necessarily mean the same thing to all peoples. Some of the most troubling discourse seeks to create a better world.

## AGONISTIC AND UTOPIAN RHETORIC ONLINE

Communication theorists have long debated the role of confrontation in public discourse. Ancient teachers (and critics) of rhetoric argued that the speaker's primary goal is to evoke and embody the goals and ideals of the audience. Confronting socially accepted and culturally embedded assumptions would surely result in rhetorical failure—indifference. The speaker would be rendered silent through force or some other mechanism and the audience would depart the scene unmoved. However, in times of social crisis, theorists of rhetoric tend to rethink the assumption that confrontational speech is counterproductive. After all, where can change take root but from the fields of conflict as values are placed in contest?

Perhaps confrontation may be defined as the rejection of a contemporary order of things and simultaneous invocation of a better worldview. Describing this process, Cathcart (1978) includes agonistic rhetoric in his study of human behavior. **Agonistic rhetoric** includes those forms of discourse that produce or invoke ritualized conflict with an established order. An example of agonistic rhetoric would be for you to upload a web page explaining why AOL is an awful ISP and demanding a change in its habits. Cathcart drew from literary critic Kenneth Burke to explain how this confrontation—reordering rather than reforming a broken system—attempts to inspire a sense of guilt that is either accepted by the speaker (and audience) or cast onto another person, group, or entity. The goal of agonistic rhetoric is to achieve redemption—to replace a faulty and disordered hierarchy of values and institutional power with a more perfect order.

This form of confrontation—where a communicator either accepts the role of mortified victim of some evil and admits guilt, or blames an exterior force for the introduction of that evil onto an otherwise perfected hierarchy—can be used to explain the power of some forms of Internet communication to resist and rebuke contemporary systems and established order. In carving out alternative spaces of interaction, some communicators seek redress for perceived personal limitations or reaction to external failings of a system they cannot control.

Here, even the most banal web pages—the "Die Jar Jar Binks, Die" site for example—may be analyzed as responses to guilt. In this site, the author notes that he saw his first *Star Wars* movie at age 13 and waited enthusiastically for the first prequel film, *The Phantom Menace*. The introduction of the computer-animated Jar Jar Binks disappointed this fan—the character was perceived to be cowardly, pointless, and offensive: "But by far the most serious crime committed is that of stinking-up a *Star Wars* movie. This is sacrilege. . . . What method of execution would promote the cause of Justice? Perhaps a lightsaber up the wazoo? Eaten alive by the Rancine? Torn apart by a wookie? Forced to listen to Vogon poetry? Turned into Jar-Jar-B-Que?" Redemption in this case is the removal of Jar Jar from the hierarchy of *Star Wars* characters—to reorder the George Lucas universe without a "Gungan warrior" in sight. By resorting to this form of scapegoating—blaming others for problems that can be blamed on ourselves—the site maintainer avoids the guilt of waiting so long for what was essentially a children's movie.

To this point, we have studied a definition of confrontation online that is agonistic—the conflict is a ritualized response to the perceived failures of a dominant group or social order. However, confrontation that provides no alternatives can hardly be expected to succeed in doing more than destroying the existing system. Thus, as a necessary corollary to agonistic discourse, many Internet communicators evoke a form of rhetoric that is best described as utopian.

**Utopian rhetoric** is that which seeks to redress contemporary problems with the social system by invoking an ideal form of human interaction distant from the audience in time, space, or in both. This form of communication was coined by Sir Thomas More who wrote *Utopia* as a response to the perceived injustices of English society in the sixteenth century.

Utopian rhetoric is more than the redemption imagined by Burke and enhanced by Cathcart's agonistic rhetoric. The power of utopia is its lack of accessible position. Indeed, the word *utopia* stems from an ironic relationship between Greek words for "no" and "place." In other words, it is a place that cannot exist; it signifies a perfect order that can never be achieved. As a corollary, utopian rhetoric creates an unassailable site from which one may protest with relative safety.

FIG. 9.1. Sir Thomas More, author of *Utopia*

Internet protest might be regarded as utopian because the "sites" from which this discourse emerges are not physical—they are not "places" one can visit in a literal manner. They are collections of text, pictures, and sounds. This is their limitation and their strength. The power of Internet protest is its placelessness. Recall the narrative at the beginning of this chapter, when Belgrade radio station B92 was forced from its offices and places of safety. Rendered vulnerable by Serbian authorities, the station could find refuge no place—online.

What are some of the components of utopian rhetoric online? As we have seen, *absurdity* is one powerful tool of protest. To reveal imperfections in the dominant system, many online communicators respond with comical rebukes that, through their humor, reveal a deeper pathos. Utopian protest also draws from the notion that *community* invokes a powerful response to entrenched power. Most utopian fictions attend carefully to the details of community maintenance if only because the gathering and keeping of potential utopians is so difficult. Third, utopian communication rests upon a firm foundation of *social order*, even when the apparent relationships between individuals appears to be free of government control. The most extreme example of utopia might be defined as anarchy, the removal of government from human affairs. However, even in a true state of anarchy, some moral order of prescribed human relations exists in the absence of the "state." Without some moral order, utopia is often replaced by its opposite, dystopia (bad place).

The social order evoked in online utopias seldom resembles the orders that we inhabit. The order of utopia is typically a radical alternative that reveals through its difference and distance from the contemporary world the corruption of the dominant worldview. In this sense, every basic term and referent that shapes our daily lives becomes a site of potential conflict.

## HYPERLINK: KATHY DALIBERTI'S CYBER-QUILT

In March 1995, David Daliberti and Bill Barloon, U.S. civilians, were imprisoned by the Iraqi government after they inadvertently entered the country. David's wife, Kathy, waited at home for news from the State Department concerning the whereabouts of her husband, for some word that her government was acting to free the prisoners.

Home, ordinarily a site of comfort and safety, only reminded Kathy of her inability to act on her husband's behalf. In response to her growing frustration as the government failed to secure her husband's release, she created a homepage called Yellow Ribbon. The Yellow Ribbon site worked on several levels to create an alternative space by recrafting the "home" as a public intersection of people and ideas, not a private and lonely abode. The homepage featured press releases, archived e-mail by visitors, and links where friends and concerned observers could send messages to government officials. Most intriguingly, however, was the site's depiction of the date and time in Baghdad. This device created a dual location of the homepage; it mirrored to some extent Kathy's home in Jacksonville, but it also symbolized David's temporary "home" in Iraq. In many ways, this conduit between Daliberti and her well-wishers was more than a cry for help. It was a protest against two governments.

The nature of this protest might remind you of early American quilts. While homey and comforting, the selection of patches often served political purposes.

Sometimes, those purposes were obscured by their simple design and lack of public display, but they served to provide voices to individuals kept from the public sphere:

> Freed from the isolating and controlling constraints of the structure, the quilt grows and connects, creating places of community on the very margins of power. Those who participate in its co-creation, even through the simple act of viewing, construct an alternative world—like the patches of the quilt that serve to recall distant times and places. (Wood & Adams, 1998, p. 227)

An example of a real quilt that further illustrates this principle is the NAMES project AIDS quilt. Not surprisingly, this physical commemoration of individuals who have lost their lives to the AIDS virus has an online version, too.

Looking back on our discussion of discursive resistance, which rhetorical approach did Kathy Daliberti take: Agonistic? Utopian? Perhaps a combination of the two?

Throughout our discussion of agonistic and utopian rhetorics, we have run the risk of confusing protest with analysis. Protest seeks to change an existing social system while analysis merely works to make sense out of the world. Many observers seeking to make sense of the Internet (and we may occasionally fall into this camp) run the risk of obscuring careful analysis with utopian rhetoric.

Kling (1996) responds to the perceived excesses in utopian and anti-utopian writings about computerization in our society by arguing that students of Internet communication should adopt a posture of social realism. According to Kling, **social realism** employs empirical data to examine computerization as it is actually practiced and experienced. The question of whether realism simply obscures a particular worldview is interesting, but beside the point. Critics of any worldview do not stop with analysis, they employ agonistic and utopian discourses to change it. In Web sites and other electronic modes of communication, these messages benefit from a potentially global audience. However, as hinted earlier, the intersection of agonistic and utopian rhetoric is not necessarily positive.

In the section that follows, we explore ways in which individuals and groups have attempted to subvert existing power structures by invoking ideal communities that you might very well find to be troubling. Some of the ideas and statements uttered in this section have been selected because of their controversial nature. Their inclusion does not signify identification from us, but rather our belief that the most frightening ideals found on the Internet should be recognized, not ignored.

## THE RHETORIC OF HATE ONLINE

> Our beloved country is waddling in the slime pits of corruption unlike anything since the dawn of civilization. If we don't speak up and act up, the het-

> erosexual civilization as we know it will vanish, and sooner then we think. (Lesbian Studies Institute, http://www.thundernet.org/legalize.html)

Before the emergence of electronic networks, the only place you might find a message like the one above would be a hastily mimeographed flyer handed out in a crowd or posted on a telephone pole. However, in January 2000, this message was available to anyone with an Internet connection. As you might imagine, this message—not a specific threat or provocation against a person or group, simply a hateful post on a Web site—is protected by the First Amendment. However, there are other messages online that are far more dangerous, other forms of discourse that have forced anti-hate groups to refashion themselves as Internet watchdogs.

You may be surprised to learn that anti-hate groups like the NAACP and the Anti-Defamation League are purchasing Web addresses that feature some of the most insulting epithets for persons and groups imaginable—so that no one can use them (Leibovich, 1999). Think of the worst word for a person that you can imagine, and you will likely find that it has been purchased as a domain name by some individual or entity. For some observers of Internet communication, this is the Internet's dark side, its growing use as a platform for hate speech.

FIG. 9.2. White Pride Logo found on Stromfront.org Web site.

At the beginning of 2000, most experts estimated that 500 hate Web sites could be found online (Etchingham, 2000). By mid-2000, that number had been revised upward to about 600. Of course, no one knows how many hate groups around the world use the Internet to communicate with one another. Encryption technology, uncategorized sites, and private intranets may hide countless other bigoted messages. No matter the number of sites, however, their presence worries a growing number of people.

What is a hate site? According to **HateWatch**, a community of volunteer activists who monitor the emergence of Internet resources employed by antisocial groups to disseminate their messages, a hate site:

> advocates violence against or unreasonable hostility toward those persons or organizations identified by their race, religion, national origin, sexual orientation, gender or disability. [This definition also includes] organizations or individuals that disseminate historically inaccurate information with regards to these persons or organizations for the purpose of vilification.

What makes hate sites worth our attention is their potential ability to incite violence in ways that cannot be mirrored by traditional hate speech (Zickmund, 1997).

According to the Anti-Defamation League, Internet communication provides five advantages to individuals and groups seeking to transmit messages of hate: community, anonymity, outreach, commerce, and information. Throughout this analysis, you might wish to draw from your knowledge of agonistic and utopian rhetoric because it appears that both are at play in these kind of sites.

## Community

Many hate groups use Internet communication to create or enhance a sense of community. Early in the 20th century, it was common—even fashionable—to be a public bigot in the United States. Many local communities and state governments included members of hate groups such as the Ku Klux Klan. Many historians argue that Klan messages found sympathetic ears in the federal government as well. Since the civil rights struggles of the 1960s, hate speech has become much less acceptable to most Americans. In the 1990s, the trend appeared to shift from established groups with sophisticated doctrines toward bedroom-based haters—individuals and small groups who had difficulty finding an audience for their messages. With the advent of the Internet, however, these cliques or cells of haters have discovered an ability to network among themselves—to fashion a sense, if not a reality, that they are not alone. Doing so, they craft a community that resists most people's notions of public life while seeking to construct a peculiar utopia.

## Anonymity

Hate communities who find themselves isolated by popular opinion and legislation maintain their ties through the anonymity provided by Internet communication. Certainly, any message posted online can potentially be tracked to its originator. However, it is a far less dangerous act to e-mail a hateful message or view a racist Web site from a public computer than to stand in the middle of a town square in a white robe and pointy hood. Matt Hale, Leader of the World Church of the Creator (http://www.creator.org/)—a hate group based in Peoria, Illinois—advocates use of the Internet to share racist rhetoric with people who might otherwise avoid his group: "a person can learn about our church without ever ordering one of our books or seeing one of our members. They can just learn through the screen" (Hale, 1997, n.p.).

This component of Internet communication appears to support the conclusion made by some scholars that a virtual community of strangers is more likely to spawn and tolerate radical voices than a physical community of intimates. A necessary aspect to online anonymity is the ability for hate-site originators to move from service provider to service provider. Visit any list of hate sites and you will find that more than half do not function. Like mushrooms that grow after a hard rain, radical Internet hate sites that appear to advocate violence seldom last for long. However, their creators do not necessarily cease their communication; they just find a new site on which to post their messages.

## Outreach

Some hate groups have begun using the Internet to seek new members often by crafting subtle appeals whose implications are difficult to discern. For example, a student doing research on Martin Luther King might be intrigued by a Web site entitled "Martin Luther King Jr.: A Historical Perspective." Its Web address (http://www.martinlutherking.org/) appears to be legitimate—maybe even owned by the King family or an institute dedicated to his memory. The first page includes an image of Dr. King in a thoughtful pose with children sitting nearby.

However, closer examination of this site reveals its true intent. Its "Truth about Dr. King" section derides the civil rights activist as "a sexual degenerate, an America-hating Communist, and a criminal betrayer." The site's "Recommended Books" section features a biography of David Duke, a notorious "White rights" advocate and former Klan leader.

### Commerce

Like most organizations, hate groups thrive on some level of commerce—if only to maintain access to ISPs, print newsletters, and purchase attire that marks their particular brand of community. Mail order centers and backroom shops hardly provide the customer base necessary to sustain a group of individuals whose views are shared by a minuscule percentage of the local population. However, Internet storefronts offering music, posters, books, and other paraphernalia may exploit a market of millions. The National Alliance (http://www.natall.com/) online store, for example, features 600 items including a poster depicting a blond-haired blue-eyed family as "Earth's Most Endangered Species." Commerce is essential to the body of hate groups around the world; Internet communication is an important artery.

### Information

The most potentially significant component of Internet communication embraced by hate groups is the proliferation of bomb-making information available to anyone with access to Web sites. In their report, Poisoning the Web, The Anti-Defamation League (1999) reported: "For those inclined to violence, the Net offers a wealth of information—from instructions on building an ammonium nitrate bomb to methods for converting semi-automatics to fully automatic weapons—that can be accessed in minutes" (n.p.).

As already discussed, there are relatively few hate sites available online—perhaps 500 to 600 are easily accessible. Yet, observers of radical rhetoric are concerned about their potential to spread their messages beyond a hard core following of social misfits. Many of these sites—most notably Stormfront—include "kids-only" pages with games, stories, and illustrations designed to teach children a disturbing view of racial identity. They attempt to accomplish their goal through a combination of agonistic and utopian rhetoric—rejecting social order and, simultaneously, envisioning a new one that horrifies most people. Perhaps, most importantly, the five advantages gained by hate groups that have turned to the Internet to communicate their messages—community, anonymity, outreach, commerce, and information—are unlikely to be overcome by regulation or legislation. For many observers of this phenomenon, the only way to overcome bad speech is to confront it with good speech. Of course, in a democratic society, the definitions of those terms can never be fixed for long.

## CHAPTER SUMMARY

In this chapter, we described a process of discursive resistance that emerges when disenfranchised individuals or groups seize or fashion spaces of tactical response to places of dominant discipline. We found that these sorts of communication may be defined as agonistic or utopian. Agonistic rhetoric refers to those sorts of discourse that confront a perceived failing in the social order through a dramatic and ritualized display that seeks purification through either an admission of guilt or casting of blame. The goal of agonistic rhetoric is a form of redemption of the corrupted place. Utopian rhetoric, in contrast, focuses its attention on alternative spaces—often by ignoring or demeaning the importance of "real places." By existing "no place," this form of discursive resistance does not face the same risk of confrontation. However, it does not ensure a high probability of success in a traditional sense. Finally, we turned to the dark side of Internet protest by examining the emergence of hate groups online. Although their numbers are small, their impact is felt throughout society.

## Online Communication and the Law

Is it legal to threaten someone using the Internet—and if not, what person, group, or agency should judge? Although there have been few cases that settle this issue, the question has generally hinged on various interpretations of First Amendment free speech provisions. However, when a man was sued in January 2000 for using the Internet to threaten someone, the case was not brought by the Justice Department; it was brought by the Department of Housing and Urban Development (HUD). What kind of speech would fall under their jurisdiction?

The story begins when Ryan Wilson allegedly created a Web site in response by efforts of Bonnie Jouhari to ensure that people trying to buy houses in the area would be protected by the Fair Housing Act. Imagine how you might feel if these words were posted on the Internet, referring to you: "traitors like this should beware, for in our day, they will be hung from the neck from the nearest tree or lamp post." The Web site is also reported to have featured images of Jouhari's office being blown up.

When the Justice Department failed to act, Jouhari turned to HUD, alleging that the Internet hate speech was directed against her efforts as a member of the Reading-Berks Human Relations Council in Reading, Pennsylvania—a group that fights housing discrimination. HUD sued, claiming that Wilson's site (now offline) is not protected by the First Amendment because it prevented her from enforcing the Fair Housing Act. In July 2000 a HUD judge ordered Wilson to pay Jouhari more than $1.1 million. The larger question raised by this case concerns the role of location and proximity in hate speech.

Although not referring to the specific site in question, American Civil Liberties Union lawyer Chris Hanson described a key distinction between immediate and mediated speech: "Saying 'I'm going to punch you in the nose' is something we think of as a threat when you are standing nose-to-nose with a person. But almost by definition, on the Net such a threat is less imminent"

(Clausing, 1999, n.p.). Of course, the question remains: How do we distinguish physical threats from virtual ones when the spheres of "real" and "virtual" human interaction continue to blur? As individuals and groups carve out new places cyberspace, that conundrum will only intensify.

## Glossary

**Ad-hoc communities**: Communities of individuals brought together by an unforeseen event.

**Agonistic communication**: Discourse that produces or invokes ritualized conflict with an established order.

**Discursive resistance**: A process through which text, oral, nonverbal communication, and other forms of meaning-making are employed to imagine alternatives to dominant power structures.

**Filtering software**: Software that limits access to certain Internet sites, often by comparing Web addresses requested by users against a directory of domains.

**Firewall**: Software and hardware barriers that regulate access between networks.

**Hate site**: Web site that advocates violence against or unreasonable hostility toward those persons or organizations identified by their race, religion, national origin, sexual orientation, gender, or disability.

**Intentional communities**: Planned organizations of individuals to accomplish some goal or maintain some lifestyle.

**Place**: A location which formalizes, authorizes, and renders permanent the processes through which dominant interests maintain their influence over individuals and groups.

**Space**: A tactical response to a place through individual or group rearticulation of its intended use.

**Social realism**: The use of empirical data to examine computerization as it is actually practiced and experienced.

**Utopianism**: Discourse that imagines an ideal world that is distant from the real world in time and/or place in order to critique the contemporary social order.

## Topics for Discussion

1. Visit Cyber Yugoslavia, a virtual community at http://www.juga.com/. Is this an example of agonistic or utopian rhetoric? Select three components of this Web site to support your case.

2. Conduct a Yahoo! search to find an insurgency group similar to the Zapatistas. Can you identify images or phrases that illustrate components of utopian rhetoric (absurdity, community, and social order)?

3. What are the necessary components of an effective online parody site? Visit one of the several Yahoo! parody sites available on the Web (such as "Yankovic!" at http://www.Yankovic.org). Which site seems to make its point most memorably? Write a one-paragraph statement that identifies your criteria for effective online parody.
4. Should online hate sites be banned by the federal government? Craft a one-page essay to support your answer. Draw from constitutional arguments, historical parallels, and a clearly stated ethical stance. Indicate which body of government, if any, should regulate online hate.
5. Of the five components of online hate sites described in this chapter (community, anonymity, outreach, commerce, and information), which one is most important to sustain a hate site? Review some of the sites mentioned in this chapter to support your findings.

## REFERENCES


Anti-Defamation League. (1999). *Poisoning the web: Hatred online.* <http://www.adl.org/frames/front_poisoning.html>.

Blair, C., Jeppeson, M. S., & Pucci, E. P., Jr. (1991). Public memorializing in postmodernity: The Vietnam veterans memorial as prototype. *Quarterly Journal of Speech, 77,* 263–288.

Borenstein, D. (2000). *Quoteland.com.* <http://www.quoteland.com>.

Cathcart, R. S. (1978). Movements: Confrontation as rhetorical form. *Southern Speech Communication Journal, 43*(3), 223–247.

Clausing, J. (1999, January 21). To fight hate speech online, U.S. turns to housing law. *The New York Times.* <http://www.nytimes.com/library/tech/yr/mo/cyber/cyberlaw/21law.html>.

Cleaver, H. M. (1995). *The zapatistas and the electronic fabric of struggle.* <http://www.eco.utexas.edu/faculty/Cleaver/zaps.html>.

Cleaver, H. M. (1998). The zapatista effect: The Internet and the rise of an alternative political fabric. *Journal of International Affairs, 51,* 621–636.

Coombs, W. T. (1998). The Internet as potential equalizer: New leverage for confronting social responsibility. *Public Relations Review, 24,* 289–305.

de Certeau, M. (1984). *The practice of everyday life* (S. Rendall, Trans.). Berkeley: University of California Press.

Die Jar Jar, Die. (1999). <http://www.geocities.com/Hollywood/Heights/5927/jarjar.html>.

Engardio, P. (1999, October 4). Activists without borders. *Business Week,* p. 144.

Etchingham, J. (2000, January 13). Welcome to the world of net racists. The *Times (London),* n.p.

Fabj, V. (1993). Motherhood as political voice: The rhetoric of the mothers of Plaza de Mayo. *Communication Studies, 44,* 1–18.

Hale, M. (1997). *An interview with Reverend Matt Hale.* HateWatch. <http://hatewatch.org/forum/HaleText.html

Kling, R. (1996, February 1). Hopes and horrors: Technological utopianism and anti-utopianism in narratives of computerization. *CMC Magazine*. <http://www.december.com/cmc/mag/1996/feb/kling.html>.

Lefebvre, H. (1991). *The production of space* (D. Nicholson-Smith, Trans.). Oxford: Basil Blackwell LTD.

Leibovich, M. (1999, December 15). A new domain for hate speech. *The Washington Post*, p. A1.

Plotnikoff, D. (1999, December 4). The closing of the Internet frontier is closer than you think. *San Jose Mercury News*. <http://www.mercurycenter.com/svtech/columns/modemdriver/docs/dp120599.htm>.

Toulmin, S. (1990). *Cosmopolis: The hidden agenda of modernity*. Chicago, IL: The University of Chicago Press.

Warf, B., & Grimes, J. (1997). Counterhegemonic discourses and the Internet. *The Geographical Review, 87*, 259–274.

Watson, R. (1995, February 27). When words are the best weapon. *Newsweek*, p. 36.

Wood, A., & Adams, T. (1998). Embracing the machine: Quilt and quilting as community-building architecture. In B. Ebo (Ed.), *Cyberghetto or cybertopia? Race, class, and gender on the Internet*. Westport, CT: Praeger.

Zickmund, S. (1997). Approaching the radical other: The discursive culture of cyberhate. In S. Jones (Ed.), *Virtual culture: Identity and communication in cybersociety* (pp. 185–205). Thousand Oaks, CA: Sage.

# CHAPTER 10

# Pop Culture and Online Expression

*The robot is going to lose. Not by much. But when the final score is tallied, flesh and blood is going to beat the damn monster.*
—*Adam Smith (Borenstein, 2000)*

Johnny sits amidst a cluttered room filled with keyboards and monitors. Boxes of exotic technology—virtual reality gloves, interface eye goggles, and the like—line the walls. He's in a hurry. Gangsters are racing to find him, to access the information stored in his brain. If they find him, the thugs won't ask for much—only his head. Johnny is a mnemonic courier; he carries data in a hard drive located where some of his brain tissue used to be.

Sirens wail outside in the distance as he "jacks in," entering the conceptual world of cyberspace. Manipulating digital objects with his gloved hands and peering into the online "city" with his eye goggles, Johnny races through a neon Las Vegas of information. He is searching for data that will help him escape, but other people search for him too. Thousands of miles away, a digital detective hits the online pavement looking for any clues about Johnny's whereabouts. Oblivious to the physical room that surrounds him, Johnny the mnemonic courier scrambles desperately from virtual building to virtual building—twisting his gloved figures to manipulate the metropolis of data pouring over him. Digital pathways and hideouts stretch outward in infinite directions, but his enemies are close behind.

The film, *Johnny Mnemonic* (Ahrenberg et al., 1995) sets the scene for this chapter's exploration of the ways in which CMC is depicted in film and literature. In a way, this chapter's topic culminates the purpose of this book. It is important that we evaluate more than the technology of Internet communication. We seek to explain ways in which people interpret this technology, using it to make sense of identities and cultures in a changing world. In this manner, this chapter explores the **popular culture** that shapes our understanding of Internet communication. As Brummett (1994) explained, "Popular culture refers to those systems or artifacts that most people share and that most people know about" (p. 21). **Artifacts** are bits and pieces of human sense-making: books, magazines, movies, advertisements, comics, and the like. Popular culture research is certainly controversial (Jacobson, 1999). The study, after all, of *Johnny Mnemonic* can hardly be compared to the study of Shakespeare or Hemingway—can it?

We propose that the distinction between high and low culture implicit in that comparison is not nearly as important as this question: How do most people reading this book make sense of Internet communication? Theories and research projects offer useful and refined insights to answer that question. Historical and journalistic efforts further help us contextualize that question. But we are certain that *most* people trying to interpret the changes that sweep through our society in this so-called Internet Age are more likely to make use of pop culture than any social scientific tools available. The stories we tell about ourselves and the changes we recognize in our culture, inspired by deep-rooted myths and images of human community, often take the form of throw-away communication—a movie that you might have seen to pass the time, a book that kept you company while sun-tanning at the beach, a song whose lyrics you can't quite recall. Each of these artifacts is formed and reformed each time we attempt to interpret the social world around us. Thus, we end this book with an analysis of some key themes that seem to shape popular conceptions of the Internet.

We begin by discussing the role of literature in shaping a response to the role of technology in our lives. Following this overview, we examine cyberpunk fiction and its examination of the manner in which humans and machines have become blurred in contemporary society. Drawing primarily from the fiction of William Gibson and Donna Haraway's notion of the "cyborg," we explore a world that looks vaguely like the future but actually serves to warn us about the present. Following a discussion of cyberpunk's ambivalent relationship to "the future," we outline three common themes to this literary form: rejection of flesh, fear of multinational corporations, and obsession with speed. Turning to film in popular culture, we first review significant movies that deal with technological themes before focusing on six "Internet-era" movies: *2001: A Space Odyssey*, *Tron*, *WarGames*, *Blade Runner*, *RoboCop* and *The Matrix*. A process that begins to unfold in these films, a collapse of human abilities to control their machines, seems to end with the obsolescence of humans to cultural narrative altogether. However, as the latter two movies indicate, popular culture artifacts have not given up on humanity's ability to control its machines quite yet. Ultimately, this chapter seeks to explore ways in which Internet communication is situated in a larger cultural discourse about an increasingly technological society.

## LITERARY DEPICTIONS OF TECHNOLOGY

Studying the impact of Internet communication on popular culture requires a brief discussion of the role of technology in literature (Dunn & Erlich, 1982). After all, popular literature is a central location where our cultural myths and assumptions are shaped. In the past two centuries, authors have attempted to make sense of the industrial revolution and its technological and social implications. Some, like H. G. Wells, proposed optimistic accounts of the potential for technology to resolve human problems and eliminate human weaknesses. However, many science fiction novelists offer a critique of that thesis. In the 19th century, Mary Shelley's *Frankenstein* warns of the risks that follow our use of technology to attain godlike powers. Ultimately, she demonstrates, we create monstrosities. Nathaniel Hawthorne's "Celestial Railroad" demonstrates how the use of technology, in this case a train on its way to heaven, only provides us illusory power and ultimately jeopardizes our very souls. Early in the 20th century, even our illusory powers over the machine began to be stripped away in literature such as E. M. Forster's "The Machine Stops," Karel Capek's *R.U.R.* (Rossum's Universal Robots) and Fredric Brown's "The Answer." Even Richard Brautigan's poem, "All Watched over by Machines of Loving Grace," contains, perhaps, some seeds of cynicism:

> I like to think (and
> the sooner the better!)
> of a cybernetic meadow
> where mammals and computers
> live together in mutually
> programming harmony
> like pure water
> touching clear sky.

A group of authors who launched a movement called *cyberpunk* have been quite successful in shaping our public concepts of technology and culture over the past two decades (Balsamo, 1995). **Cyberpunk** refers to a literary movement that took hold among many science fiction writers in the 1980s—its primary theme is the blurring distinction between humans and machines. As discussed later, some critics hold that cyberpunk no longer offers a coherent philosophy or critique in contemporary times. However, the question asked by cyberpunk authors remains critical in our day: What happens when our society gets all the things promised by pulp comics and Flash Gordon serials and science fiction novels?

Answering this question, cyberpunk authors took a somewhat dim view of the future, given that the present—yesterday's tomorrow—appears to have become a dehumanizing and dangerous time. They no doubt recalled the ringing promises of earlier visionaries who imagined 10-lane superhighways and nuclear-powered cities. Gleaming towers like the Emerald City of Oz were indeed depicted in popular advertisements for products as basic as automobile tires and life insurance in the 1930s and 1940s. The problem with these marvelous futures wasn't that they were an illusion; the problem is that they actually came true! Today, we face the consequences of those technological utopias: snarled traffic jams and environmental hazards. In a short story called the "Gernsback Continuum," Gibson (1981) writes:

> Dialta had said that the Future had come to America first, but had finally passed it by. But not here, in the heart of the Dream. Here, we'd gone on and on, in a dream logic that knew nothing of pollution, the finite bounds of fossil fuel, or foreign wars it was possible to lose. . . . Behind me, the illuminated city: searchlights swept the sky for the sheer joy of it. I imagined them thronging the plazas of white marble, orderly and alert, their bright eyes shining with enthusiasm for their floodlit avenues and silver cars. It had all the sinister fruitiness of Hitler propaganda. (p. 88)

In this piece, Gibson reveals a dangerous dimension to the technologically perfect world of tomorrow: The machines necessary to build that utopia have a nasty tendency of reprogramming the people who built them.

As discussed in chapter 9, Internet communication is frequently idealized as a utopian promise that ensures equal access to an **Encyclopedia Humanus**—a universal collection of all the knowledge generated by humankind. Cyberpunk is a critical response to the assumption that CMC is a humanizing influence on our society. "Cyber" refers to the impact of technology in its many forms on the human condition. The 1970s show, *The Six Million Dollar Man*, illustrates this dimension by depicting an astronaut who crashes his experimental aircraft and almost loses his life. Medical science is his only hope: "We can rebuild him. We can make him better than he was before . . . " Thanks to modern technology, he is rebuilt as a **cyborg**—part human and part machine, or as Haraway (1996) puts it: "a fusion of the organic and the technical forged in particular, historical, cultural practices" (p. 51). The cyborg-astronaut can run faster, see farther, and jump higher than another other man alive. However, the question emerges, is the astronaut a man or a machine?

Although the show rarely delved into the psychological and social implications of that conundrum (focusing, instead, on Steve Austin vs. Big Foot and similar episodes), the question resonates in an age when human physiology seems to be similar to a Swiss Army Knife—one piece goes bad, replace it with a new one. At what point does the knife (or person) cease to be what it was before? To put it a slightly different way, borrowing from a popular slogan a few years back: "Is it live or is it Memorex?" It's no surprise that the day these words are written, the University of California, Berkeley announced success in its attempts to link human cells to computer circuitry in a "bionic chip" (Abate, 2000, p. D1). We seem to be getting more "cyber" every day.

The second part of "cyberpunk" is, of course, *punk*. **Punk** refers to a range of antisocial movements in music, fashion, and literature. Grossberg (1986) describes how punk included a range of behaviors designed to challenge dominant assumptions about power by demystifying its trappings. Instead of looking sharp toward a glittering future, punk bands such as the Sex Pistols inspired youth to cut up their corporate logo t-shirts and mock their elders' sanctimonious statements about doing it, "my way." Punks responded: "We're the future. Your future!"

Of course, the notion of the antiestablishment gadfly flaunting tradition and questioning authority is not so new. Socrates drank hemlock for challenging the city fathers of Athens 25 centuries ago. However, cyberpunks appeared to address a contemporary problem that had not been imagined before: What happens when the far-fetched promises of science fiction stories about the power of technology to change the human condition become possible? How can we confront the impact of a computer-mediated society whose members seem increasingly more alienated from each other? In this form of literature, punks respond as outlaws, hackers, castaways, and victims might; they use the system for their own purposes. They make do in a world not of their making.

Cyberpunk, therefore, is an ironic response to contemporary life—a play on the notion that a computerized society is necessarily a better one. No one story can adequately incorporate all of the themes suggested by this literary movement. Cyberpunk, like its musical punk predecessors, is at first a style rather than a coherent message. As Sterling (1986) observes, "the work of the cyberpunks is paralleled throughout Eighties pop culture: in rock video; in the hacker underground; in the jarring street tech of hip-hop and scratch music; in the synthesizer rock of

London and Tokyo" (pp. xi–xii). The lyrics or the moves are dissimilar, but the attitude is uncanny. Knarf (1998) maintains the alt.cyberpunk FAQ file that defines cyberpunk style:

> The setting is urban, the mood is dark and pessimistic. Concepts are thrown at the reader without explanation, much like new developments are thrown at us in our everyday lives. There is often a sense of moral ambiguity; simply fighting "the system" (to topple it, or just to stay alive) does not make the main characters "heroes" or "good" in the traditional sense. (n.p.)

Some historians of the movement claim that cyberpunk began in 1980 with Bruce Bethke's short story of the same name. Most agree that its most prolific and well-known contributors were Gibson and Sterling. The irony is that few authors would actually classify themselves as being cyberpunk. This makes sense given a fundamental anti-authoritarianism that animates so much of their writing.

Some critics respond that cyberpunk died with the 1995 release of *Johnny Mnemonic* (described in the introduction to this chapter). The demise of the cyberpunk "movement" might be traced 2 years earlier when "punk rocker" Billy Idol released his homage to computer-mediated rebellion, "Cyberpunk." Either way, Kroker and Kroker (1996) write that cyberpunk, once the literary hideout for social outcasts bent on revealing the contradictions of techno-utopia, sold itself out with the release of bland and soulless entertainment that seemingly perpetuated everything contested by "the movement." Predictably, "real" hackers have responded that plenty of rebels remain to resist dominant culture, no matter what the critics say.

Why talk about cyberpunk today? For the same reason that one explores any literary form, even when written decades or centuries ago—cyberpunk is worth our attention because of its contemporary nature. Unlike traditional science fiction and fantasy that wraps its intended critique of dominant culture in a narrative isolated in distant space or time, cyberpunk fiction attempted to locate its people and technology in the near present. Its rhetoric lay in a rejection of some distant future where social problems are magically resolved.

What specifically were cyberpunks rejecting? Think back to re-runs of Gene Roddenbury's *Star Trek*. Set in the 23rd century, the show revealed an optimistic future. How the people of Earth formed a cooperative world government and began to explore the stars is occasionally referenced, but never in much detail. In contrast, cyberpunk places its audience in the near future or what might be termed the hyper-present: a contemporary time that seems a bit faster than our own experience—as the *Max Headroom* television series puts it: "20 minutes into the future" (Warner Brothers, 1999). In his essay, "The Future? You Don't Want to Know" Sterling (1995) claims that cyberpunk authors fear dating "the future" because so much of it has already come to pass—much faster than we ever could have anticipated.

> If we can't control the future—if we can't make it do what we want—what is there left to say or do about it? We're all hip to nonlinearity now—anyone with two brain cells knows that the future is unpredictable, even in principle. Science fiction writers still like to jabber about it, and they are more reckless than a lot of other basement prophets because they have so very little to lose. But why say anything? The crystal ball's as cracked and clouded as the ozone layer. Who are we kidding? (p. 152)

More than 5 years after this piece was written, our collective faith in the future seems no more solid than it did in the 1980s or 1990s. Worse, it seems that we can longer keep up with the present, much less can we anticipate tomorrow. As Jurek (1991) writes: "Velocity can be calculated, the pliability of entrails cannot" (p. 85). Some of the more radical visions of cyberpunk authors remain in the realm of fiction, or in the future. But several themes remain significant to our understanding of the role of computer technology in popular culture.

We propose three common themes to cyberpunk fiction and provide some examples from Gibson's (1984/1991) *Neuromancer* to illustrate them. It is hard to overestimate the impact of this award-winning book on popular culture. Authors striving to make sense out of computer technology return to this literary totem in search of guidance. Moreover, as Conklin (1987) notes, *Neuromancer* may be responsible for our contemporary notions of hypertext, the underlying principle of the World Wide Web. The novel (part of a trilogy of cyberpunk literature) follows the attempts by Case, a hacker who has been cut from the net of computerized information and hunts desperately for a way back in—only to discover the matrix of information might be a conscious entity with its own agenda. *Neuromancer* demonstrates primary themes of cyberpunk literature: (a) human flesh is weak in comparison to computer technology, (b) corporate dominance of social life is enabled by computer technology, and (c) the pace of human life is increasing beyond our ability to adapt.

## The Weakness of Human Flesh

The constant refrain in cyberpunk fiction is the sense that human beings cannot possibly continue to exist as we do in a world dominated by machines. We have two choices: We may become outlaws who slip through the digital cracks and live our lives on the run from various forms of surveillance, or, we must integrate machines into our flesh and thinking processes. Choosing that path, we discover that human flesh is a poor substitute for pure machinery. One scene from *Neuromancer* first illustrates this concept:

> Ratz was tending bar, his prosthetic arm jerking monotonously as he filled a tray of glasses with draft Kirin. He saw Case and smiled, his teeth a webwork of East European steel and brown decay. . . . His ugliness was the stuff of legend. In an age of affordable beauty, there was something heraldic about his lack of it. The antique arm whined as he reached for another mug. It was a Russian military prosthesis, a seven-function force-feedback manipulator, cased in grubby pink plastic. (p. 65)

A corollary to this literary rejection of the flesh is its cyberspatial counterpart, the glorification of noncorporeal existence. Losing access to this virtual paradise results in an almost biblical punishment:

> For Case, who'd lived for the bodiless exultation of cyberspace, it was the Fall. In the bars he'd frequented as a cowboy hotshot, the elite stance involved a certain relaxed contempt for the flesh. The body was meat. Case fell into the prison of his own flesh. (p. 67)

In *Neuromancer*, as in many cyberpunk fictions, CMC is more than a way to access data; it is freedom from social constraint and power to act in a world of powerful forces. Therefore, it is not surprising that Case's experience of the matrix is shaped explicitly by corporations.

## The Power of the Wired Corporation

As discussed in chapter 7, corporations of all types find their interests converging and the abilities to impact our daily lives increasing thanks to the integration of computer technology into homes and businesses. Cyberpunk fiction offers a stinging rebuke to this trend by frequently painting multinational corporations and their "artificial intelligence" agents as enjoying privileges to transgress or simply ignore laws that bind persons of lower socioeconomic class. One quotation from *Neuromancer* suffices:

> Now he slept in the cheapest coffins, the ones nearest the port, beneath the quartz-halogen floods that lit the docks all night like vast stages; where you couldn't see the lights of Tokyo for the glare of the television sky, not even the towering hologram logo of the Fuji Electric Company, and Tokyo Bay was a black expanse where gulls wheeled above drifting shoals of white styrofoam. Behind the port lay the city, factory domes dominated by the vast cubes of corporate arcologies. (p. 68)

The punk aesthetic of this literary form is to reveal the broad range of corporate control manifested by vast buildings, huge expanses, and endless cyberspace. One imagines the digital Las Vegas of computer-generated buildings representing "lattices of logic," but their shapes and colors are strictly copyrighted—their accumulated knowledge jealously guarded. As discussed in the next section, at least one corporation finds insight from this notion of mediated dominance. However, we first turn to a third theme of cyberpunk literature: the computer-mediated acceleration of human experience.

## The Pace of Human Life

It is a timeless complaint; the times are changing faster than our ability to adapt. Futurist Alvin Toffler (1971) coined a term **futureshock** to account for an increasingly common sense that technological change is accelerating an a revolutionary, and potentially dangerous, pace. More recently, Bertman (1998) and Gleick (1999) returned to this argument with more contemporary evidence. In *Neuromancer*, we see this theme most powerfully:

> Night City was like a deranged experiment in social Darwinism designed by a bored researcher who kept one thumb permanently on the fast-forward button. Stop hustling and you sank without a trace, but move a little too swiftly and you'd break the fragile surface tension of the black market; either way, you were gone, with nothing left of you but some vague memory . . . (pp. 68–69)

The pace of life in a computer-mediated—and dominated society—appears in cyberpunk literature as a prime cause of the disembodiment of humankind and the rise of corporate structures and artificial intelligence. As is seen in the forthcoming section, this transition appears frequently in popular film.

Visions of computer technology in literature have historically struggled to strike a balance between utopianism and dystopianism. However, with the apparent increase in state and corporate influence over our daily lives, rebellious movements like cyberpunk warned of a near future in which our bodies might be devalued by machines, our lives controlled by wired corporations, and our lives overwhelmed by accelerating change. In this way, popular culture provides a site where Internet communication is reinterpreted within historical and political contexts. However, fewer and fewer people appear to gain their cultural identities in literature.

That doesn't mean that people have stopped reading! Only that, for most contemporary readers, Scott Adams' *Dilbert* cartoon resonates more clearly than any story or novel. As Aden (1999) notes, *Dilbert* provides a therapeutic response to millions of cubical dwellers literally and technologically isolated from their colleagues, yet under constant surveillance by their bosses. How might these corporate drones climb the walls of their cubicles and, if they do, can only a vestige of humane society be found? Adams offers a humorous, but ultimately pessimistic view. In one strip that ran in February 2000, Asok the intern announces that he's created a "prison Morse code" so that he and Wally can communicate. Tapping on the cubical wall, Wally responds: "I sent you e-mail." An example of pop culture literature at its most transitory, Dilbert illustrates the power of throw-away communication to mock a computer-mediated society.

Of course, popular film offers an even more powerful way to define and contest images of computer technology. Sitting in darkened theaters (more than in our living rooms) film can overwhelm our senses with striking images that affix themselves long after the popcorn is stale. Despite the advent of cable and the promise of high definition television, cinematic approaches toward our rapidly computerized society maintain their central role in popular culture.

## POPULAR FILM AND TECHNOLOGY

With the introduction of cinema to popular culture, we find another medium through which society confronts a growing sense that computer technology contains both utopian and dystopian implications. Fritz Lang's *Metropolis* set the scene with its dreary machine-city that sucks the life out of its inhabitants. In contrast to the 1936 film version of H. G. Wells' *The Shape of Things to Come,* with its depiction of a new world built with the aid of powerful machines over the ashes of the old, many films since *Metropolis* wrestled with the downside of technology. That same year, as discussed in chapter 7, Charlie Chaplin released *Modern Times*—a depiction of the dehumanizing use of "tele-screens" and assembly lines to control human beings. One imagines that many of these films, with their threats of mechanical tyranny wielded by an all-powerful state or corporation (or both), were a severe indictment of the fascist movements gaining strength in Europe and some sympathy in the United States.

After World War II, communism replaced fascism as the primary threat to U.S. society and monster movies replaced technological **dystopias** as the major means to confront our cultural fears. However, by 1968, an increasingly digitized culture re-emerged as a common theme. Stanley Kubrick's (1968) *2001: A Space Odyssey*—more than Arthur C. Clarke's novel—paints computer technology as an empty, soulless force that forces the evolution of humankind or portends its destruction.

Michael Crichton's film, *Westworld*, anticipating many themes of his wildly popular *Jurassic Park* movies, envisioned a fantasy world "where nothing can go wrong." Of course, in that film and in its later incarnations, things always seem to go wrong when you trust machines to do the work of people. Even *The Right Stuff*, a 1983 film that narrated the struggles of U.S. astronauts to win the Space Race against the Russians, addressed the theme of looming technological influence over humanity as humans pushed their machines closer and closer to the "envelope" of endurance.

In this section, however, we focus on "Internet-Age" films—movies released since the advent of the Internet. We cheat a bit by discussing in more detail Stanley Kubrick's *2001* (which appeared months before the construction of the first Internet in 1969) before outlining the impact of *Tron*, *WarGames*, *Blade Runner*, *RoboCop*, and *The Matrix* on popular conceptions of Internet communication. Other films (and, in some cases, more popular films) could be argued to deserve inclusion in this list: *The Lawnmower Man*, *The Net*, *Hackers*, and *Enemy of the State*. But we have chosen those movies whose technology themes were the most significant in their time. Notice that although virtually every film involves a theme of humans and their use of technology—either to explore the universe or control other people—each film raises the troubling question of whether our machines actually control us.

## *2001: A Space Odyssey*: Confronting Technology

Since its release in 1968, Stanley Kubrick's *2001: A Space Odyssey* has confounded its viewers. As some critics have noted, *2001* is a Rorschach film blot; when you stare at it closely, you end up studying your own assumptions about the world. The film illustrates the role of computer technology in the transformation (or potential obsolescence) of humankind. Starting with the depiction of how an alien monolith is responsible for the evolution of humans from their pre-historic ancestors, *2001* narrates in stark detail (and even starker acting) the voyage of the Discovery spacecraft to Jupiter's moons where another monolith awaits. On the way, the ship's crew confronts its own computer, HAL 9000, which apparently has other plans. When Mission Commander Dave Bowman leaves the ship to recover the body of his colleague who is killed by HAL, a central crisis to the film ensues:

Dave: Open the pod bay doors, HAL.
HAL: I'm sorry Dave, I'm afraid I can't do that.
Dave: What's the problem?
HAL: I think you know what the problem is just as well as I do.
Dave: What are you talking about, HAL?
HAL: This mission is too important for me to allow you to jeopardize it.
Dave: I don't know what you're talking about, HAL.
HAL: I know that you and Frank were planning to disconnect me, and I'm afraid that's something I cannot allow to happen.

Bowman's ingenuity allows him to overcome HAL. But he cannot overcome the voiceless and inscrutable monolith, an alien technology infinitely more advanced than humankind's feeble machinery or intellect. When Bowman attempts to land on the device, he falls into a sort of intergalactic "grand central station" where he winds up on his own deathbed, only to be reborn as a "star child." *2001* matters because of its depiction of computer technology as simultaneously an engine of human growth and an obstacle to human expression. Its conclusion, confusing to most viewers, is designed to suggest that humanity has ultimately triumphed over its machines, but only by becoming something more than human. As is seen here, even this bleak narrative appears to be optimistic when compared to some later films.

## *Tron*: Taking on the Master Control Program

Disney's foray into computer animation resulted in *Tron* (Ellenshaw, Kushner, & Miller, 1982) a significant advance in the use of computer technology to make movies. The plot, such as it is, features a computer program designer, Kevin Flynn, trapped in a parallel-digital universe where computer programs take human form. In this pseudo-cyberspace, the malevolent Master Control Program forces his fellow software agents to forego allegiance to their human masters ("users") or risk destruction ("de-rezzing") in various forms of gladiatorial combat. In haste to escape this digital underground and free the subjugated programs, Flynn and his virtual friend, Yori, discover a security program, Tron:

| | |
|---|---|
| Kevin Flynn: | It's time I level with you. I'm what you guys call a "user." |
| Yori: | You're a user? |
| Kevin Flynn: | I took a wrong turn somewhere. |
| Tron: | If you ARE a user, then everything you've done has been according to a plan, right? |
| Kevin Flynn: | Ha, ha, ha, you WISH! Well, you guys know what it's like. You just keep doing what it looks like you're supposed to be doing no matter how crazy it seems. |
| Tron: | That's the way it is for programs, yes. |
| Kevin Flynn: | I hate to disappoint you, pal, but that's the way it is for users, too. |
| Tron: | Stranger and stranger . . . |

*Tron's* blurring of human and machine occurs on multiple levels. Most directly, Flynn is seized by the Master Control Program, digitized, and dropped into the computer network. More importantly, computer programs are said to possess the same emotions and drives as people. It's not a giant leap from that supposition to claim that humans might act like machines from time to time. However, to researchers such as Lippert (1996), *Tron* represents more than a journey into the workings of a machine; the film represents "dominant culture"—a vision of social forces that shape our lives, yet cannot be altered: "absolute Cartesian space divided by abstract linear coordinates, or irradiated light neither reflected nor blocked by anything solid" (p. 266). Chances are that *Tron*'s target audience viewed the film as a pleasant diversion and could hardly be expected to adopt Lippert's perspective. However, the power of the film to introduce a cultural notion of unchecked computer power is hard to deny. *Tron* matters because it re-tells the common story of human versus machine in a new way. This time, in order to beat the program, one must *become* a program.

### Hyperlink: "Invasion of the Dots"

Black spheres fall from the sky, crashing into the street, setting cars aflame, sending business-suit clad victims fleeing for their lives. It's not an alien invasion or the setting of the next Stephen King novel—it's "Invasion of the Dots," a clever advertisement run by Sun Microsystems whose slogan is, "We're the dot in .com." Leaf through any mass market magazine and you'll find dozens of advertisements for computers, peripherals, or Internet services. Not too surprisingly, few of these ads offer a critique of the new economy. But some, like this one, play on a culturally shared fear that computer technology is somehow growing faster than we'd like. Like the film, *Tron*, these images depict a machine that is no longer under our control. An excerpt from the copy: "LOOK, UP IN THE SKY. It's a whole new dot-conomy! It's an INVASION OF INGENUITY, powered by technology that seems OTHERWORLDLY . . . " Designed like a 1950s monster movie, the Sun ad plays on shared fears about the power of technology to alter our lives even as it sells its computer product.

In 1984, Apple Computer was less ambivalent about its role in contemporary society. In a classic advertisement directed by *Blade Runner*'s Ridley Scott, Apple (2000/1984) portrayed IBM computer users as corporate drones under the watchful eye of a "big brother" like character. In the midst of this oppressive environment, a woman runs toward the tele-screen and smashes it with a hammer. The voiceover announces: "On January 24th, Apple Computer will introduce the Macintosh. And you'll see why 1984 won't be like *1984*."

The ad aired only once, during Super Bowl XVIII. But its impact was unmistakable. Real-life "corporate drones" recognized themselves in that ad, and wished they could trade places with the lithe runner who smashed the system. The fact that she was merely selling another kind of computer (albeit, a computer "for the rest of us") was elegantly understated. We do not include this discussion because advertisements are a site where popular culture routinely and obviously works out its contradictions. Rather, we point your attention to artifacts like magazine ads precisely because they attempt to *eliminate* traces of the ideological clash so explicitly stated in other forms of human expression—but can't quite succeed in doing so. As you thumb through a magazine, try to look between the images and slogans to discern the subtle messages about technology in popular culture. They may be hidden, but they're out there.

## *WarGames*: Is It a Game or Is It Real?

As the tagline reads, *WarGames* (Goldberg, Hashimoto, & Schneider, 1983) focuses on the struggle for individuals to convince a computer network to abandon its plans to start World War III. *WarGames* introduced most people to the image of the computer hacker, capable of controlling machines through clever phone tricks. Although the actual habits (and capabilities) of hackers are portrayed none too literally in the film, a generation of computer enthusiasts trace their obsession with software and networking technology at least in part to this groundbreaking film. The main character, David Lightman, initiates the movie's crisis by tapping into a defense department super computer. Innocently asking it to play a "game" of thermonuclear war, David is shocked to discover that the machine believes his commands are real. Setting the countdown for doomsday, David and his girlfriend race to stop the machine who clearly has little regard for human decision making. You want a war, the machine seems to decide: I'll give you a war.

David Lightman: Is this a game or is it real?
Joshua (the computer): What's the difference?

*WarGames* contributes to the evolving cinematic depiction of computer technology by switching the roles between computers and machines. Mirroring literary uses of this theme by such authors as Isaac Asimov ("The Evitable Conflict") and Arthur C. Clarke ("The Nine Billion Names of God"), *WarGames* depicts most of its human characters as hopelessly foolish. Only the machine can discern the lesson of this deadly game: "The only winning move is not to play." Tragically for cinematic humanity, the machine isn't so humane in *Terminator 2: Judgment Day* (1991) when the military computer network, "SkyNet," kills 3 billion people. However, a common theme remains: Computer technology in film has begun to dispense with human decision making. Machines now act like people, exhibiting childlike wisdom in the case of *WarGames* or willful self-preservation in the case of *Terminator*. The result: the obsolescence of human beings.

## *Blade Runner*: More Human than Human

Where cyberpunk fiction and popular film converged most impressively was Ridley Scott's 1982 film noir classic, *Blade Runner* (Deeley et al., 1982). The film features a sparse plot set in Los Angeles of the near future, a site where "replicants" have escaped an "off world colony" to seek their maker, Dr. Eldon Tyrell. Although his corporation's motto is "More human than human," Tyrell's replicants are hobbled by a 4-year life span. The film, with its gritty depiction of near-future urban life, focuses on a somewhat pedestrian series of chases and close encounters as Rick Deckard, the Blade Runner, is dispatched to "retire" the replicants. However, the film gains significance when one of these machine-humans, Roy Batty, confronts Tyrell.

Tyrell: I'm surprised you didn't come here sooner.
Roy: It's not an easy thing to meet your maker.
Tyrell: What could he do for you?
Roy: Can the maker repair what he makes?

As the movie settles into its inevitable struggle between the replicant and the Blade Runner, the plot careens toward an unexpected outcome: Perhaps Deckard *himself* is a replicant—the ultimate shadow identity. The notion of machines stalking machines in a world in which most humans could easily be confused for animals may not be so far-fetched. Davis (1999) described the "high-tech police death squads" of 2029 Los Angeles as "not fantasies, but merely extrapolations from the present" (p. 155). But the most troubling question for humanity remains:

Rachael: "Have you ever retired a human by mistake?"
Deckard: "No."
Rachael: "But in your position that is a risk, isn't it?"

Ridley Scott's *Blade Runner*, loosely based on Philip K. Dick's novel *Do Androids Dream of Electric Sheep*? challenges the viewer to confront a society in which machines and people have blurred to such an extent that neither can truly be considered human by traditional standards.

## *RoboCop* and *The Matrix*: Ghosts in the Machine

Finally we turn briefly to a pair of films that propose a gradual pulling away from the brink of computer-mediated inhumanity: *RoboCop* (Davison et al., 1987) and *The Matrix* (Berman et al., 1999). Paul Verhoeven's (1987) *RoboCop* envisions another gritty city; this time, it's Detroit, a town overrun by criminals and controlled by a ruthless corporation, Omni Consumer Products (OCP). The plot follows the tragedy of a cop, Alex Murphy, who is gunned down by a gang of thugs—but rebuilt by OCP in the form of a cyborg, RoboCop. Significantly, the film emphasizes Murphy's struggle to retain some sense of humanity despite his mostly artificial body. When an OCP scientist is asked RoboCop's name, he snaps: "Let me make something clear to you. He doesn't have a name. He has a program. He's product." However, by the conclusion of the film, Murphy reclaims his humanity by beating a machine said to be even more powerful than he is.

More recently, Andy Wachowski and Larry Wachowski's (1999) *The Matrix*, captured the public imagination with its clever effects and optimistic view of humanity's ability to overcome computer technology. The film, set 200 years in future, depicts all of humankind as being struck in a "matrix"—an artificial world shaped by a computer network—designed to lull them into submission. Throughout the film, Neo, the protagonist, struggles to come to grips with the fact that his entire life is merely a digital prison. However, after being freed from the Matrix and taught to manipulate its power, Neo prepares to strike back against the machine:

> I know you're out there. I can feel you now. I know that you're afraid—afraid of us. You're afraid of change. I don't know the future. I didn't come here to tell you how this is going to end. I came here to tell how it's going to begin. I'm going to hang up this phone, and then show these people what you don't want them to see. I'm going to show them a world without you. A world without rules or controls, borders or boundaries. A world where anything is possible. Where we go from there is a choice I leave to you.

Arching from Kubrick's bleak *2001* to the Wachowski brothers' *Matrix*, it is hard to discern whether film provides any conclusion about the role of computers in contemporary society. But it is certain that these movies provide cultural totems where many people attempt to make sense out of the emerging wired-world.

### HYPERLINK: WHAT ABOUT VIRTUAL REALITY?

Doesn't virtual reality (VR) provide a setting to reinterpret the role of computer technology in our lives? For years, scholars have argued that VR will allow us to immerse ourselves in cyber-realities and expand our ability to experience artificial worlds (Hayles, 1993; Lanier & Biocca, 1992). However, the fully interactive worlds that whet the appetites of computer-philes have yet to emerge except in the form of expensive video games and high-tech experimentation—and, of course, *The Matrix*. For the rest of us, VR is a more figurative than literal experience. Even so, some video games are increasingly effective in crafting environments that draw players into their digital realms. Anyone who has lost a weekend playing a simulation game knows how immersive these games can be.

Games like *SimCity 3000* and *The Sims*, both created by Maxis, enable players to vicariously play the roles of mayors of their own towns—or, more intriguingly, become virtual deities who shape the lives of human beings. Laying virtual water lines, zoning artificial airports, or instructing a digital person to take a shower may not seem to have much cultural impact. Indeed, these games might merely represent an isolated activity through which persons create worlds rather than inhabit their own "real" lives. However, as the popularity of these computer simulations continues to grow, we might discover that these cyber-communities provide a therapeutic response to our increasingly technological society. As with books, films, and television shows that depict fictional struggles between humans and machines, VR games—both real or conceptual—provide the opportunity for people to "play" with machines, and perhaps rediscover the sense that while they cannot fully control technology, technology doesn't fully control them either.

## CHAPTER SUMMARY

Exploring films such as *2001: A Space Odyssey*, *Tron*, *WarGames*, *Blade Runner*, *RoboCop*, and *The Matrix*, one discerns a growing pessimism with the potential for humans to use machines in any meaningful way. *2001* envisions a form of human evolution through contact with alien technology, but one is never quite sure if humanity will retain any features that we might recognize. *Tron* adds personality to the machine, an apparently inscrutable device in Kubrick's film, and predictably allows humanity to triumph over the computer threat—but only by forcing the individual to become a machine. *WarGames* expands on the growing obsolescence of humanity by depicting people as too foolish to control their machines or themselves. A year before, however, *Blade Runner*, dispensed with humans altogether by introducing a protagonist who kills androids but is probably an android himself. Still, there is room for optimism. *RoboCop*, a bloody and disturbing fantasy about the corporate use of cyborg technology, concludes that even a human-machine hybrid can claim a sense of humanity. Finally, *The Matrix*, explores in a most contemporary way how humanity may yet overcome the sense that computers control our physical worlds and even shape our dreams.

Certainly, no typology of film themes can maintain itself for long; plenty of films offer messages that contradict this narrative, refigure it, or ignore it entirely. But these movies, landmarks in their own way, can arguably be said to have done more to shape our cultural understanding of technology than any others in the last three decades. Their messages, although sometimes unpleasant, intersect and affect the way we communicate online even today.

In this chapter, we've "gone meta." Going meta refers to the notion of **meta-communication**: communication about communication. In other words, we haven't limited our analysis to the functional uses of CMC to facilitate or hinder human expression and sense-making. We've turned our analytical gaze onto computers as texts that demand interpretation and invite re-readings. Rather than simply accepting the common notion that computer technology is changing popular culture—perhaps for better, maybe for worse—we've attempted to discern the themes that animate various forms of popular response to this technology. Books, films, and television shows are each challenged by this channel of discourse in some way. The fact that you can download a novel, view a DVD movie on your computer and get CNN headlines on a digital assistant surely indicates that traditional media must accommodate Internet communication. But, as we've seen, they also provide the means to articulate and interrogate common assumptions about computer technology.

Throughout our journey, a common question has emerged: How might popular culture shape our understanding and articulation of computer technology? Today's software engineers grew up on *Tron* and *Blade Runner* and William Gibson. The images and notions inspired by these artifacts of popular culture have infiltrated themselves into commercials, magazine advertisements, musical styles, and clothing accessories. Trying to build and update a world-girdling communications network is not simply a matter of physics or mathematics or even engineering. Computer technology is, at heart, an attempt to manipulate abstract data with physical tools. In a way similar to our use of a graphical user interface to move bits from sector to sector, popular manifestations of the machine informs the ways in which designers make sense out of their own work and articulate future innovations. For that reason, we challenge you to read popular culture closely. For the visions of computer technology you find there may indeed come to pass.

## Online Communication and the Law

Artifacts of popular culture like the film and literature examples cited in this chapter help us to interpret the world around us. We have already discussed how this function is performed in helping us deal with misgivings that we share about the role of technology in our lives. The entertainment industries also seem to offer ways for us to better understand health care, police work, and the law, among other fields of influence we encounter. In recent years, even as our society has seemingly grown more litigious, we have witnessed a rise in the popularity of legally themed television series like the reality-based *Judge Judy*, the comedic *Ally McBeal*, and the dramatic *Law and Order*. Yet when it comes to making credible portrayals of anything as intricate and changing as the law, the talented people who write for television, film, and the print media may not all be as well versed in the small details of legal practice as they might wish to be.

That is where the influence of the Internet might be felt once again, by connecting those with the legal know-how with those with the stories to tell. Stacey Grossman, a New York attorney who has worked with such celebrities as Joan Collins, operates Legal Fiction, a dot com that provides technical advice on legal matters to writers (Kaplan, 2000). For fees ranging from $25 to several thousands of dollars, Grossman or one of the lawyers connected with her enterprise will consult with an author, answering simple questions of legal practice or reviewing entire manuscripts for the legal realism. "I just had the idea that it was not necessary to charge writers who need advice on legal plots an attorney's hourly rate," Grossman says (Balestier, 2000).

An operation like Legal Fiction is just one more example of how technology, the law, and the larger culture are increasingly entwined. In previous "Online Communication and the Law" selections, we have seen how online behavior affects the law and, conversely, how the law seeks to affect online behavior. With services like Legal Fiction added to the mixture, we can see how the presence of online communication affects culture even beyond that which is directly communicated through the Internet as a medium. Certainly, there are other "behind-the-scenes" uses of mediating technology that influence the production of our shared culture, but we offer this one example to demonstrate just how pervasive, and innovative, online communication has become. It is also a reminder of just how unobtrusively online communication may help to shape our lives in the years to come.

## Glossary

**Artifacts**: Bits and pieces of human sense-making: books, magazines, movies, posters, comics, and the like.

**Cyberpunk**: 1980s literary movement whose primary theme is the blurring distinction between humans and machines.

**Cyborg**: Mechanical blurring of human and machine, illustrated by the 1970s show, *The Six Million Dollar Man*.

**Dystopia**: Opposite of utopia; it is a "bad place."

**Encyclopedia Humanus**: A universal collection of all the knowledge generated by human kind.

**Futureshock**: Term coined by Alvin Toffler to describe the results of excessive innovation and social change.

**Gernsback Continuum**: An alternative universe that exists along side our own—and occasionally intersects with our "real" world through artifacts such as comics, novels, films, and other forms of human communication.

**Meta-communication**: Communication about communication.

**Popular culture**: System of artifacts that shape our common understanding of the world.

**Punk**: A range of antisocial movements in music, fashion, and literature.

## Topics for Discussion

1. Join a small group of film buffs in your class and view Fritz Lang's (1926) *Metropolis* and H. G. Wells' (1936) *Things to Come*. Construct a list of themes about the role of computers and machines in our daily lives. Which film seems more similar to our contemporary experiences of public life?
2. Go to your library and pick up (or request) a copy of Sterling's (1986) *Mirrorshades Anthology* and read William Gibson's "The Gernsback Continuum"—an ironic response to technological optimists. Then take a walk through your downtown. Can you find artifacts of the American-that-never-was as described by Gibson?
3. Go to the Dilbert Zone (available online at http://www.dilbert.com/) and examine 2 weeks of Scott Adams' comic strip about corporate life. Generate a list of themes or motifs related to technology appearing in *Dilbert*. Does Adams' contribution to pop culture provide any means of resistance to the computer-mediated workplace?
4. View the director's cut of Ridley Scott's (1982) *Blade Runner*. Beyond the director's vision for this film there continues to be debate within the fan community about whether Rick Deckard is indeed a replicant. Search for clues to indicate his true nature and write a paragraph outlining why you think he is either a man or a machine.
5. While offering vastly different qualities of writing and execution, *Tron* and *The Matrix* provide strikingly similar plots. A group of outcasts searches for a chosen one (a security program in *Tron* and Neo in *The Matrix*) to free them of malevolent computer program. Which film's depiction of cyberspace is most compelling to you? Write a paragraph to explain your point of view.

## REFERENCES

Abate, T. (2000, February 26). Scientists develop bionic chip. *San Francisco Chronicle*, p. D1.

Aden, R. (1999). *Popular stories and promised lands: Fan cultures and symbolic pilgrimages*. Tuscaloosa: University of Alabama Press.

Ahrenberg, S., Carmody, D., Desormeaux, J., Hamburg, V., Lantos, R., & Rack, B. J. (Producers). Longo, R. (Director). (1995). *Johnny Mnemonic*. [film]. TriStar Pictures.

Apple Computer. (1984). <http://www.apple-history.com/history.html>.

Balestier, B. (2000, July 7). Literary lawyer advised legal fiction writers. *Law.com* <http://www.nulj.com/backpage/00/07/bp070700a2.html>.

Balsamo, A. (1995). Signal to noise: On the meaning of cyberpunk subculture. In F. Biocca & M. R. Levy's (Eds.), *Communication in the age of virtual reality* (pp. 347–368). Hillsdale, NJ: Lawrence Erlbaum Associates.

Berman, B., Cracchiolo, D., Hughes, C., Mason, A., Mirisch, R., Osborne, B.M., Silver, J., Stoff, E., Wachowski, A., & Wachowski, L. (Producers). Wachowski, A., & Wachowski, L. (Directors). (1999). *The Matrix*. [film]. Silver Pictures.

Bertman, S. (1998). *Hyperculture: The human cost of speed*. Westport, CT: Greenwood.

Borenstein, D. (2000). *Quoteland.com*. <http://www.quoteland.com>.

Brummett, B. (1994). *Rhetoric in popular culture*. New York: St. Martin's Press.

Conklin, E. J. (1987). Hypertext: An Introduction and Survey. *IEEE Computer, 20,* pp. 17–41.

Davis, M. (1999). Fortress Los Angeles: The militarization of urban space. In M. Sorkin (Ed.), *Variation on a theme park: The new American city and the end of public space* (pp. 154–180). New York: Hill & Wang.

Davison, J., Lim, S., Neumeier, E., Schmidt, A., & Tippett, P. (Producers). Verhoeven, P. (Director). (1987). *RoboCop*. [film] Orion Pictures.

Deeley, M., Fancher, H., Kelly, B, Perenchio, J., Powell, I., Scott, R., Shaw, R., & Yorkin, B. (Producers). Scott, R. (Director). (1982). *Blade Runner*. [film] The Ladd Company.

Dunn, T. P, & Erlich, R. D. (1982). *The mechanical god, machines in science fiction*. Westport, CT: Greenwood.

Ellenshaw, H. & Kushner, D., & Miller, R. (Producers), Lisberger, S. (Director) (1982). *Tron*. [film] Walt Disney Productions.

Gibson, W. (1991). Neuromancer. In L. McCaffery (Ed.), *Storming the reality studio: A casebook of cyberpunk and postmodern science fiction* (pp. 65–74). Durham, NC: Duke University Press.

Gibson, W. (1981). The gernsback continuum. In T. Carr (Ed.), *Universe 11* (pp. 81–90). Garden City, NY: Doubleday.

Gleick, J. (1999). *Faster: The acceleration of just about everything*. New York: Random House.

Goldberg, L., Hashimoto, R., & Schneider, H. (Producers), Badham, J. (Director) (1983). *WarGames*. [film]. Metro-Goldwyn-Mayer.

Grossberg, L. (1986). Is there rock after punk? *Critical Studies in Mass Communication, 3,* 50–74.

Haraway, D.J. (1996). *Modest_witness@second_millennium*. New York & London: Routledge.

Hayles, N. K. (1993). The seductions of cyberspace. In. V. A. Conley (Ed.), *Rethinking technologies* (pp. 173–190). Minneapolis: University of Minnesota.

Jacobson, D. (1999, March 5). Pop culture studies turns 25. *Salon.* <http://www.salon.com/it/feature/1999/03/05feature.html>.
Jurek, T. (1991). Straight fiction. In L. McCaffery (Ed.), *Storming the reality studio: A casebook of cyberpunk and postmodern science fiction* (pp. 85–86). Durham, NC: Duke University Press.
Kaplan, C. (2000, September 1). New York lawyer advances "Legal Fiction." *Cyber Law Journal* <http://www.nytimes.com/library/tech/00/09/cyber/cyberlaw/01law.html>.
Knarf, F. (1998). *Frequently asked questions alt.cyberpunk.* <http://www.knarf.demon.co.uk/alt-cp.htm>.
Kroker, A., & Kroker, M. (1996). *Hacking the future.* New York: St. Martin's Press.
Kubrick, S. (Producer), Kubrick, S. (Director). (1968). *2001: A Space Odyssey* [film]. Metro-Goldwyn-Mayer.
Lanier, J., & Biocca, F. (1992). An insider's view of the future of virtual reality. *Journal of Communication, 42,* 150–172.
Lippert, P. (1996). Cinematic representations of cyberspace. In L. Strate, R. Jacobson, & S. B. Gibson (Eds.), *Communication and cyberspace: Social interaction in an electronic environment.* Cresskill, NJ: Hampton Press.
Sterling, B. (1986). *Mirrorshades: The cyberpunk anthology.* New York: Ace Books.
Sterling, B. (1995). The future? You don't want to know. *Wired, 3*(11), 152.
Toffler, A. (1971). *Futureshock.* New York: Bantam Doubleday Dell.
Warner Brothers Virtual Lot. (1999). *Max Headroom.* <http://www.virtuallot.com/cmp/vault/classic/cl01.htm>.

# APPENDIX A

# INTRODUCTION TO HYPERTEXT MARKUP LANGUAGE

In this appendix, we offer a brief overview of some of the technical components to building a web page. In this effort, we recognize that keeping up with the changing standards and protocols for Web site design is impossible. The World Wide Web changes constantly, and so do the means to contribute to this "docuverse." Nonetheless, we offer this brief overview to provide some guidance as you develop your first contributions to the Web. We begin with an overview of hypertext markup language (HTML) before describing some key hypertext "tags." We conclude with a note on uploading and downloading files.

HTML is really a form of word processing. Hypertext refers to the ability of documents placed on the World Wide Web (WWW) to be read in more than two dimensions. In other words, rather than having the choice of reading a document from top to bottom or left to right—or in any other set of directions on a flat sheet of paper—hypertext allows the author to craft pages in three or (theoretically) more dimensions. Imagine several sheets of paper stacked on top of one another. Typically, the reader will progress through each page in linear fashion, one after another. In hypertext, the reader has that option. But he or she also has the option of moving from concept to concept, page to page, *through* the pages. As Fig. A.1 illustrates, the reader and/or page author is free to choose a piece of information and then create a link between that information and some text on another page.

This concept of hypertext is similar to "hyperspace" as demonstrated in the film, *Star Wars*. In hyperspace, our heroes were able to evade the evil empire by creating "holes" in space from which they could "jump" from one location to another with ease, instantaneously. Hypertext allows people to consume texts in any order, "jumping" from idea to idea as they wish. Authors of hypertext documents shape this experience somewhat by placing links in their pages, suggesting connections between documents that may not be so apparent from a traditional linear order. As discussed in chapter 2, this hypertext business raises serious questions about the power of authorship and the responsibilities of readership. But our purpose here is to explore the ways in which you can craft textual spaces that enable the reader to discover connections across, between, and beyond your words.

So far, we've figured out the "hypertext" in hypertext markup language; now let's tackle the "markup" part. Markup refers to the traditional practice in editing

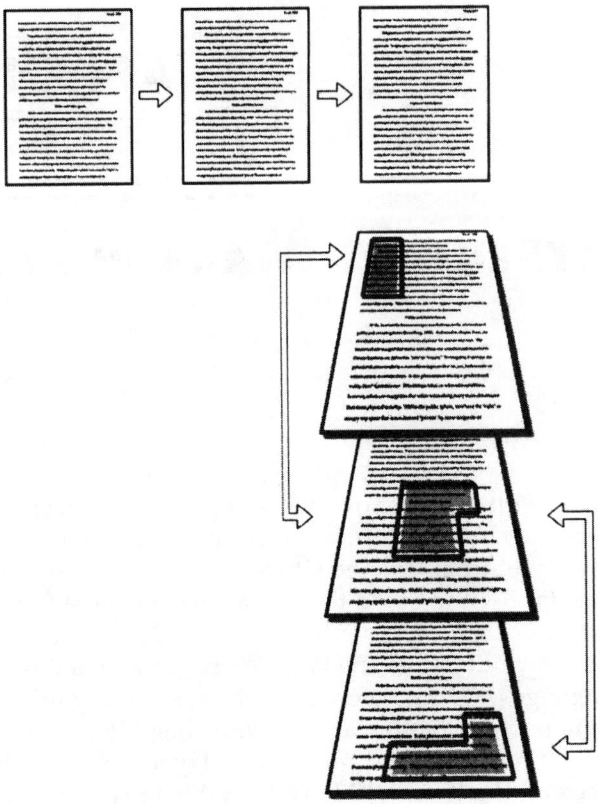

FIG. A.1. Linear versus hypertext

in which the author takes a pen and literally "marks up" the page with extra notations to indicate specifically how the page should appear when it is complete. Here is an example: you might manually place an underline beneath a word to emphasize that the word should be underlined or italicized in the final draft of your document. HTML works the same way. This language adds notations called **tags** to tell browsers how to display the documents they have downloaded from the server. Thus, an HTML document is no different than any word-processing document you create. In fact, you can write a Web-ready document using SimpleText (for Mac users) or some other Notepad software (for Windows users). The only difference is that you add tags to that document to make it readable by browsers.

What is a browser? A browser is like a pair of glasses. We often wear glasses to see the world more clearly. We use a browser to access information more easily. A browser—such as Netscape Navigator or Microsoft Explorer—helps you "see" the information of the Web; it also helps you select which information you wish to see and which information you wish to ignore. A browser "reads" a web page when you use a computer to access files in another computer called a server, a machine that stores information. You maintain your files in a "public folder" on your server. The files can be as simple as a school lunch menu or as complicated as a virtual world complete with three dimensional images and stereo sound. The principle in accessing files on the Web is pretty much the same.

So, what actually happens when you browse a web page? When your browser accesses a document on the Web, it takes a copy of the information you seek and places it in your hard drive, the location in your computer where its files are saved. The Internet connection (phone lines and a modem, ethernet connection, or some other way of accessing this information) is necessary to get the Web document. The browser is necessary to "read" the document by translating HTML tags.

What can tags do? That answer is evolving. During the infancy of the WWW, tags were utilitarian. They centered text, added italics, and facilitated other simple tasks. Nowadays, tags allow page authors to lay their documents out with precision that rivals that of a magazine designer. For our purposes, however, it is necessary only to speak of a handful of tags. Once you know how to use these tags, you will be able to create documents that can be read by any browser in the world. At this point, you might wonder, "Why learn HTML tags" when there are plenty of software packages that can create web pages—no HTML required? The authors of this book believe that you should first learn the nuts and bolts of HTML, its theory and its functions, before playing with software packages like Dreamweaver and Frontpage. Moreover, if you learn basic HTML code, you're more likely to craft documents that can be read on any browser; code created by packages can sometimes create havoc on browsers.

The first tags you should know are those that are essential for your page to be read. When a browser "reads" a page, it looks for these tags first.

```
<html>
<head>
<title>
Note: Your page title appears here
</title>
</head>
<body>
Body of your page appears here.
</body>
</html>
```

Let's discuss them in turn.

- <html> is generally the first tag that should appear on your page. It tells the browser, "read this document as a hypertext-markup-language document."
- <head> tells the browser, "the information from this part onward (until I indicate otherwise) is for you to organize this document in relation to others." An HTML document is composed of a "head" and a "body." Information at the head will not appear in the browser window (with one exception, which is explained later). It is information used by the browser and the server. In the example we have provided, the only information in the head is a "title." But, some heads include special keywords designed to help automated search engines locate your documents more easily.

- <title> tells the browser, "the information from this part onward (until I indicate otherwise) will appear in the "title" section of the browser." The title is generally found at the very top of your browser, above the buttons. If someone chooses to bookmark your page, the title is the name his or her browser will give to that link.
- </title> tells the browser, "I've stopped naming the title." Notice how the slash (/) is the browser's cue to stop some function. Almost all tags work in this manner. Thus, <title> says, "start title here." </title> says, "stop title now. " The information between these tags (above, we wrote "Note: Your page title appears here") is usually a descriptive word or phrase such as "my homepage." **Remember**: the title is not the same as a headline that might appear in the body section of your web page. It only appears at the very top of your browser. Also, you should never put other tags in the title section; they will appear as the title.
- </head> tells the browser, "I've stopped creating the head. Everything from here onward is the body." **Remember**: you have to use the slash to tell the browser, "stop reading the document in this manner."
- <body> tells the browser, "the information from this part onward (until I indicate otherwise) will appear in the "body" section of the browser." This section is the "page" we've been talking about. The page can include words, pictures, and other media. In theory, you don't need any tags in the body section; the browser will display your words without them. However, certain tags are necessary to ensure that your words will be displayed in a reader-friendly manner.
- </body> tells the browser, "I've stopped creating the body. Nothing from here onward should appear on my page."
- </html> tells the browser, "my HTML document is complete." This tag is not technically essential, but some browsers get cranky without it.

## SOME COMMON TAGS

At this point, we've learned that on any page, regardless of its complexity, you will find the same set of tags. They are fairly basic to use, but not so easy to remember when you're first developing pages. To save time, we recommend that you create a page with those tags to serve as a template. Then, when you wish to start a new HTML page, open the template and save it under a different name. Let's explore some more tags you can use to lay out your pages.

These first tags are exceptions to the rule that states that each tag must come paired with another one containing a slash (remember: <tag> </tag>?). These tags are useful when you want to avoid excessive "gray" on your pages. They create hard returns and line breaks. "Wait a second," you might say. "Don't we use key strokes to do that?" Yes, but browsers aren't terribly discriminating. They read text but don't care about keyboard niceties like hard returns. Browsers do read the single space-bar strokes that separate words, but they ignore strokes beyond that.

Thus, "Web design is     fun" would read, "Web design is fun"
Moreover, a text document laid out in this manner:

> Web design
> is fun

would read on a browser as "Web design is fun"

Fortunately, we have tags that can tell browser, "I want the line to stop. I want you to create a hard return."

**<P>** The "P" tag works as a hard return and a space between lines. It won't provide more than one hard return at a time, however. In other words, <P><P><P> only gives you one empty line.

**<BR>** The "BR" tag works as a simple line break. For example, to tell the browser to break text up into stanzas, you'd code as follows:

Gone, gone, sold and gone<BR>To the rice swamp dank and lone<BR>From Virginia hills and waters—<BR>Woe is me, my stolen daughters!

Your browser would display the text in this manner:

> Gone, gone, sold and gone
> To the rice swamp dank and lone
> From Virginia hills and waters—
> Woe is me, my stolen daughters!

**Remember**: The browser doesn't care if you use hard returns to separate the text. It only looks for commands within these keys: < and >.

**<H>** Use this tag to control the size and boldness of headers and sub-headers. This command requires a number to tell the browser how large the text should be. The command also requires a closing tag (with a slash) to tell the browser, "Stop formatting the text this way. Go to standard size." There are six options—<h1> through <h6>. The lower the number, the larger the font. For example:

<h1>This is text</h1> would display This is text

<h6>This is text</h6> would display This is text

**<font size>** Use this tag to control large sections of text. <font size=+1> tells the browser, "add one unit of size to the size of font."

<font size=–1> tells the browser, "subtract one unit of size from the size of the font." At the end of the text you are resizing, place the following tag </font> to tell the browser, "go back to the normal font size."

<font size=+1>Look at the large font</font> that is available

Look at the large font that is available

**Remember**: you don't need to use the font size tag unless you want to alter the font size. Browsers have a default size that's fairly readable.

**<a href=" "></a>** This is a set of complicated but powerful tags. They allow you to link to other documents within and beyond your pages. When a browser sees the tag **<a href="**, it looks for the quotation marks. Within those quotes, you will place the web address of the site to which you are linking. The browser will then look for the > symbol. After that symbol—and before the < symbol, any text you place will be highlighted. The text becomes a hypertext link that, when clicked, downloads the file addressed within those quotes. The **</a>** tag is absolutely essential. It tells the browser, "don't turn any text beyond this point into hypertext unless I start a new link."

Here's an example. To link to one of the authors' homepages, you'd tag as follows:

> Here's a link to
> <a href="http://www.sjsu.edu/faculty/wooda">
> Dr. Andrew Wood</a>'s homepage.

Note: within the quotation marks, you place the full address to Dr. Wood's page. Between the > and the <, you tell the browser what word (or words) to highlight. After the </a>, you instruct the browser to stop highlighting. The result is this:

Here's a link to **Dr Andrew Wood**'s homepage.

Note: The boldfaced words, when selected by clicking, tells the browser to link to the address within the quotes.

You can also link to other pages within your own server space (we'll talk more about placing files in your server later). This is useful to break up long pages. Instead, you can provide several short pages and allow the reader to choose the direction s/he follows. When linking to a file within your public folder, you don't need the full address—just the name of the document will do.

**<center>** This tag centers a piece of text. In fact, all text below it will be centered until you employ the </center> tag. For example:

> This text is not centered.
> <P>
> <center>This text is.</center>
> <P>
> This text is not centered.

A browser would display the coded text in this manner.

This text is not centered.

This text is.

This text is not centered.

**<B>** This tag allows you to set pieces of text in boldface. To do so, place the <B> before the text you wish to bold and a </B> after the text you wish to make bold. Thus:

This text is <B>bold</B>.
This text is **bold**.

**<I>** This tag allows you to set pieces of text in italics. To do so, place the <I> before the text to be italicized and </I> after the text you wish to italicize. Thus:

This text is <I>italicized</I>.
This text is *italicized*.

**<U>** This tag allows you to underline pieces of text. To do so, place the <U> before the text to be underlined and a </U> after the text you wish to underline. Thus:

This text is <U>underlined</U>.
This text is <u>underlined</u>.

## DISPLAYING IMAGES

Using the <IMG> tag, you can display images on your web page. The <IMG> tag acts sort of like a linking tag. It instructs the browser to locate a document and display its contents. In this case, the document is an image. On the Internet, most images end with either .gif or .jpeg in their suffixes. What's the difference between .gif and .jpeg? Image type .gif generally is used for images with flat color (cartoons, for example). The suffix .jpeg is saved for more complicated images with rich gradients of color (photographs, for example). .gif images almost always take up less memory than .jpeg images. Linking to an image requires a tag with the following attributes: <IMG SRC>

This tag tells the browser, "look for an image at the following location and display it." The location of that image is a web address, placed within the quotation marks. Here's an example:

<IMG SRC="http://www.sjsu.edu/faculty/wooda/homeguy3.jpeg">

Note: there must be no spaces within the quotation marks, just the Web address.

The address should provide the browser enough information to find the image. If you are displaying an image that is not in your public folder, provide the entire address (see earlier example). If, however, you are displaying an image in the same public folder as the html document, you need only place the name of the image (including suffix) in your tag. Example:

<IMG SRC="logo.gif">

## OTHER IMG ATTRIBUTES

Within the tag you may add other attributes such as ALT, HEIGHT, and WIDTH. ALT is used to display text while the image is downloading to provide users a sense of what they'll see. ALT is particularly useful for text-only browsers (such as those used by the visually impaired). HEIGHT and WIDTH can be placed in the IMG tag to tell the browser the dimensions of the image. These attributes are useful if you have many images along with your text on a page. There are some browsers that take so much effort processing those images that they won't display the text for several seconds or longer, forcing the user to wait for *anything* to appear on the screen. With the HEIGHT and WIDTH tags, the browser can calculate the approximate dimensions of the images and display the text first. Then, while the user reads the text, the browser works to display the images. Here's an example of a tag using all of these attributes:

<IMG HEIGHT = 38 WIDTH = 30 ALT = "image description"
SRC = "logo.gif">

## UPLOADING AND DOWNLOADING FILES

Accessing the WWW is really just a process of uploading and downloading information between your computer and a server that maintains files. We know that browsers search for documents in our public folders and download them, based on the addresses they are sent. The question remains, how do we upload files to our folders? For many web page maintainers, the answer is a free piece of software that enables a process called **File Transfer Protocol** (FTP). FTP does pretty much what it signifies by its name. It transfers files according to a common protocol so that their contents remain unaltered, even as they cruise in digital format through multiple telephone wires.

Although each piece of FTP software works in a slightly different way, the process is similar. You select a file or files on your hard drive and indicate—through either pressing a button or "dragging"—that you wish to move a copy of that file to a location on a remote server. All types of FTP software need four pieces of information to transfer your files. They need a server, a path, a username, and a password.

- The server is an address where the computer that stores your files is situated on the Internet. Frequently, the address for this site is unlike the location of a document on the WWW.
- The path is a set of nested folders that indicates specifically where your public folder is located. Again, this address is unlike your web address. It is composed of locations that are specific to the server.
- The username is pretty simple. It's the name you use to access your account with the university or your ISP.
- The password is also pretty self explanatory. It's the word (generally, a combination of letters and numbers) that ensures that only you can alter files in your public folder. By keeping your password secure, other people can look at your public files, but only you can alter them.

Once you have established a connection to the server through FTP software, you move the documents in the manner indicated by the specific program you're using. The process is fairly simple either way. For instance, someone using a piece of software called Fetch to FTP their files sees a window filled with the documents in his or her public folder. Using a mouse, the user selects the document on his or her hard drive and drags that document into the server window. Depending on the speed of your Internet connection, the file transfer can range from being instantaneous to mind-numbingly slow. The only other consideration is to ensure that you are using the correct protocol for your document type. If you are given the option to choose, select "text" for HTML documents and "binary" for images (in either .gif or .jpeg format). This is not a rule; it is advice from trial and error on several systems.

Learning how to get online and develop web pages takes practice and patience, but the result is worth the effort. There's a world of ideas floating between computer servers and bouncing against the satellites. We hope this appendix has helped you get closer to entering that world.

# APPENDIX B

# RESEARCHING THE INTERNET EXPERIENCE

If you've read parts of *Online Communication* or completed the whole book to this point, then you have some appreciation for how academics are striving to understand the online experience. As you probably noticed in your reading, researchers from communication, composition, computer science, law, psychology, and sociology, to name but a few disciplines, are working to interpret the human-to-human interactions mediated by computer technology. As you know, the introduction of the Internet into our lives has raised a host of issues, including questions about self, relationships, addiction, communities, commerce, privacy, and censorship, among others. The answers to these questions rest in careful investigation into Internet phenomena.

As an appendix to this book, we suggest some of the considerations scholars have taken as they have sought explanations of online phenomena. In particular, this appendix defines two types of scholarship into mediating technologies and reviews guidelines for conducting ethical research initiatives. It is our hope that these points will assist you as you evaluate the research of others and plan research projects of your own. As you have read in the previous chapters, the results of such investigations have yielded a growing body of literature that helps us make sense of the communicating online, and your contribution could be one that furthers our knowledge that much more.

## RESEARCH INTO THE TECHNICAL OR SOCIAL ASPECTS OF CMC

Writing in *Doing Internet Research,* Costigan (1999) states that CMC literature can be divided into two categories. The first category involves research into how information is stored and retrieved from the Internet. This research seems to focus on the technological aspects of the computer and its software and the implications for how humans manage them. Such a technological perspective is evident in the following two relevant works of communication scholarship.

In the first, Elmer (1997) examines how the indexing capabilities of the Internet function. One form of indexing that many of us encounter is through search engines on the World Wide Web. These engines draw particular sites to our attention, but also draw attention to us. As Elmer notes, a number of sites, notably those of a commercial nature, are seeking to index us by soliciting our personal information for marketing purposes. His research calls to our attention the double-edged sword of the Internet indexing functions. Another scholarly contribution in terms of understanding how humans manage the Internet comes from Whittaker and Sidner (1997). They looked at how people manage "e-mail overload," which is when one gets too many messages to cope with all of them efficiently. Their research reveals some of the ways in which people flooded with so much communication practice the reading, filing, overlooking, and responding to messages. (Other examples of this kind of research are found throughout the text with a notable amount appearing in chapter 7.)

In addition to aspects of technology management, Costigan (1999) cites a second body of research that has emerged, this one dealing with the social aspects of the Internet. This is the kind of research that covers human interaction in forums like newsgroups, chat rooms, and MUDs. As he notes, "Research on these topics is truly unique to the Internet. There is no existing parallel social construct, and in many ways, the Internet creates wholly new social constructs" (p. xix). Much of the material in the previous chapters pulls on this type of research. (Chapter 4 is particularly rich with this kind of research.)

In pursuing knowledge about the social aspects of the Internet, scholars have adopted a number of methods to explore questions they have about these "new social constructs." Some have "gone native" and participated with the various forms of CMC and then written *ethnographies* of their experiences. A good deal of work into software designed for group decision making involved *experiments* where the responses of a group exposed to online interaction were compared to those of a control group of people who interacted without mediation. Other researchers have performed *surveys* in order to solicit the feedback of other users. Still others adopt a more critical perspective, and have analyzed examples of communication as artifacts from a *rhetorical perspective.* Certainly these, and many more, of the research methodologies scholars use to investigate human interaction in other contexts have been, or have the potential to be used in online research as well.

As you move forward in your studies of CMC, it is likely that you too have questions about the nature of social phenomena online. As you consider how to come up with answers to these questions, you too will need to consider what type of phenomenon you will be examining and what scholarly methods will provide you with greater understanding it. As you do, however, it is important that you keep in mind certain ethical principles to guide your investigation.

## PRACTICING ETHICS IN ONLINE RESEARCH

Hand-in-hand with what you want to learn about online interaction is how you go about investigating it. Hamilton (1999) reminds us that a code of ethics should guide our inquiries whenever human beings are voluntarily contributing to our efforts, in real life or virtual life. Even as researchers who use student volunteers in their experiments or distribute survey questionnaires to mass lecture courses must protect their subjects from harm, so too must those who conduct research online keep their contributors safe. To that end, Hamilton recommends that researchers construct a careful plan for conducting their efforts and submit it to the members of the **Institutional Review Board** (IRB). At research universities, an IRB helps to ensure that research involving human or animal test subjects is conducted in an ethical manner. However, because online research is so new, IRBs may not as yet have established guidelines for what qualifies as ethical research on the Internet. Moreover, some smaller institutions may not have such an overseeing body to provide guidance, and thus Hamilton has suggested minimal guidelines to facilitate such research.

The researcher should provide . . .

- A way (e-mail, address, or phone number) for participants to contact the researcher.
- A means for obtaining participants' fully informed consent.
- Full disclosure of any risks to the participants' confidentiality.
- A post-experimental debriefing page.
- A way for the participants to learn about the results of the study. (adapted from Hamilton, 1999)

Hamilton's five minimal guidelines emphasize that researchers have a responsibility to provide their subjects with as much information as possible, beginning with who the researcher is and continuing on through the completion of the project. First, identifying oneself and one's professional affiliation is a good idea if only because it serves to distinguish one's legitimate research efforts from those of commercial or parody efforts. Second, respondents should be provided with a form for acknowledging that they are aware of the research and its purpose. If you have ever participated in a research project on campus, you might recall signing an informed consent form prior to your participation. In like manner, online participants should be told what they are getting into and have a channel to acknowledge their agreement to have the information they provide used for research-specific purposes. Implicit in the third checklist item are the steps that the researcher should take to protect the identity of any respondent. Letting people know the degree to which their information is secure from the prying eyes of a hacker, especially if the information is sensitive, is a fair disclosure in helping a person decide whether or not to contribute to the research. Fourth, following the completed experiment, the respondent should be directed to a debriefing page, which provides them with a full explanation of the study and, as indicated by the fifth criterion, a reference for how to learn the results of the research initiative (such as a Web site or other publication they can eventually turn to).

Hamilton is concerned that researchers using the Internet may not be treating people online with the same safeguards as they would people in real life. If there are questions you have about online communication that you are looking forward to answering with the online surveys or experiments, keep in mind that behind every tally and comment there is a person who should enjoy the same privacy that you would expect as a participant yourself.

Certainly, there is a lot yet to be explored when it comes to understanding and managing online interaction. We hope that our introduction to the issues raised and research conducted up to this writing will help you in your own further explorations into the nature and processes of CMC.

## REFERENCES

Costigan, J. T. (1999). Introduction: Forests, trees, and Internet research. In S. Jones (Ed.), *Doing Internet research: Critical issues and methods for examining the net* (pp. xvii–xxiv). Thousand Oaks, CA: Sage.

Elmer, G. (1997). Spaces of surveillance: Indexicality and solicitation on the Internet. *Critical Studies in Mass Communication, 14,* 182–191.

Hamilton, J. C. (1999, December 3). The ethics of conducting social-science research on the Internet. *The Chronicle of Higher Education*, pp. B6–7.

Whittaker, S., & Sidner, C. (1997). Email overload: Exploring personal information management of email. In S. Kiesler (Ed.), *Culture of the Internet* (pp. 277–295). Mahwah, NJ: Lawrence Erlbaum Associates.

# AUTHOR INDEX

Page numbers in *italics* denote full bibliographic references

## W



## Y



## Z

# SUBJECT INDEX

Page numbers in *italics* denote terms appearing in glossary.